Police
Stories

Police
Stories

Vikki Petraitis

LAKE PRESS

LAKE PRESS

Lake Press Pty Ltd
5 Burwood Road
Hawthorn VIC 3122 Australia
www.lakepress.com.au

Some of these stories have been
previously published.

This edition first published 2020

Printed and bound in Australia at McPherson's
Printing Group, Maryborough, Victoria 5 4 3
LP21 384

Photo credits
Cover photo copyright ©Darren McNamara
Photos for 'Danger and death on the frontline'
courtesy of Chris Glasl
Photos for 'Searching for Sarah MacDiarmid'
courtesy of the MacDiarmid family
All other photos courtesy of South Australia Police
and Victoria Police

A catalogue record for this
book is available from the
National Library of Australia

For Steve Petraitis, husband and tea-maker.
And as always, for my mum, Helen Burke, who has forever
been my champion, my biggest fan and my honorary publicist.
Even after proofreading my books, Mum reads them over and
over again. She's the best fangirl a girl could have.

CONTENTS

AUTHOR'S NOTE

It has been a delight to revisit this collection of stories and to add new ones into the mix. For this book, I approached police officers working in different fields to ask for their best stories. In a world of big stories, frontline police officers have the biggest. These stories span the twenty-seven years I've been writing crime and collecting police yarns. Over time, they become a barometer, a time capsule of crime.

Crime stories are captivating, and the impact isn't lessened if the people involved are called Fred Smith or Jill Brown. Accordingly, some names in some stories have been changed.

The helicopter makes and models were correct at the time of writing. New models would have replaced these by now. All ranks and positions of police were correct at the time of the interviews. These also will have changed. And years on from when I interviewed some of these police officers, many will be enjoying a well-earned retirement.

We thank them for their service and understand that sometimes, the toll was too high.

Vikki Petraitis, August 2020

Chapter One

DANGER AND DEATH ON THE FRONTLINE

In the early 1990s, the police station in Davey Street, Frankston was old and dilapidated but the cops who worked there had a fondness for the character of the place. They were packed in the tiny correspondence rooms and tiny locker rooms, but it seemed to work. There was little security and it wasn't uncommon for an offender to escape through the interview room window if left alone for too long. Senior Constable Chris Glasl would arrive for his shifts and enter into a cloud of cigarette smoke – smoking was permitted inside buildings in those days – and it wasn't uncommon to witness gun target practice in the long hallway where officers were known to fire guns down the hall into a phone book (when the bosses weren't around). It was only when rounds were fired into the wall of the Frankston branch of the Commonwealth Bank that the senior sergeant had some stern words with the boys and the guns were holstered for a while.

By the time Chris Glasl had been at Frankston for half a dozen years, he and the other local cops would spend time together in their off-duty hours. They worked together and played together, going to the pub after work, and hanging out. One of his mates was another senior constable at Frankston whose nickname was Sharpie. Since Chris's surname rhymed with razzle-dazzle, every time Sharpie saw Chris, he'd say, 'Hey Razzle-Dazzle Glasl!' Over time, 'Raz' stuck and became Chris's nickname.

Sharpie was a fun guy. He didn't take life too seriously and was always the one to make a joke out of anything. He had one of those captivating personalities that drew people to him. He got along with everyone and everyone liked him in return. He wasn't overly tall, but he was stocky enough to have a natural presence in the job.

Sharpie was in his mid-twenties and had just moved into an apartment above an office in a building almost directly across the road from the police station. Chris and the other blokes joked to Sharpie that he couldn't take a sickie. The bosses will walk over and check, they said. The building fronted onto Davey Street and had a car park at the rear. Elevated above the end of the car park was a narrow laneway. Its name, Bay Lane, made it sound fancier than what it was – a strip of bitumen barely wide enough for a car.

One night, Chris was working with Sharpie's best mate, Harves – a cop whose nickname was simply a shortening of his surname, since it was almost a crime to call anyone their whole name.

Chris and Harves were in the divvy van when they got the call over the police radio.

'Frankston 3-11, we have a report of an off-duty member being stabbed at his address in Davey Street.' D24 gave the full address. The member had disturbed two car thieves in the car park behind his house and been stabbed as he confronted them.

'That's Sharpie's place!' Chris said with a flash of panic.

One of their own was down. It was lights and sirens all the way to Sharpie's place. The marked police sedan – 2-11 – was right behind them and they both pulled up in convoy about a minute later.

Chris's van screeched to a halt, and he jumped out and ran up the front stairs of the old post-war brick building. The front door to the second-storey apartment was open. Chris ran through it and saw Sharpie straightaway; he was lying on the floor in the lounge room with some shocking injuries. Chris tried to process what he was seeing. The phone was off the hook, receiver dangling. Made sense, since Sharpie himself had called in the stabbing. Sharpie was wearing a pair of grey trackie pants and nothing else – no shoes, no top. Chris knelt down beside him.

'Sharpie! Sharpie! Are you with me?' Chris shouted. It looked like Sharpie was drifting in and out of consciousness. Chris resisted touching his felled colleague to try to rouse him. He could see knife wounds, injuries on his arms. Both shoulders were sliced open and wounds were gaping – Chris could see muscle and sinew.

Chris also noticed a lack of blood, which was strange. The thought occurred to him that maybe Sharpie's body had gone into survival mode and forced blood away from extremities and towards major organs to keep him alive.

Even though the shoulder wounds looked really bad, it was the chest injury that worried Chris the most. The stab wound looked deep.

Harves and the two cops from 2-11 had followed Chris into the lounge room. As Chris looked up from Sharpie, he saw Harves standing frozen as a statue, like he was planted on the spot. Suddenly, logic came rushing back. They didn't know what had happened. Someone had obviously attacked Sharpie and that person could be in the house.

'Harves, clear the rest of the house!' Chris said in a voice loud enough to rouse Harves, but not jolt Sharpie.

Harves didn't move.

Chris felt a rising panic. If there was anyone in the house, they were all in danger.

'Harves! Clear the fuckin' house!' Chris felt such a surge of anger, he added: 'And if there's anyone else here, shoot 'em!' Chris was mad enough that if someone emerged from another room with a knife, he would have shot them himself. His anger got Harves moving too.

Chris turned his attention back to Sharpie. 'Sharpie, stay with us!' Chris's mind reeled with what to do next, desperately trying to remember his first-aid training. *Should I put him in the coma position? Should I move him? Put pressure on the wounds?*

'Raz,' Sharpie whispered almost inaudibly; his eyes flickered. He knew Chris was there.

'Mate, stay with us.' Chris could hardly bear to see his mate like this. The fun guy. The joker. *Who would do this to him?*

Moments later, Harves returned and said the house was clear. Sirens sounded. Then the thump of feet on the stairs. Ambos. Chris moved from his position beside Sharpie and let the ambos do their job. There was no mucking around once they saw his injuries. They loaded him onto the gurney and carried him down the flight of stairs to the waiting ambulance. As the sirens screamed their way to the hospital, police from everywhere converged on Sharpie's house.

A command post was quickly set up in Davey Street, and Sharpie's place became a crime scene and the area was sealed off. Soon the place was teeming with the brass and detectives, who took over the investigation. The flapping police tape was a grim reminder of what had happened to their colleague.

Regular updates were passed down from the bosses and from the members who had gone with Sharpie to the hospital. Sharpie's life was in peril. Word went around that he had to be brought back from the brink of death three times on the way to the hospital. Chris understood. He'd seen him. Seen the injuries.

In the hours after the stabbing, Chris guarded the front of Sharpie's building and Harves was stationed at the rear car park where the stabbing had happened. Chris kept a log of who came and went. In the dead of night, Chris wandered around to check on Harves. He and Sharpie were close mates. Chris couldn't get the image out of his mind, of Harves standing over his mate, frozen.

'How you doing, mate? You okay?' Chris kept the inquiry simple. They were tough cops. They'd be okay. He didn't want to open any kind of Pandora's box or start a floodgate of emotion.

'I'm okay,' said Harves, perhaps for the same reasons. Even if he wasn't.

It was a tense night. Guarding the scene. Keeping a lookout for two offenders. Sharpie's life in the balance. Reports filtered through that he had come out of surgery and was alive and in intensive care.

Chris was supposed to finish his shift at 7 am but when his senior sergeant mentioned it, Chris was firm.

'Nah, I don't want to go home,' he said. Sharpie was a mate, but it was more than that. He was a police officer and he had been attacked. It was a police solidarity thing.

It wasn't until Chris came off shift, twenty-four hours after he'd started, that he felt heavy with tiredness and a desperate need for sleep.

The story of the attack came in drifts and snippets and was further pieced together by detectives and the crime scene examination team.

Sharpie had been in bed and heard a noise coming from the rear car park. Looking out a back window, he saw two thieves breaking into his car. He'd grabbed a golf club and gone down the front stairs rather than the back stairs, maybe to creep up the side driveway and around the back to surprise them. He confronted two youths in the car park. Once he saw how young they were, he dropped the golf club and a scuffle started. A fistfight. Sharpie was winning until one of them pulled a knife. In the heat of the battle and with a rush of adrenaline, Sharpie didn't know he'd been stabbed until after the kids ran off. He picked up his golf club and made his way back around to the front of his building. When he started climbing the stairs up to his apartment, he noticed a labouring in his breathing, then collapsed halfway up the stairs. He managed to get himself to the top of the stairs, grab the phone and dial triple 0.

Listening to the tape of the call later, Chris heard the faintness of Sharpie's voice. 'I'm an off-duty member and I've been stabbed.' He'd identified himself and that sent the troops running.

Right from the start, police were looking for two offenders. Chances were, they'd jumped up from the lower car park at the back of Sharpie's place into Bay Lane and had taken off through an adjoining car park that bordered Frankston Park.

An extensive police search failed to find them.

A couple of days later, Chris visited Sharpie at Monash Hospital in Clayton. Chris didn't know what state he'd find his mate in, considering how he'd looked the last time he'd seen him. Chris took a deep breath and walked into the ward where Sharpie was. It was a large ward with a number of beds and patients. Sharpie was in a bed in the far corner with a curtain drawn around it. Chris braced himself, trying to push out of his mind the memory of Sharpie badly injured on the lounge-room floor.

To his pleasant surprise, Chris saw Sharpie sitting up in bed looking fine. A hospital gown covered all of his injuries and his colour had returned. Chris had resolved not to talk about what happened on the night of the attack because he knew Sharpie would have been interviewed enough already.

'Can't wait for you to get out, Sharpie,' Chris said brightly, levity prevailing. The knife had missed his heart by centimetres. He would recover. Medically, Sharpie was fine, therefore, he *was* fine. There was no discussion about his near-death experience. No talk about fear, or the aftermath. Just mates having a chat over a hospital bed, ignoring the fact that one had seen the other lying on his lounge-room floor sliced open with a stab wound to his chest.

It was kids who'd attacked Sharpie. Blond hair. Shoulder length. Short, lean. School age. Police from Frankston visited every secondary school and got class photos of students in that age bracket.

Sharpie reckoned he'd recognise the kids if he saw them again. When he was well enough, he pored over hundreds of photos of blond teenagers until he found the young man who'd stabbed him.

The boy was brought in for questioning and without much prompting, he named the boy who was with him at the time. Both were arrested and charged. The one who stabbed Sharpie reckoned he only did it because he was getting beaten up.

Chris had no sympathy. They could have run. They could have chosen not to break into cars in the first place. They chose to pull a knife, to bring a knife to a fistfight, chose to carry one in the first place. In Chris's mind, they deserved everything they got. And more.

The kid who had stabbed Sharpie received a custodial sentence.

Chris Glasl was always a cautious cop. When he went to a job, he always had his hand poised to go for his gun. After Sharpie's attack, he became more so. But there was anger there as well – if the offender had been in the house that night, Chris wouldn't have hesitated to shoot him. Any incident like that weakens a cop's basic trust in people.

The attack on Sharpie opened the door to the possibility that none of them were really safe; before that, they'd felt bulletproof behind the blue uniform.

Chris's next stop would be with the police Special Operations Group (SOG), the specialists who deal with counterterrorism and other critical incidents – the men in black. It had been a life goal of his.

And, of course, the SOG gave its members the body armour and any number of deadly weapons to reduce their vulnerability to the most hardened of crims. Or teenagers wielding knives.

Chris never forgot the moment at his police academy graduation when the then Chief Commissioner Mick Miller shook his hand. The Chief had asked Chris what he wanted to achieve in the job.

'SOG, sir,' Chris had replied without hesitation.

Miller had looked him up and down. 'Well, you're certainly big enough.'

The SOG was a world away from Frankston. Within a couple of years of joining the SOG, Chris would see what it looked like when the tables were turned, and the cops outnumbered the bad guys.

Chris was on the SOG on-call A-team on Wednesday 11 February 1998. When the phone woke him up at 2 am, he wiped the sleep from his eyes and noted down the job details in a notepad he kept by his bed.

The job was a siege. Male person in Wandin, holed up in his house. He was armed with a .22 rifle and was shooting up the house. He had also set fire to the family car. Chris imagined the job would be another surround-and-contain situation in line with the latest force command philosophy after a spate of police shootings. Most likely, he and his SOG colleagues would surround the target premises and wait it out while the police negotiator talked the suspect into a voluntary surrender. It usually took hours, sometimes days to negotiate a peaceful resolution. For cops trained for action, these hours of inaction were tedious.

Chris dressed in his black coveralls and kitted himself out with his equipment. Riding in the armoured vehicle he'd taken home while on call, Chris placed his shotgun on the passenger side, on the floor space facing upwards. When he arrived at the location around 3 am, he saw that the other on-call crews had been deployed too. They had all gathered on a narrow, unsealed road about a kilometre from the house where the siege was taking place.

SOG Team Leader Sergeant Welsh was giving a briefing on the situation. The rural property in Wandin was around ten acres in size. Snipers had been deployed to surround the house and get as close as they could without breaching the stretch of open area immediately around the house. The man inside the house – Robert Anthony Hall –

was known to be unpredictable and violent, with prior convictions for armed robbery and assaulting police. The day before, he had reportedly attacked his mother and threatened to shoot his girlfriend.

The sergeant explained the SOG role would be a surround-and-contain – just as Chris had suspected – while the negotiator attempted to talk Hall out of the house. The premises had gone quiet and no shots had been heard for over an hour, so Chris would just have to wait out the negotiations. The fact that Hall had a gun was a concern, but the SOG operatives surrounding the house had guns too. Bigger guns.

At the end of the briefing, the team double-checked their equipment and climbed into the back of the armoured vehicle. The negotiator sat up front next to Chris.

Chris drove along the unsealed road towards the target property. Eerily, a full moon illuminated the road enough for him to keep the headlights off. The driveway to the property was about sixty metres long; Chris turned in to it and immediately disabled the brake lights. It was important to try not to draw attention to their approach.

The driveway was bordered by fenced paddocks on either side. Chris could see the farmhouse up ahead, a weatherboard with a wraparound veranda. There were lights on in the house, but no movement. As the armoured vehicle moved towards the open space at the end of the driveway, Chris could see the family car that Hall had set on fire. Small flames were still licking the burnt-out shell and there was black smoke rising from it. Something about the smouldering wreck made Chris realise that this might not be an ordinary job. Hall obviously meant business. Setting fire to your family car was an act of rage, not reason. An angry man. Armed. The powder keg was lit.

Chris drove into the large open space at the end of the driveway with a cluster of several large trees in the middle, maybe twenty or thirty metres from the house. Chris didn't pay much attention to them. He turned the armoured vehicle to face the house and came to a stop around twenty metres from the steps leading up to the veranda and the front door. He kept the engine running. There was still no visible movement from inside the house. The team surrounding the house had not reported any movement either. They had night-vision goggles and hadn't spotted him leave.

Welsh directed one of the operatives to exit the rear of the vehicle and position a loudspeaker near the front of the house. The negotiator would attempt to contact Hall via a microphone from the safety of the armoured vehicle. Chris was worried about the operative who had to position the loudspeaker. Out of the vehicle, there was no cover. He stayed silent though. SOG members did as they were instructed. The operative exited the rear of the armoured vehicle and Chris watched as he walked past the driver's-side window to the front of the vehicle. He placed the speaker about ten metres from the house.

Chris's mind raced with possibilities. He braced himself for shots to ring out while his colleague was so exposed. Thankfully, the operative retreated to the rear of the armoured vehicle, and Chris breathed a sigh of relief once the doors were again locked.

With the loudspeaker in place, the negotiator began his script. 'This is the police. We will not hurt you. Come out of the house without any weapons and with your hands above your head. You will not be harmed.' He repeated the same thing over and over. 'We wish for this to be resolved peacefully. We can help you. Come out with your hands raised. We will not harm you.' This went on for several minutes with no response whatsoever. Welsh instructed the negotiator to keep trying.

After several more fruitless minutes the negotiator turned to Chris. 'When we drove down the driveway,' he said, 'I think I saw movement in those trees.' He indicated the ones behind them.

Chris was incredulous. *What the hell?* Expletives flew. If Hall was *outside*, the whole team was at risk – especially the guy who had exited the vehicle. Chris quickly reversed the vehicle and swung it around to face the trees in question. He halted around ten metres from the trees. Despite the full moon and the breaking dawn, the trees cast a long shadow and the area was dark. Chris hit the headlights and illuminated the trees.

That's when he saw Robert Anthony Hall.

He was lying in a hammock strung up between two of the trees, wrapped in a blanket, looking straight at the armoured vehicle full of SOG operatives. Chris felt a sudden chill. Hall had been watching them the entire time.

As soon he was caught in the spotlight, Hall sprang into action. He jumped out of the hammock, moving so fast it took Chris by surprise.

The guy was fit looking, toned and lean. Maybe five foot ten. Close-cropped hair. Pale complexion. Probably late twenties or early thirties. Wearing tracksuit pants and a light-coloured T shirt. Hall's eyes were wide, almost deranged. In the glare of the headlights, Chris could see his anger, his fury. Hall started yelling and screaming and waving his arms around. He obviously had no fear – so much so that Chris wondered what drugs he might be on. His first thought was amphetamines.

It took Hall seconds to cover the distance between the trees and the armoured vehicle. He yanked on Chris's door handle, trying to pull it open. It was locked. Chris watched incredulous as the man began smashing his fist into the driver's window with all his might. The assault had no impact on the protective window but having the deranged man right next to him, only separated by glass, was unsettling to say the least.

Chris could hear him screaming.

'I'm going to fucking kill you! I'm going to put a bullet in your head!' Hall was out of his mind.

After realising trying to open the door was futile, Hall moved to the front of the vehicle and tried pulling off one of the aerials attached to the bull bar. Once again, he was unsuccessful, but he didn't give up. He continued moving around the car, trying the passenger door and the rear doors, smashing his fists into the side of the car and continuing with his threats.

'I'm going to fucking kill you all!'

Hall wasn't going away. He was on a mission. Chris's entire attention was focused on Hall. As loud and aggressive as he was, he was also unarmed and in the open – making it an opportune time to subdue and arrest him. The armoured vehicle had a hatch on the roof so gas could be deployed to the outside while the members were protected on the inside.

Hall's attack on the armoured vehicle went on for several minutes.

Chris wondered why it was taking so long to order the gas. 'What's taking so long?' Chris called into the back. 'Gas him!'

But apparently, the team needed permission to gas a suspect. It didn't make sense to Chris. They were wasting time. All the member tasked with the gas had to do was pop up through the hatch and spray Hall with a decent dose of OC spray and this would all be over.

Hall was still screaming and doing his best to pull the armoured vehicle apart with his bare hands when TJ, one of the snipers surrounding the house, suddenly appeared dressed in camouflage gear and armed with a Steyr AUG 5.56 mm fully automatic long-arm. By this stage it was getting brighter as dawn was breaking. TJ was just behind the tree line, with his weapon raised towards Hall from a distance of maybe ten metres. Chris heard him yell, 'Police, don't move!' several times. That's when Hall's attention was diverted away from the armoured vehicle and directed towards TJ.

Oh, fuck, Chris thought.

Without a word, Hall turned away and began striding towards TJ. This was a situation that could end very badly. TJ was on his own and facing a man who was pumped up and angry. Chris's hand hovered over the door handle, his brain computing possible courses of action. He wanted to jump out of the armoured vehicle to go to TJ's assistance because any second, he was going to need help. Fighting the impulse was the thought that it was his task to drive the armoured vehicle. If he jumped out, he would leave it driverless.

Chris was torn. *Do I? Don't I?*

All this in the space of two or three seconds.

But time seemed to slow down. As Hall stormed towards TJ, Chris could see TJ pointing his weapon at Hall, screaming, 'Police, don't move! Get on the ground!'

Hall closed the gap quickly, getting so close that TJ began kicking out at Hall in an attempt to keep him at a distance. The whole situation had turned to shit and it was happening before Chris's eyes. His hand hovered over the door handle. TJ needed help!

Chris opened his door and climbed out just as the rest of the team burst through the vehicle's rear doors. In seconds, the entire arrest team had weapons drawn, aiming at Hall. Most members were armed with Benelli M4 Super 90 semiautomatic shotguns, as well as Heckler & Koch 40-calibre semiautomatic handguns. Chris's shotgun was still in the passenger well of the armoured vehicle, so he drew his 40-calibre handgun. All of them moved towards Hall, screaming, 'Police, don't move! Get on the ground!'

Hall turned his attention towards the men coming towards him. He began moving towards them. From five metres away, Welsh gave the order: 'Gas him!'

The gas was contained in a large fire extinguisher, so it had a good range and there was lots of it. The team worked like clockwork. Even though the job had turned pear-shaped, they all still knew what to do. They knew where to stand or where not to stand, and how to avoid the line of fire of the gas.

A thick plume of gas enveloped Hall and for an instant he disappeared. As the cloud dissipated, they could see Hall was still standing. Most people would have dropped to the ground; the gas takes your breath away and causes severe eye pain and temporary blindness. But Hall seemed unaffected. Chris wondered again if he was high on drugs, which would explain why the spray had no effect. If anything, though, the gas made Hall angrier. Still threatening. Still coming closer. Welsh gave the instruction to gas him again and he was hit with a second burst. It still had no effect.

The second cloud dissipated, and Hall was still standing there. He let out a huge scream. For a split second, Chris thought he was going to charge towards the team again, but instead, he turned and ran back behind the two trees where his hammock was strung up. Chris and the rest of the arrest team took off after him, falling into a natural formation, all the while yelling at him to get on the ground.

Everything from that moment happened in slow motion. As Hall ran behind the tree, he stooped and grabbed a .22-calibre bolt-action rifle leaning up against one of the hammock trees and suddenly, the crazed man was armed.

The situation had escalated quickly. The entire team realised the danger. Dawn was breaking and visibility was now quite good. Hall ran towards the middle of the paddock and into open space. Chris saw another one of the advance crew had joined the chase as Hall attempted to escape. The problem Chris saw immediately was that the new member was in a crossfire position with the arrest team. SOG operatives trained diligently to avoid crossfire situations, but they still happened.

Hall spotted the member and, while still running, raised the .22 rifle and aimed it at him.

Welsh screamed, 'Gun!'

Gone was any chance to call on Hall to surrender.

Hall had raised his weapon at a member and the situation escalated to the use of deadly force.

The operative raised his own weapon and discharged a couple of rounds at Hall. Chris felt a bullet whiz past his head. The bullet hit the armoured vehicle, lodged in the side of the cabin. Chris knew that if his squad mate's bullet nearly hit him, then he too was in the crossfire and Chris couldn't fire at Hall without risking shooting the guy who had nearly shot him. He moved to the cover of the armoured vehicle. Meanwhile, six other members also opened fire, each believing it was the only option.

The explosion of firearms should have rendered the team temporarily deaf, but adrenaline diverts the senses to the focal point and Chris hardly even registered the sound of the shots ringing out – even though they were so loud they were recorded by a news crew a kilometre away.

He watched as the bullets thumped into Hall's body. He had always thought it ridiculous in the movies when someone is shot and remains standing – until he saw it with his own eyes. As the bullets tore into Hall's torso, he remained upright, his body jerking and convulsing.

He's not going down, Chris thought.

It wasn't until the final shot rang out that Hall finally collapsed backwards onto the ground. His firearm fell beside him. The echoes of gunshots faded and the SOG team cautiously approached Hall's body. As they stood over him, Chris could see his eyes were lifeless. Multiple gunshot wounds were evident. Hall had a lot of tattoos, including a tattoo of a devil on one of his arms. A shotgun pellet had penetrated the eye of the devil.

Despite shooting him moments earlier, it was the duty of the SOG operatives to attempt to keep Hall alive even though it was a lost cause. One of the members knelt and began performing CPR chest compressions. With each compression, Chris could see blood oozing from Hall's mouth. Blood was seeping into the soil beneath his body.

It was an eerie moment. Dawn had broken and a soft mist hovered over the ground. The pump of the chest compressions broke the silence and the rhythm was soon joined by the sound of birds chirping and tweeting their welcome to the new day.

By contrast, the team of SOG operatives stood over the lifeless body, watching as one of their own tried in vain to revive him.

When it was all over, Chris turned away and began to walk back towards the armoured vehicle. There was still work to be done – the area needed to be fully cleared. He moved to the rear of the armoured vehicle, pointed his firearm towards the house and yelled, 'Covering!' At the same time, other members of the team lined up behind him. Four altogether. The shoulder squeeze came from the back to the front to indicate everyone was ready to go and they moved off, guns drawn, up the steps to the front door and into the house. Usually they would go in fast, everyone yelling, 'Police! Don't move!' But this situation was different. They didn't need the element of surprise. Anyone left in the farmhouse already knew they were there.

They moved silently through the house, nodding when a room was cleared, indicating cupboards that needed opening and beds that required clearing underneath. None of them needed to speak. They all knew what to do just from a nod or a glance.

The house was quickly cleared and the scene secured. The team exited the house and made their way to the armoured vehicle where the rest of the team had congregated. Hall's body remained where it had fallen.

Chris asked TJ if he was all right and he nodded. Everyone checked over everyone else and made sure they were all okay. They were. None of them had been shot by Hall or caught in the crossfire. Chris didn't know if Hall had managed to fire. It didn't matter. He'd raised the weapon at police. That was enough.

Chris found the obvious mark on the side panel of the armoured vehicle near the driver's door. A .223-calibre round was wedged roughly at head height and maybe two feet to the left of the driver's door. It was the round Chris had felt whiz past his head. He had come inches from death and the realisation hit him as his adrenaline began to subside. He stopped at that moment and took his pulse as Welsh moved up to take a look.

'Are you okay?' he asked after inspecting the damage to the armoured vehicle.

Chris's pulse was still rock solid at seventy beats per minute. He nodded to his boss. 'Yep.'

Once the scene was secure, the ambulance could be called inside the cordon and so could the senior sergeant. The ambos couldn't do anything for Hall – it was just procedure. The boss asked if everyone was okay and handed around a mobile phone for them to call their families before they woke up to the news on the TV and radio.

Later, detectives from the Homicide Squad arrived and the SOG operatives were all stripped of their weapons, which were bagged and labelled for forensic examination. Their hands were swabbed for gunshot residue and then they were all taken to the Homicide Squad office to give statements.

The day after the shooting, members of Robert Anthony Hall's family were quoted in the press praising the police, saying, 'They've done well, they've done an excellent job.' At the coronial inquest, SOG members were cleared of any fault or liability in the death of Robert Anthony Hall. His family wrote a letter of appreciation to the squad, expressing their gratitude and relief that all of them were okay. They said they knew the SOG had no choice but to take the action they did. The letter brought a tear to Chris's eye, even though he had no issues with the action they took. The shooting was completely justified under the circumstances. But the SOG took a life that day. No-one could turn back time and change things. Hall made the decision to point the firearm at armed police.

Two decades after the event, Chris has come to terms with it. But it doesn't stop him wondering how things might have turned out for Hall if he had surrendered that day.

Chapter Two

THE BLACK WIDOW

On Wednesday 25 May 1994, at the Millicent police station, Sergeant Steve Chapple returned from leave. Millicent lies about an hour's drive into South Australia from the Victorian border. Mount Gambier with its famous Blue Lake is the closest major town.

When he was in his late thirties, Steve Chapple had taken a promotion from the Port Pirie Criminal Investigation Branch (CIB) and was now back in uniform doing general duties. But in uniform or not, there's an old saying: *once a detective, always a detective*. Over the next few days, Chapple had no idea how important his past investigative experience would be.

Not long after he'd arrived at the new single-storey Millicent police station, Chapple received a telephone call from a local woman, Gina Agostinelli. Chapple knew Gina from the Lakeside Caravan Park and Deli. She and her husband Angelo had taken over the business the previous August. It was the closest shop to his house and Chapple regularly dropped in to buy milk and a newspaper.

When Gina said her husband was missing, Chapple drove straight to the caravan park to take an official missing person report.

Angelo and Gina shared a shabby on-site caravan close to the sandy-coloured brick deli overlooking a huge artificial lake, which too much chlorine had turned the same shade as a public swimming pool – which looked odd in a lake.

At thirty-five years of age, Gina Agostinelli was an attractive but somewhat tragic figure: her first husband had died aged twenty-seven, after a short and mysterious illness that had baffled doctors, leaving her with two young children. Now, she sat in front of the sergeant explaining how her second husband of five years was missing. Gina's voice carried slight traces of her Italian heritage as she explained how she and Angelo had argued one night a week earlier and he had stormed out of the caravan. She hadn't seen or heard from him since. Chapple pulled a missing person form from his folder and began to take down the details.

Angelo Agostinelli was thirty-three years old and Chapple ticked his appearance as 'southern European'. Angelo had dark hair and a thick moustache; his photographs bore more than a passing resemblance to tennis player John Newcombe. Gina explained that $5000 was missing from their safe. While the money was gone, Angelo hadn't taken his Toyota 4Runner four-wheel drive, which was still parked behind the deli.

Chapple asked Gina about the argument that precipitated Angelo's disappearance. It had occurred on the night of 18 May. Angelo had said he was bored with his life and had become aggressive and Gina said she had told him to, in her words, 'piss off'. Chapple studied Gina as she spoke. He sensed annoyance rather than concern in her voice.

Before he left, Gina said she heard Angelo make a quick phone call – to whom, she didn't know. Angelo had said two words – *Meet me* – and then hung up. Gina said she hadn't reported her husband missing earlier because he had left her before after an argument. In February, he had been stressed and aggravated; they had argued, and he left to stay with his family in Adelaide. He'd returned when he calmed down. But on that occasion, Angelo had told her two sons where he was going. He chlorinated the artificial lake and then left in his car.

'Was Angelo suicidal?' asked Chapple. Gina didn't think so.

Chapple asked if there were any other women who Angelo may be involved with and Gina quickly volunteered that she had seen her husband in conversation a couple of times with a local woman called Sandra. He could have gone off with her, but Gina wasn't certain. Angelo had not taken any extra clothes, his car or his keys. Gina said she was at a loss as to where he could be.

Chapple returned to the police station and began to make inquiries. He telephoned two of Angelo Agostinelli's friends, who both told him that they hadn't seen the missing man recently. They also confirmed that Angelo had gone to Adelaide in February after an argument with Gina.

Next, Chapple telephoned members of Angelo's family. His disappearance came as a surprise to them – they had no idea that he was missing. They hadn't heard from him for a couple of weeks.

After Chapple knocked off for the day, a couple of other officers continued the investigation. One officer visited Sandra but found no-one at her address. Another officer spoke once again to Angelo's family, who had telephoned everyone they could think of. No-one had seen or heard from him.

The following day, having ruled out that he was staying with close friends or immediate family, the search for Angelo Agostinelli began in earnest. Chapple obtained further photographs of Angelo, and Gina agreed for the media to be used in the search for her husband.

Sitting at his desk at the Millicent police station, Chapple continued the phone chase. Speaking first to Angelo's sister-in-law, he got other names and numbers of friends and family and then spent another couple of hours on the phone, eventually calling as far away as Papua New Guinea. Apparently, Angelo had a friend there who he'd spoken of visiting, but the friend hadn't heard from him for some time.

Drawing a blank, Chapple went back to the Lakeside Caravan Park and Deli to have a more thorough look around. As far as he was concerned, there were only a couple of possibilities: that Angelo had gone off with another woman; that he had suicided; or that he had met with foul play.

While Gina looked on, Chapple searched through the Agostinellis' caravan, finding nothing of value to the investigation. He noted that Angelo's passport was still in the safe, which ruled out overseas travel. Chapple took down the names of yet more friends from a teledex he found in the caravan and then he took a look around the deli. Gina followed him as he searched. She repeated her story about last seeing her husband just before midnight on 18 May. They fought. He made a phone call. Then he left.

According to Gina, when he left, Angelo had been wearing a dark jumper with the words 'Lakeside Deli' printed on it, long bone-coloured trousers and black boots. There had been no transaction on the bank accounts since Angelo had disappeared – Gina had checked. Aside from a couple of disputes with caravan park residents over unpaid rent, Angelo had no troubles with anyone that Gina knew about.

During Chapple's visit, Gina wasn't alone. A man in his late forties called Gary Lewis sat and watched the proceedings. Gary explained that he was a friend of both Angelo and Gina and he and the Agostinellis regularly played cards. He lived in one of the tiny cabins in the caravan park. Gary Lewis was a butcher at the Millicent Woolworths store; he told Chapple that he had last seen Angelo on 18 May. He said Angelo came into Woolworths and was loud and agitated and he had paced the floor before leaving.

When Chapple asked Gary if he and Angelo had ever had any difficulties, Gary explained that he had once intervened when he thought Angelo was going to hit the children – but apart from that, they were on good terms.

Using the teledex numbers, Chapple once again spent hours on the phone, always to be told the same thing – no-one had heard from Angelo since his disappearance and no-one knew where he could have gone. As a matter of course, police checked all motels and pubs in the surrounding areas to see if Angelo had rented a room, but these investigations drew a blank.

Finally, ten days after Angelo disappeared and three days after he had been reported missing, Chapple knew it was time to call in detectives from the Mount Gambier CIB. Chapple had covered every angle and had come up with nothing. The odds of Angelo voluntarily disappearing without taking his car or contacting his family seemed slim and the sergeant knew that if Angelo had only taken $5000, it wouldn't last him forever.

Senior Detective Joe Ryan from the Mount Gambier CIB had worked eight years as a detective around South Australia after having spent seven years on uniformed patrol in Port Adelaide. He had seen a lot in his years as a police officer, but nothing more bizarre than a love triangle where one of the men was killed by another. What made the case stay in Joe Ryan's memory was the fact that the murder house had been literally awash with blood. It had been classic horror movie stuff. His short chat to Steve Chapple gave him little indication that another bizarre case was in the offing.

Ryan arrived at Millicent on Sunday 29 May. He spoke to Chapple in the late afternoon about Angelo Agostinelli. The two officers discussed the case at length and Ryan agreed it was definitely a case the Mount Gambier CIB should take a look at.

Earlier in the day, Chapple had met with Angelo Agostinelli's family, who held fears for his safety. According to them, Angelo wasn't into drugs, didn't owe any money and wouldn't disappear without telling them. Angelo's family also expressed concerns about Gary Lewis. It seemed that whenever they tried to speak to Gina, Gary was always there. They weren't sure whether the two were having an affair, but they did think his perpetual presence odd. Chapple told Ryan that their suspicion of an affair wasn't the first time such a rumour had surfaced. Others had also hinted at a relationship between Gina Agostinelli and Gary Lewis.

On Tuesday 31 May, Sergeant Ron Hope and Senior Detective Alan Rodda arrived in Millicent to examine the growing file on the Agostinelli disappearance. Sixteen of the twenty-six years Ron Hope had been in the job had been spent in various South Australian CIBs. This type of case was unusual. While Hope's turf in Mount Gambier had investigated two murders in the last six years, if Angelo Agostinelli had met with foul play, it would be the first murder in Millicent since 1956. Life in the two towns was fairly tame, although Hope remembered a particularly violent assault where a man had tortured his ex-girlfriend with a car cigarette lighter, tried to run her over, then left her naked to walk six kilometres to find help. It proved that every now and again, the most extreme violence could visit even the sleepiest of country towns.

After a briefing with Steve Chapple, Ron Hope and Alan Rodda knew Gina's side of the story. On the short drive to the caravan park, they wondered whether there would be any inconsistencies when they spoke to her. Gina was in the delicatessen when the two officers arrived and she led them over to her caravan. Setting a micro tape recorder on the kitchen table, Hope began the interview. Gina spoke in a strong voice, showing little emotion or concern for her husband as she went through the details again. A couple of minutes into the interview, Hope asked, 'Have you been having a relationship with a fellow who is a butcher from Woolworths?'

Without hesitation, Gina replied firmly. 'No, I haven't.' There was no trace of surprise in her voice and she didn't sound the slightest bit indignant as she told the detectives they were all just 'very good friends'.

When Hope asked about the telephone call Angelo had made before he left, Gina told him that Angelo had said, 'Meet me,' before hanging up. It had been around 11.45 pm. Hope told her that he would check Telecom records the next day. Gina said she had heard Angelo open the safe before he disappeared, and she assumed at the time that he was taking the $5000. It was the first inconsistency in Gina's story. She had told Chapple that she hadn't heard the safe being opened the night Angelo left and had only discovered the money missing the day after he vanished. Hope asked about life insurance policies. Gina said there were probably three or four, but she said she didn't know how much they were worth.

Another aspect to the disappearance was the fact that Angelo Agostinelli had made inquiries about joining the local branch of the State Emergency Services (SES) and had asked a couple of times about getting the forms to join. One of the local police officers, who was an SES volunteer, had spoken to Angelo shortly before he disappeared. Angelo had told him that he no longer wanted to join because it 'was too late now'. Was Angelo contemplating suicide? Or was he simply annoyed because the SES hadn't sent him the forms to join? Gina could shed no light on the subject.

After the interview finished, Hope and Rodda left Gina and went straight to see Gary Lewis in his cabin. Gary was a small man with short hair parted down the middle and greying at the sides. He invited the detectives into his cabin and offered them a chair at the kitchen table. After they were settled and had explained that they were investigating the disappearance of Angelo Agostinelli, Alan Rodda asked bluntly, 'Were you having a relationship with his wife?' Gary repeated Gina's words that they were just good friends and they all used to play cards together. Gary said that he had a wife from whom he was recently separated and that they were still trying to sort things out.

By his own admission, Gary Lewis was one of the last people to see Angelo alive. He had come into the Woolworths where Gary worked on the day he disappeared. Gary told the detectives that Angelo had been agitated and had paced up and down saying he was bored. According to Gary, Angelo used to visit him regularly at work and the two would often have lunch together. Gary described him as good one day and difficult the next. Apparently, he had a fiery temper with almost everyone he knew, although Gary said that Angelo had never argued with him.

The three men discussed the rumour that Angelo had been seeing the woman called Sandra. Gary said that the previous weekend, he and Gina had driven to Sandra's house to see if Angelo was there. But no-one was home.

Gary also admitted staying in the annex of Gina's van on occasions when she had called him saying that she was scared. He discussed going on nightly walks with Gina but stressed they were innocent in nature.

Alan Rodda was again blunt. 'I suppose the thing that enters our suspicious minds is that you and Gina have got together, had an affair, and done away with Angelo.'

Gary laughed at the suggestion and said coppers always thought the worst. But after chatting for another half-hour, just when the detectives were about to leave, Gary told them he was worried about Gina and her two children and asked if it was all right for him to stay with her in her caravan. Incredulously, they asked if he thought it was a good idea considering the rumours already circulating. Finally, Hope told Gary that the decision was ultimately up to him and Gina.

On the short drive back to the Millicent police station, Hope turned to Rodda and said, 'What do you think?'

Rodda shrugged.

With Gina Agostinelli, it was hard to gauge the truth, but one thing both detectives agreed on was that her account of the phone call Angelo made was strange. To simply say, 'Meet me,' without saying where or when was unlikely. To leave without his car was also unlikely, especially since Gina was adamant she hadn't heard another car pick him up. And then there was the inconsistency about hearing him going to the safe to get the $5000. Angelo's disappearance was definitely strange and both detectives thought there was a distinct possibility that Gina and Gary were having an affair.

The following day, Ron Hope and Alan Rodda contacted their superiors about the Agostinelli disappearance. They also contacted Telecom to check Gina's phone records but apparently the line wasn't connected to the right dispatch, and calls couldn't be checked. They tried to catch Sandra at home and, although there was no sign of anyone there, a neighbour told them that she hadn't seen any men at Sandra's house – let alone anyone fitting Angelo Agostinelli's description.

Hope and Rodda finally located Sandra on Thursday and questioned her about Angelo. Sandra was surprised at the rumours. She admitted to chatting to Angelo a couple of times when she went to the deli, but that was the extent of the friendship.

Another Mount Gambier CIB detective, Kurt Slaven, joined Hope and Rodda in the investigations on Friday 3 June. Slaven had been in the CIB for two and a half years and had come from the Drug Squad. He had seen enough of the seedier side of life and was interested in the Agostinelli case. On the same day, detectives from the Mount Gambier CIB were advised by their superiors not to waste too much time on the search for Angelo Agostinelli. Resources were limited and there were other pressing matters that required their attention. As far as the powers that be were concerned, it was a simple case of a man leaving his wife – probably for another woman, taking $5000, and not wanting to be found. But Ron Hope and his team had a collective gut feeling about this one. They decided to do just a little more checking to see what they could turn up.

Hope, Rodda and Slaven went to the caravan park to speak to Gina again but she had taken her young son who was suffering a sore throat to visit the doctor. While they were waiting for her, they spoke to a woman who worked for Gina and Angelo in the deli. They learned that on the night Angelo had disappeared, Gina had told the woman she had cut her arm on the deli's meat slicer. She had asked her to come in to work the following day.

When Gina returned, Kurt Slaven introduced himself by saying, 'We hear you cut your arm.'

For the first time, Gina's demeanour showed signs of cracking as she nervously rolled up her sleeve to reveal a deep jagged wound.

'How did that happen?' Slaven asked.

Gina led the men outside the deli before explaining that Angelo had in fact inflicted the wound on the night he disappeared. They asked her why she didn't tell them before, but Gina said that she didn't want Angelo to be in any more trouble than he was already in. According to Gina, she'd told Gary Lewis about the injury and he had taken her to the local hospital then stayed for a short while afterwards for a coffee back at her caravan. Hope instructed Rodda to take a statement from Gina in her caravan while he and Slaven went to see Gary Lewis in his cabin.

Gary admitted straightaway that Gina had been injured on the night of Angelo's disappearance, but he hadn't said anything earlier because Gina had begged him not to. He said that he had stayed in her caravan until five o'clock the following morning.

Slaven put a number of scenarios of foul play to Gary Lewis but he calmly denied them all – so calmly, in fact, that the detectives were immediately suspicious. Slaven would say later, 'If that were me, I would have been jumping up and down denying everything and calling for a lawyer.'

Because Gina had been injured and Angelo had disappeared, the detectives called in crime scene examiner Senior Constable Phil Argy. South Australia crime scene examiners did everything from collecting evidence to fingerprint dusting and photographics. Argy had spent eight years as a crime scene examiner and his experience was considerable.

On his arrival at 8.30 pm, Argy met Gina for the first time. He thought she looked nervous as she bared her arm with the jagged scar for the camera. Rodda remained in the caravan with Gina while Slaven brought Argy up to date: they had a missing husband, a woman who said she was cut in the kitchen area of the caravan, and a possible accomplice in Cabin 1. As the crime scene examiner, it was Argy's job to find evidence to prove or disprove Gina's story.

As he examined the caravan, Argy wondered why anyone who had $5000 in the caravan safe could live in such a hovel. The caravan was tiny and old and the two young boys slept in a covered-in annex.

Argy questioned Gina closely to see where she had been standing when Angelo cut her. The cut was deep enough to look as if it had almost penetrated to the bone. It would have bled profusely. Gina took a large knife out of the kitchen drawer and said it was the knife Angelo had used. She said he had stabbed her near the kitchen bench, but when Argy tested the surrounding areas, he found no traces of blood.

Outside, using torchlight for illumination, Argy tested Angelo's Toyota 4Runner. While the four-wheel drive was fairly clean, a small stain in the rear luggage section tested positive for blood.

Using this information, Gina was questioned closely about which vehicle Gary Lewis had taken her to hospital in. She said that Gary had driven her in Angelo's four-wheel drive and she had sat in the front passenger seat with a green towel wrapped around her arm. The detectives didn't tell her that they had found traces of blood in the back, but they did ask her if at any time she had been anywhere else in the vehicle apart from the front seat. She said she hadn't. Argy asked if anyone else could have bled in the car. Gina couldn't think of any occasion, except when their dog was injured and they had to take it to the vet. But on that occasion, they hadn't used Angelo's car.

Argy asked to see the green towel that Gina had used but she said she had given it to another resident of the caravan park, Helen Miller. Mrs Miller had taken the towel to wash it for her but she had recently left for Perth on a holiday and Gina hadn't got the towel back.

The four police officers figured that if Gina and Gary Lewis had killed Angelo, they could easily have transported his body in the back of the four-wheel drive and dumped him somewhere. The question was where.

But theories were one thing and proof was another – one small spot in the four-wheel drive reacting positive for blood didn't really prove anything. The detectives reluctantly left the caravan park, leaving the vehicle there. They didn't alert Gina to the fact that they had found anything in it. Argy returned to the police station to arrange for Central Crime Scene officers to assist in the further examinations, while Hope and Slaven called in to the local hospital to check Gina's story. One of the doctors remembered suturing a deep cut on Gina's arm on the night in question.

Over the weekend the police, together with SES members, scoured the area surrounding the caravan park looking for Angelo's body.

On Monday 6 June, Kurt Slaven and Phil Argy went back to the caravan park with officers from the Central Crime Scene Section. They brought more advanced equipment for blood testing and the officers went straight to the four-wheel drive. To Argy's dismay, the small spot in the back had been scrubbed clean. But on the positive side, if someone was worried enough to scrub the tailgate, there must be something to hide. He and his fellow officers knew they needed to go over the four-wheel drive with a fine toothcomb. If Angelo's body had been in the back, there should be other blood evidence, so they focused the search around the back of the vehicle.

Argy shone a torch down the slim space where the back window went down inside the tailgate and saw blood. After that, it was plain sailing. The crime scene officers found tiny streaks of blood on the protective metal strips around the tailgate, and when Argy lifted the inside handle that opened the tailgate, he found large globules of thick congealed blood underneath the handle. He called to the others and saw Slaven punching his fist in the air crying, 'You bloody beauty!'

While Slaven and Argy were carrying out their examinations at the caravan park, Alan Rodda telephoned the Adelaide Coroner's office to check into the death of Gina's first husband. According to their records, the young man died of adult respiratory distress syndrome (ARDS) and a 'presumed viral infection (nature not known)'. According to records, doctors at the time seemed happy to certify his death as a viral infection and he was buried without a post-mortem examination.

Rodda spoke with Angelo's family to see if he had ever donated blood. The blood found in the back of the car would need to be tested to see if it was his. Failing that, it was also possible to test the blood against members of Angelo's immediate family. If the blood was Angelo's, the DNA could be matched with that of his parents or siblings. The whole family agreed to give blood – by now they were sure there was foul play involved in Angelo's disappearance and they were eager to help.

At the caravan park, the next step for Slaven and Argy was to go inside and tell Gina Agostinelli they were seizing the car. She seemed calm enough and handed over the keys, saying she had no idea how the blood could have got there. Argy studied her carefully, considering what they thought she had done. He had a strong feeling that she would come up with some sort of explanation for the blood in the car and wondered what it would be.

The crime scene examiners searched the deli for anything that could be considered evidence. They found a bottle marked 'Poison' in the shop and bagged that as evidence. Gina also handed them a green towel – the one she had given Helen Miller on the night her arm was cut. Helen had given it back to her.

Alan Rodda and Kurt Slaven paid a visit to Helen Miller in her on-site caravan. Helen was in her late forties. She lived in the caravan with her husband Henry, who was in his early sixties. The two detectives noticed Henry's badly scarred face and Helen explained that he had skin cancer. Once settled inside the caravan, the detectives asked her how she came to wash the blood-soaked towel for Gina Agostinelli. Helen said she had arisen around 5.30 am on the morning after Angelo disappeared. She was on her way to the caravan toilet block when Gina called her over explaining she had hurt her arm and asking Helen if she could help her in the deli that day. Helen also offered to help with the washing and it was then that Gina had handed her the blood-soaked green towel. Helen had just returned from Perth and had given the towel back to Gina.

Rodda and Slaven took down her statement.

The following day, both Gina Agostinelli and Gary Lewis were escorted to the local clinic for blood tests. Both went willingly.

A couple of hours later, Argy wasn't surprised when he was called back to the caravan park to examine and photograph a number of pop rivets in the window of one of the hire caravans. Helen Miller's husband, Henry, had come forward with a story about Angelo cutting himself while he was drilling in the rivets. According to Henry Miller, Angelo had backed his four-wheel drive up to the caravan and was using the tailgate as a workbench. He had cut himself on the drill and Miller said that, although the cut was superficial, Angelo had a small trickle of blood running down his arm. Miller also had something interesting to add – he said he had come forward with his story after Gina had told him about the blood found in the back of the four-wheel drive. It appeared that Gina was working behind the scenes.

The only problem with Miller's timely story was that it didn't account for the large amount of blood they had found.

With the police circling in on the inconsistencies in Gina's stories and her close association with Gary Lewis, Sergeant Ron Hope made an application to the Major Crime Squad in Adelaide for listening devices to be installed in both Gary Lewis's cabin and Gina's caravan in the hope that the two would discuss the investigation. Gina had her two young sons and her parents staying with her in her caravan so Hope figured it was more likely she would speak candidly with Gary in his cabin.

On Thursday 9 June, Ron Hope organised a briefing at the Millicent police station to discuss the evidence so far. Eleven police officers involved in the case discussed strategy for nearly three hours. The general feeling was that Gina and Gary were both involved in Angelo's disappearance, but the blood in the car was the only solid evidence against them.

Authority was given for the planting of listening devices, and Gina and Gary were both picked up for questioning again while the technicians made their way to the caravan park. Unfortunately, Gina's children and her parents were in her caravan at the time, but the technicians were successful in planting a listening device in Lewis's cabin.

Over the next couple of days, detectives from the Mount Gambier CIB played a waiting game. Frustration levels were high. Every day, Kurt Slaven and Alan Rodda made the fifty-kilometre drive to Millicent to review the tapes of conversations in Gary Lewis's cabin. Gina and Gary said little about the case, but Gina did say to Gary, 'I think I love you,' and the detectives listened to sounds of the couple having intercourse. At least they now had evidence that rumours of the affair were true. The detectives also maintained a constant presence at the caravan park. They questioned Gina and Gary almost daily, but the couple remained cool, calm and collected.

On Sunday 12 June, five members of Angelo's family met Kurt Slaven and Alan Rodda at the Millicent police station. Although they agreed to meet Gina at the caravan park to film a televised plea for Angelo to return, one of Angelo's brothers was initially reluctant. He said quietly to the detectives, 'I don't want to see her because she killed my brother.'

A local reporter covered the story while a cameraman filmed Gina flanked by Angelo's family outside the deli. Gina looked toward the camera and said in an emotional voice, 'Come home, Angelo; we're all hurting.'

When Slaven and Rodda reviewed the listening device tapes on Tuesday 14 June, they discovered a new twist to the case. Helen Miller had visited Gary Lewis in his cabin and told him that she wasn't strong enough to cope with what had happened. Gary then spoke to her about yoga and how he used it to keep his wits about him.

Slaven looked at Rodda. *Was Helen Miller involved too?*

The following Wednesday, detectives finally orchestrated the opportunity for Gina's listening device to be installed. The whole family was kept busy in the deli while a technician crept into Gina's caravan and installed the device. It didn't lead to anything. Gina was usually with her children and members of her family, so the recorded conversations had nothing to do with Angelo's disappearance.

On Sunday 19 June, Ron Hope organised a search of the Canunda National Park. He figured that if Angelo had been murdered and his body dumped, the national park was the closest place to effectively conceal a body. The search failed to turn up anything, but all the detectives involved thought it highly likely that Angelo was in there somewhere.

Two days later the four detectives – Hope, Rodda, Slaven and Joe Ryan – sat down around the cluttered desks of their office and discussed what evidence they had. At the end of the meeting they decided that Helen Miller was the weak link in the whole thing. Her cryptic conversation with Gary Lewis certainly indicated that she knew more than she was letting on. They decided to call her in for questioning. If they could shake her up a bit, she may well implicate Gary and Gina in Angelo's disappearance. Sure enough, a nervous Helen broke down almost immediately and told her story. She explained that Gary had come to her caravan around 1.00 am on the night Angelo had disappeared. Gary told her that there had been an accident and asked her to come and sit with the children. Once inside Gina's van, Helen learned that Gina and Angelo had fought and that he had cut her arm. Helen had minded the children while Gary drove Gina to hospital. When they had returned, Gary told Helen that Angelo was dead and that he (Gary) had shot him through the head right there in the caravan although there was no blood around. According to Helen, Gina had said very little, suffering from the after-effects of her injury. However, she did urge Helen not to tell the police about what happened that night and together, they concocted the story about Helen first seeing Gina the morning after Angelo had been murdered.

This was the breakthrough the detectives had been waiting for. They now had something more solid against Gary and Gina. Helen was scared and the detectives thought it best that she and her husband leave the caravan park and stay with relatives.

Detectives Alan Rodda and Joe Ryan went to Gina's caravan while Ron Hope and Kurt Slaven went to Gary Lewis's cabin. Kurt Slaven said to Gary, 'You told Mrs Miller that you killed Angelo.'

Gary looked at the two detectives with disdain. 'Is that right?' he asked dryly before settling into a sullen silence.

Gina and Gary were taken to the Mount Gambier CIB offices and arrested for the murder of Angelo Agostinelli. Both requested a solicitor.

Following the arrest, the four detectives again tried the weak-link strategy. Of the two, they felt Gina was more likely to crack. All along, Gary Lewis had been abnormally calm. They doubted if he would ever crack. They decided to read Helen Miller's statement to Gina.

'I honestly don't know where the body is,' she said after listening calmly to the statement. 'I want to see a solicitor.'

When the solicitor arrived, he spoke first to the detectives. They made it plain to him that they needed the location of the body. But neither Gina nor Gary wanted to talk.

The following day, there was a rush of activity. Crime scene examiners went back to the caravan park to give Gina's van another thorough going over. Alan Rodda interviewed a car detailer who told him that Angelo's car had been thoroughly cleaned and detailed nine days before he disappeared. This meant that any evidence found in the car was likely to have occurred after the cleaning since all the carpets had been shampooed, including the area in the back. Another officer spoke to Gary Lewis's boss at Woolworths, who told him that Gary had borrowed some strong cleaning detergent a little while ago.

The detectives also went back to see Helen Miller. She handed them a piece of paper. On it, she had written details about the night Angelo died. Gary had shot Angelo in the head and stabbed him. According to Helen, Gina was holding Angelo while Gary stabbed him and he had cut her arm accidentally.

Ron Hope called in members of the STAR search and rescue team from Adelaide. He found out that there was an offal pit at the Canunda Tip that adjoined the national park. Local butchers all had a key to the pit, which they used to dump their waste. Twenty-five people were used in the search for Angelo's body, but they found nothing.

Kurt Slaven again spoke to Gina's solicitor. He told him that if Angelo's body was found, it would be better for Gina and it would also ease the suffering of Angelo's family. Later that afternoon, the solicitor called back saying that Gina would lead them to the body on the condition that she be asked no questions. Slaven readily agreed. A short time later, he was driving down the dirt roads of the Canunda National Park with two detectives from the Major Crime Squad and Gina with her solicitor in the back seat of the police car. Gina was emotionless as she gave scant directions in a monotone. Crossing a small bridge on the Bevilaqua Fort Road, she said it looked familiar but minutes later, she suddenly told Slaven to stop.

'This isn't the road,' she snapped. Slaven was angry. She knew where the body was and now she was playing games. He was about to say as much when her solicitor stopped the proceedings and requested that they be taken back to the police station. Slaven did a U-turn and he suddenly realised that this must be the place. Gina had led them right to it and then she had backed down. Later that evening, he and Phil Argy returned to the place with their powerful police torches. They knew that a thorough search would be instigated the next day, but they couldn't wait. They found nothing.

On Saturday 25 June, the detectives contacted Gary's solicitor. He told them that Gary was ill and couldn't assist them with the search, but he was willing to pass on directions. It didn't surprise Kurt Slaven when Gary's directions matched the exact area where Gina had told them to stop.

Fifteen police officers drove to the national park, pulled their vehicles to the side of the dirt road and began walking along, peering into the thick scrub on either side. They only went 200 metres further than the point where Slaven and Argy had suspended their search the night before when Slaven smelt a foul, rotting odour. Without even looking, he knew that the month-long search for Angelo Agostinelli was over.

'We've got it!' he yelled, sending the others rushing over.

Crouching down and peering into the heavy undergrowth, Slaven saw a boot. He reached in to try to feel if there was a body attached. There was.

'How the hell did they get him in there?' Slaven asked, looking through the thick foliage.

Ron Hope joined the throng with a great sense of relief. He was in charge of the investigation and now it was over. He radioed for a pathologist to attend the scene and got the SES workers to clear a path through the bush to the body. Using their equipment, they hacked through the thick bushes towards the body, which had been partially covered by broken branches. Those venturing close enough saw that the body was dressed in a dark jumper adorned with the words 'Lakeside Deli'.

When the bush was cleared, the pathologist supervised the removal of the immediate surrounding scrub while Argy photographed the proceedings. As Argy stared down at the badly decomposed body, he was thankful that he and Slaven hadn't come upon it in the dark the night before. The mouth was frozen open in a silent scream. The flesh was rotting back from his skull and what remained of the chin was a green colour. The pathologist bent down trying to breathe upwind and carefully picked off a number of maggots and sealed them in a small jar. They would be used to help determine how long the body had lain in the bush.

In this hive of police activity, a local news program filmed the police from a distance.

After the discovery of Angelo's body, Gary Lewis was prepared to make a statement. Alan Rodda and Joe Ryan conducted an interview the following day – Sunday 26 June. Ironically, Gary refused to be interviewed by Kurt Slaven because he said the detective – with his thick moustache – reminded him too much of Angelo.

Gary Lewis was in the mood to make a full admission and what he was about to say would lead to two other people being charged. He began by describing his relationship with Angelo and Gina. While he had initially liked Angelo, Gary told the detectives that he had seen Angelo acting violently towards Gina and the children and had begun to get closer to Gina because she confided in him.

'I came home from work one night and I ran into Mrs Miller and she told me that she had crushed tablets and put them in Angelo's food.'

Apparently, Helen Miller had often cooked for Angelo and Gina. Helen had also told him that her son Adrian had gone to Melbourne once to try to get drugs to feed to Angelo. Helen and her son had felt sorry for Gina too, and they had all joined forces to get rid of Angelo.

After months of procrastinating, Gina had finally decided that she couldn't take it anymore.

On the night of the murder, Gina called Gary to come over and according to him, Angelo was again abusive. Later, Gina called him again after Angelo had gone to sleep. She was hysterical and wanted Gary to kill him that night. Gary said that he had been standing by Angelo's bed when the sleeping man awoke and lunged towards him. Angelo had then tripped and – according to Gary – hit his head on the sideboard. He hadn't bled, but there was a big lump on his head. Gary had pulled the dazed man out through the caravan and loaded him into the back of the four-wheel drive, telling him they would take him to the hospital.

Gina was hysterical and yelling at him and Gary said he 'just couldn't think straight'. They had then headed off into the bush surrounding the Canunda National Park. By this stage Angelo was 'getting pretty upset' and when they slowed down near a little bridge in the national park, Angelo told Gary to stop because he wanted to be sick. They had all stepped out of the car. Gina screamed for him to 'do it' and finally Gary turned around and stabbed Angelo with a knife. 'I'll never forget his voice. He just yelled at me: *What did you do that for?* We just put him in the back of the car and drove.' Gary Lewis was adamant that he only stabbed Angelo once. He said the body-dump site was familiar because he used to go horse riding there.

Rodda asked how Gina had received the wound to her arm and Gary said, 'Apparently when I stabbed him, I hit her as well.'

Rodda asked if Gina could have been holding her husband as Gary stabbed him.

'I don't know,' he replied.

It was after the stabbing that they had loaded Angelo into the back of the car and driven to the area where they dumped him.

Alan Rodda knew the importance of pursuing the poison allegations that Gary had made earlier in the interview. Once again, he said that Helen Miller had told him that she used to crush tablets into cakes and feed them to Angelo. Apparently, discussions had been going on for 'a long time' between Helen, her son Adrian, and Gina about killing Angelo. Gary implied that Helen had spoken about 'doing in her husband as well' because he was suffering from skin cancer and was occasionally short with her. He also added that before he had entered Angelo's bedroom, Helen had joined him and Gina in discussions outside the caravan.

The interview was interrupted by a knock at the door. Joe Ryan left to take a telephone call from the pathologist who had performed the post-mortem examination on Angelo's body. He had counted five stab wounds. Angelo's head had also been crushed above and around his right eye with a weapon with a circular striking surface – probably with a hammer or mallet. The pathologist counted nine separate bone fragments in Angelo's skull. The head injuries alone would have killed him.

Gary Lewis denied that he had bashed Angelo and stuck to the story about Angelo hitting his head on the sideboard.

The following evening, Helen Miller was brought in for another interview. She in turn implicated her 24-year-old son Adrian, who was also brought in for questioning. Between the mother and son, detectives listened to an incredible tale.

The Millers said they helped Gina plan Angelo's murder.

The initial plan was to drug him and then kill him. Ideas of shooting him and dumping him in the middle of a marijuana crop were also bandied around to make the death look drug related. Gary Lewis had been involved all along. Indeed, he had got 200 milligrams of diazepam from a chemist, saying it was for his horse. He told the Millers that if it could knock out a horse, it should be able to do something to a human. The drug had been administered to Angelo via cola, coffee and port but had only succeeded in slurring his speech. On another occasion, Gina had given Adrian Miller $600 to buy drugs in Melbourne. Adrian told the detectives he was a sex worker in Melbourne and he knew where to buy drugs. He had spent the money on speed but Angelo had woken the morning after with only a headache. On a third occasion, Helen had emptied eighteen capsules of an anti-depressant into whipped cream and made cream puffs, which Angelo ate. On that occasion, he simply fell asleep.

Adrian Miller told the detectives that Gina had said to him, 'I'm not going to put up with this any longer. I don't want half of what he's got in a divorce. I want it all.' Apparently, Angelo's insurance and assets totalled nearly $400,000.

Then came the bombshell. Both Adrian and Helen admitted that Angelo wasn't the first person Gary Lewis had murdered. According to them, Gary had hired an itinerant man called Bluey to kill Angelo. Bluey had stayed with Gary at the home of Gary's ex-partner while she was out of town. Gary told the Millers that after taking a $1000 payment, Bluey refused to kill Angelo so Gary had killed him instead.

The morning after, Gary had taken Adrian and Helen to the house in Millicent and had them scrub clean the carpet in the lounge room. He told them he had killed Bluey, wrapped his body in an old waterbed bladder and dumped him in a creek bed under a bridge in Bevilaqua Ford Road – the same place where Gary later told the detectives he had stabbed Angelo.

Adrian and Helen both stressed that they had only been involved to help Gina. Helen was the motherly type and Gina had appealed to her maternal instincts. Adrian had been drawn into the plot as well. They were both simple, gullible people and it seemed to the detectives that through their confessions, they lifted a huge weight off their shoulders. They were both charged with murder.

After the interviews had finished, detectives gathered to plan a search for Bluey. Phil Argy went to the house where the alleged murder had happened and examined the lounge room. He found traces of blood in the area of carpet described by the Millers, and there were also traces of blood on the ceiling and on the top of a door frame in the lounge room, consistent with a spray of blood. In a garden shed, Argy found an old waterbed bladder cut down the middle like a body bag. It was damp inside and it too tested positive for blood.

Even though the evidence strongly suggested that the story Gary Lewis told the Millers about killing Bluey was true, searchers found no trace of a body under the bridge on Bevilaqua Ford Road. However, the search wasn't wasted. They did find a mallet that matched the size of the weapon used to inflict the wound to Angelo's skull. Opinion remained divided about the existence of Bluey. Despite extensive media coverage, detectives found no-one who knew who he might have been. All Blueys recorded as missing were checked but didn't fit the scant description they had. The Millers had never seen him and his identity remained a mystery. As indeed did his existence. Some wondered whether Gary Lewis was simply testing the Millers' loyalty.

But considering the forensic evidence, it seemed like a very elaborate hoax.

Gina Agostinelli and Gary Lewis fronted court at the end of February 1995. The terrible tale was made public. The Millers pleaded guilty to the lesser charge of accessory after the fact and made solid prosecution witnesses. Helen Miller was sentenced to a four-year jail term with a one-year non-parole period. Her son received a one-year suspended sentence and a three-year good behaviour bond.

Gina and Gary changed their not guilty pleas to guilty after the trial began. Gary's lawyer told the court that Bluey was a figment of his client's imagination. He had simply invented the idea of a hit man to stall for time because he was so reluctant to kill Angelo. Gary also denied any knowledge as to how Angelo received the crushing blows to his skull. The judge was scathing. He said there were 'very large areas of unknowns' surrounding the whole case.

When Gina's lawyer told the judge that his client was remorseful, the judge replied, 'I take that with some hesitation.'

On 26 February 1995, Gina Agostinelli and Gary Lewis were both given non-parole periods of twenty years for the murder of Angelo Agostinelli.

Not long before the trial, Sandra – the woman who Gina suggested Angelo had left town with – was found hanged at her home. Her death was ruled to be a suicide.

Nothing ever came of investigations into the death of Gina's first husband. Experts said that if he had been poisoned, there would be no traces of poison left in his remains after all that time.

Bluey was never found despite extensive searches of the Canunda National Park.

Just after the twentieth anniversary of the murder of Angelo Agostinelli, Sergeant Steve Chapple, retired by then, spoke of the murder to journalist Kate Hill from ABC South East SA.

'I think Bluey is somewhere out there in Canunda National Park,' he said.

And what did he think of Gina?

'The fact that she could so coldly kill him and not break down, not give away hints about what had really happened to him … I've dealt with a lot of people over the years, whether they've been involved in murders or other things, and she was very good at what she was doing.'

By the time the article was written in 2015, Gina Agostinelli and Gary Lewis had been released from jail.

Gary Lewis had been transferred to a Tasmanian prison in 2009 to complete his sentence and apparently had done community-based work prior to his release. His release in 2011 was cause for comment in the Tasmanian media.

Chapter Three

ON HER DEATHBED

On Wednesday 28 October 1998, Tina, a 25-year-old nurse, was working a nightshift at a small suburban private hospital. Tina was rostered on the oncology ward with patients who had cancer in its various forms or stages. The young woman was a dedicated nurse who put her patients first.

When agency nurse Darren Fary arrived a little after 10 pm, Tina divided up the beds in the ward, giving him beds 31A to 35A, and she took beds 35B to 40B. The lights were dimmed after the bustle of the day, and the nightshift was looking relatively peaceful. The patients mostly slept and Tina and Darren spent quiet times sitting and chatting at the nurses' station. Even though they'd just met, 33-year-old Darren spoke at length about himself, his friends, places he'd worked, and even his previous relationships. Occasionally, a buzzer would sound and one of them would go and answer it.

At 12.30 am, Tina told Darren that she was stepping outside for a cigarette. She had just put Mrs Vincent in room 40A on a bed pan and told Darren that she should be fine but to help her if she needed it. Tina left Darren at the nurses' station and stepped out the main door of the hospital. She was only gone a couple of minutes. When she returned, she noticed the buzzer light flashing in one of Darren's rooms, 32B, and since Darren was no longer at the nurses' station, she assumed he'd gone in to help old Mr Wentworth in 32B and forgotten to turn off the buzzer.

Tina returned to Mrs Vincent's room and when she'd finished with the bed pan, took her pulse and blood pressure. From Mrs Vincent's room, 40A, Tina could hear a rocking sound coming from one of the adjoining rooms – either 38 or 39. It was a rhythmic sound – sort of like a bed moving, rather than someone moving *in* bed. She thought it unusual and knew it couldn't be room 39 because the patient in room 39 was 68-year-old Mrs Munroe, who was dying of cancer. She had been unconscious for the past two days and was not expected to live much longer.

The buzzer from 32B sounded again and Tina went in to turn it off, figuring that Darren must have forgotten. When she walked into Mr Wentworth's room, the elderly patient asked where the other fella was. He asked if Tina was a nurse too; she assured him she was and gave him some Panadol.

Wondering where Darren had gone, Tina went looking for him. Mr Wentworth was *his* patient, and it wasn't up to her to look after his patients as well as her own.

Starting at room 31, Tina popped her head into the dimly lit room and quietly called Darren's name. He wasn't in room 31 and so she went along to each room till she got to room 37 near the kitchenette. From where she was standing, she could see into room 39. From that vantage point, she could hear the sounds again – the rhythmic rocking noises and now, she also heard soft grunting noises – a man's deep grunting. The curtain she'd left open earlier was pulled all the way around the bed in room 39. The light she'd left on had been turned off, and the room was dark. There was no reason for the curtain to be closed and the light off.

Tina suddenly knew there was something wrong and felt sick to her stomach.

She hurried into the room, turned on the light, and flung open the curtain. Darren was standing right up against the edge of the bed leaning against Mrs Munroe's buttocks. She had been curled up into a foetal position and her buttocks were hanging over the side of the bed. Darren was pressed up against her. As soon as Darren saw Tina, he fumbled around his groin area but remained pressed up against Mrs Munroe. He looked shocked that Tina had walked in and was nervous and shaking.

'What are you doing?' she said incredulously.

'Nothing.'

'What are you doing?' she repeated.

'I heard a groan and she was restless, and I was just trying to make her comfortable.'

Tina stared at him in disbelief.

'Why ... what did you think I was doing?' he asked.

'She's unconscious!' said Tina. And then she became aware of her own predicament. She was alone with a man in a ward full of very ill sleeping patients, and suddenly got scared. Tina had the presence of mind to play the situation down and keep things calm.

'How about we move her up and get her comfy?' she said in as normal a voice as she could muster.

Tina moved to the opposite side of the bed. She noticed that the incontinence sheet under Mrs Munroe had been moved – nurses sometimes move patients by sliding them on the plastic-lined sheets. As Darren helped move Mrs Munroe, he remained pressed up against the side of the bed and kept the sheet bunched up in front of his mid-section. Nonetheless, Tina noticed that when he moved slightly away from the bed, Darren's fly was undone. When Tina pulled Mrs Munroe back towards her, she saw Darren fumbling with his pants and when he moved away, she saw his fly was now half zipped up.

All the while, Darren chatted nervously, but Tina was too preoccupied with what she had just witnessed to listen to what he was saying. She believed that she had just witnessed a rape and, even though the thought made her feel sick, she was desperate to act normally and keep the situation calm.

'Can you help me with Mrs Vincent?' she asked, wanting to get out of the room and act like nothing had happened. The two nurses walked into Mrs Vincent's room and Tina told Darren that she thought the patient needed a bladder scan.

'I'll just nick upstairs and tell the coordinator to order the scan,' she said.

Racing upstairs, Tina rushed into the coordinator's office and burst into tears. She told her what had happened. The coordinator called the director of nursing who arrived twenty minutes later. The nurses then called the police.

Detective Senior Constable Sue Hughes unlocked the door to the Moorabbin Criminal Investigation Unit (CIU) offices at 6.50 am on Thursday 29 October. She was working an early shift and still had her key in the door when she heard the phone ringing. It was never a good sign when the phone rang before you even got in the door. Stumbling through the dark, deserted offices, she grabbed the phone and answered it. On the line was one of the nightshift detectives.

'We've got a situation down at the hospital,' said her colleague. To Sue Hughes, a 'situation' meant that things were complicated. An assault was an assault, a theft was a theft, but a 'situation' could mean anything – or nothing.

'What is it?' asked Hughes.

'We think one of the patients may have been raped.'

'Well surely, the patient would *know* if she's been raped,' said Hughes.

'Not this one. She's unconscious. She's a 68-year-old cancer patient who's dying.'

Sue Hughes was shocked. She wondered how anyone could do that. Her partner for the shift, Trevor McDonald, arrived as she was still on the phone and he turned on all the lights.

When the detective on the other end of the phone began giving her directions to the hospital ward, Hughes told him not to bother, she knew it well. Her father had been a patient on the very same oncology ward only a month or so earlier.

Sue Hughes and Trevor McDonald drove to the hospital and met the nightshift detectives who had gathered in a room away from the ward to discuss the best way to proceed. Darren Fary had been sequestered in a small room nearby and he sat wearing on odd selection of clothes because the nightshift detectives had bagged his clothing for evidence. The handover crew gave Hughes and McDonald the lowdown on the case.

'The female nurse heard the bed creaking. She's pulled back the curtain and he's there with his fly undone and the old lady has been pulled right over to the side of the bed and the nurse can see her bare buttocks. He's fumbling round with his fly and the nurse reckons he's raped the patient.'

'You're joking!' said Hughes, knowing he wasn't. She looked over at the suspect sitting alone in the adjoining room. She was careful to speak in low tones. 'What kind of sick piece of shit does that to someone?' When it came to talking to a suspected sex offender, Hughes knew from experience that detectives have to minimise whatever it was that an offender has done – no matter how awful – to get the suspect to open up. If sex offenders were belittled or antagonised, they tended to clam up.

As she was walking back to the ward to talk to Tina the nurse, Hughes realised the dying victim's room was two rooms down from the one her father had recently occupied. At fifty-six, her father, Tony, had recently been diagnosed with a tumour in his bowel and had come to this ward for surgery. Revisiting the ward brought it all back for the 33-year-old detective. The vibe this time, however, was different. Instead of being a daughter visiting her sick dad, she was now a detective walking past nurses who were all so shocked and disturbed by what had happened, they refused to meet her eye and bustled past doing their rounds ignoring the fact that their corridors were filled with uniform police and plainclothes detectives.

Speaking to Tina, Hughes was impressed with how forthright and sure of herself she was, even though she was very distressed and still shaken about what she had seen.

'There was no reason that Darren should have been in that room,' she declared. 'I had left Mrs Munroe on her back with the curtain open and the light on. It is not normal procedure to pull a curtain around a patient and turn the light off to move them. And if he was going to move her, it is normal procedure to ask another staff member to help. He knew where I was. He could have easily asked me to help.'

Detective Hughes asked Tina to describe what she had seen. Tina, who had by now told her story to the coordinator, the director of nursing, the uniform cops, and then the nightshift detectives, obliged by repeating what had happened. Tina described how she had seen Darren with his fly undone and how he had told her that he'd moved Mrs Munroe because she had moaned in pain.

'There is no way Mrs Munroe could have moaned or communicated in any way that she was uncomfortable. Earlier in the night, I had assessed her level of consciousness by pressing her nail for signs of pain or reaction. I checked her response to gentle shaking and verbal stimuli and she gave no reaction whatsoever. She is totally unconscious and incapable of any speech or movement.'

Hughes asked if Darren's fly could have been undone before the incident. Tina said, 'I saw Darren several times before I found him in the room with Mrs Munroe. He stood in front of me earlier and I didn't notice that his fly was undone then and I believe I would have. He didn't go to the toilet prior to me finding him at Mrs Munroe's bedside, because he would have had to walk past me to go to the toilet and I would have seen him. Even when I was out having a smoke, he still would have had to walk past where I was.'

'How long do you think it was between when you went out for a smoke and when you found him with Mrs Monroe?' asked the detective.

'About ten minutes,' replied Tina. Both women shuddered at the thought of what could have occurred during that time.

Tina said that Mrs Munroe was only dressed in a hospital night-gown with the standard back ties. Because she was incontinent, she wore no underwear. She also wasn't expected to live much longer.

Outside the dying woman's hospital room, a uniformed police officer stood keeping a crime scene log of everyone who went into the room that had now become a crime scene. Sue Hughes stepped into the room, which was quiet and peaceful apart from the raspy breathing of the dying white-haired woman who lay in the bed. Her face was slack in unconsciousness and her short hair was messed and flattened. The room bore no signs of the recent attack and questions ran through Hughes's mind. Did she suffer? Did she feel it? Could she have known what had happened? The detective was hard-pressed to think of anything more horrible than for her to be raped in her dying hours.

Soon after Hughes had finished speaking with Tina, she saw Mrs Munroe's husband arrive. He was in his late seventies and looked completely dazed. Around 6.20 am, he had been woken at home by detectives at his door telling him that his dying wife may have been assaulted at the hospital. The police needed his permission to forensically examine her. None of the detectives involved could think of a worse situation for the elderly man to be in.

By the time he arrived at the hospital, Mr Munroe was told that it would be best to wait outside while a crime scene examiner completed his work.

The next job for Sue Hughes and Trevor McDonald was to interview Darren Fary at the Moorabbin CIU offices. Fary had been taken there earlier by the nightshift crew and was waiting in the interview room.

Hughes looked at Fary with interest. A check of his date of birth revealed that he was the same age as her; they were born in the same year but his birthday was a month earlier. Hughes reflected that in her thirty-three years, she had joined the police force and become a detective; while given the same thirty-three years, Fary had become a nurse and a rapist.

'We need to have a forensic procedure done on you,' said Hughes after the preliminaries had been taken care of. 'The nature of the procedure that we seek to conduct is the taking of a blood sample, the taking of some pubic hair, and the taking of a penile swab. Do you understand all this so far?'

'Yes.'

Hughes explained that the procedure could be done with his consent or by a court order.

'Go ahead and take the samples you need,' replied Fary.

Fary sat quietly in the interview room. He was average in every way. Hughes thought – and not for the first time – that really normal-looking people were capable of doing really despicable deeds. After Fary agreed to the forensic procedure, Hughes and McDonald drove him to a local doctor's surgery and stood in the room with him while the doctor took the required samples.

The drive back to the CIU offices gave Hughes and McDonald a chance to develop a rapport with their suspect. They chatted about nursing in general and Fary seemed to open up.

'You realise that when we get back to the police station, we're going to have to talk about what happened,' said Hughes. She was driving and glanced at Fary in her rear-vision mirror. She saw his head drop down in a gesture she took to be a mixture of guilt and shame. In the unguarded moment in the rear-vision mirror, he looked small, podgy and pathetic.

Back at the station, Fary again sat in the interview room. The detectives reminded him of his rights and continued the interview after offering him something to eat. Fary said he wasn't hungry.

Hughes led the interview. She began by asking Fary to explain how agency nursing worked. She then led the questioning around to his being assigned the hospital shift the previous night, and then to the circumstances surrounding the alleged rape.

'What happened in room 39? The patient, Mrs Munroe ...'

'I don't know her name.' Fary didn't make eye contact. He stared down at his fleshy hands.

'She's a terminally ill patient suffering from cancer. Were you aware of that?'

'I would have been told what her condition was. I knew the lady in there was unconscious.'

'Can you tell me what happened when you went into her room?'

'Yeah, I went in, checked to make sure she was dry. Sort of ... I star ... I ... I ...' Nervously, Fary stumbled over his words. 'I changed her position. I was moving her around, trying to make her ... she didn't look comfortable and I was changing her position. And I don't know what happened, I really don't. I don't know why ... but I stuck my penis in her.'

'Okay,' said Hughes keeping her voice even. She had to get Fary to be more specific. Fary went into detail about what he had done and then became upset.

'Are you okay?' she asked.

'No, I feel sick.'

Hughes asked Fary if he wanted to take a break, but he didn't. He wanted to go on.

'Do you feel sick because of the nature of the allegations and how you feel about yourself ... or something else?' asked McDonald.

'I feel sick thinking about what I did.'

McDonald got Fary a drink of water.

'It's bloody disgusting,' said Fary, sipping his water. 'I've been sitting in a room mostly by myself since about half past three this morning and all I've been thinking is what the bloody hell did I do it for? I can't for the life of me ... I just don't understand it ... I didn't go into that room to do what I did. I honestly didn't. I went in there as a nurse to care for that woman and I did something bloody terrible. And I just don't know why. I don't understand it; it doesn't make any sense.'

As most rapists do, Fary tried to minimise what he had done. In

Hughes's mind, he was probably more upset by getting caught than by what he had done.

Fary explained that Mrs Munroe hadn't looked comfortable and that 'her legs were sprawled out' and all he was doing was checking whether the incontinent woman was dry.

Sue Hughes wasn't buying it.

'The other nurse said that she wasn't able to move … and that she was lying completely flat on her back with her legs down.'

Fary then resorted to: 'I just wasn't thinking clearly …' At the time, he said, '… it was very foggy …' – a much easier response than admitting a pre-meditated rape on a dying woman whom you are being paid to care for.

Trevor McDonald wanted to make the point clear for the tape: 'So, you're sure of what you saw, and what you were doing, but you're not sure what you were thinking?'

'Yeah, that's right, that's correct,' said Fary.

Describing the rape, Fary told the detectives that he 'stuck it in once or … a couple of times … I don't know, a few times, and then I just stopped and I thought, "What the hell am I doing?" You know, I stopped and I withdrew. I was pretty bloody horrified with myself.'

In Sue Hughes's opinion, the only reason that Fary stopped and didn't finish the act was because he was interrupted. Another awful realisation for the detectives was that Fary would have known that a cancer patient dying in hospital wouldn't have had an autopsy performed and naturally wouldn't be checked for signs of rape. So if he hadn't been caught, Fary may well have gotten away with it.

His attack was so slick they wondered if he'd done it before.

Having spoken at length to Tina, the nurse who had made the report, Hughes knew that the rhythmic creaking of the bed went for around ten minutes from the time she first heard it till the time she interrupted Darren in room 39. But Fary was noncommittal. He said that the squeaking sounds must have been a result of him pumping up the bed.

After a few more questions, Hughes asked Fary, 'Do you realise what you've done is you've committed the offence of rape?'

'Yeah, I do,' he replied. Fary then told the detectives that he had recently had a close friend die, and then he'd had a relationship break-up.

'So it's fair to say that you've got a few personal problems at the moment?'

'God, yeah!'

Fary's problems then became much worse when the detectives read him his rights again and charged him with the rape of Mrs Munroe.

When the interview was over, Sue Hughes returned to the hospital with her sergeant, Ken Stanlake. Now that they had an admission of guilt, they wanted to speak to Mrs Munroe's family. The matter was so delicate and fraught with horror that the detectives decided to speak to Mrs Munroe's son, who was in his early thirties, rather than speak to the elderly Mr Munroe, who still looked dazed and shocked.

Asking the son to come with them into the small visitors' room, the detectives sat him down and broke the terrible news to him. Being in this room was doubly awful for Hughes. It was in this very room, only a month or so earlier, that her mother had sat Hughes and her sister down to break the news to them that their father's cancer was inoperable and terminal. Now *she*, Sue Hughes, was the bearer of bad news.

'We've interviewed the nurse,' said Hughes as gently as she could, 'and he's admitted having sex with your mum.' She avoided using the word 'rape', feeling that it was just too awful in the context of the frail unconscious woman lying in room 39. She waited for the son to say something. Anything. He didn't. He just stared at the detectives seemingly unable to comprehend what he was hearing.

Get mad! Start crying! React! thought Hughes. Having experienced this room as a family member, she also couldn't help but think: *How would I feel if I was in his situation?* The whole thing was so utterly heartbreaking.

'Do you have any questions?' she asked, more to break the silence.

'Not right now,' said the stricken son.

Hughes handed him her business card and told him to call her if he needed to talk. The detectives left it up to the son as to what he would tell his elderly father, who was by now at the bedside of his dying wife. They had all suffered enough.

Back at the police station, Sue Hughes rang Tina, the nurse who had raised the alarm. Tina was relieved that Fary had admitted to what she knew he had done. In fact, Hughes had a hard time remembering a witness who had been *so* relieved.

Mrs Munroe died at 12.48 pm on Friday 30 October – thirty-six hours after she was raped. She never regained consciousness. Her doctor would later write in his report: '... one would have to suspect that in this situation that she would have had no awareness of the sexual assault that occurred.'

Everyone connected with the case could only hope he was right.

The confession of Darren Fary wasn't enough to build the case on and Sue Hughes and her colleagues still had to corroborate his statement with evidence. Tina made a credible witness and was clear and forthright, but Mrs Munroe's test results for traces of semen or DNA to connect her with Fary came back inconclusive. Fary had denied ejaculating into the unconscious woman and the evidence backed this. Evidentiary swabs taken from Fary were also inconclusive.

One thing that made Hughes more determined than ever to win this case when it went to court was an off-hand comment by an ex–Rape Squad detective. He told her that she didn't have enough evidence for a conviction. Fary could recant his statement, and she would have little else. It wasn't unheard of for a suspect who had confessed to claim later that he was tired or under duress and then take back his confession. Furthermore, there was no victim, since Mrs Munroe had died. Hughes was also determined to win the case because her own father's illness with cancer was worsening. He was admitted several times to the same hospital where Fary had assaulted Mrs Munroe and each time she visited him, Hughes was reminded of what had happened.

When her dying father was admitted for the final time, Hughes rushed to the hospital to be with him. All the way into the oncology ward, she said over and over, 'Not that room, please, not that room.' Luckily, he was in a ward a couple of rooms down from room 39 and its memories.

As her own father lay unconscious in his final stages of life, Hughes felt unable to leave his bedside. It wasn't that she didn't trust the nurses but ...

During the long vigil, hospital staff encouraged the family to talk to their unconscious dad as if he could hear them. And they did. During all this time, Hughes couldn't help wondering that if they assumed her father could hear his family even though he was unconscious, then what if Mrs Munroe knew ...?

Around four months after the rape of Mrs Munroe, and the day before Darren Fary was due to go to trial, Sue Hughes worked an afternoon shift at Moorabbin and took a call from a detective at the Malvern CIU.

'We've got an overdose suicide,' he told her. 'One of your crooks.'

'Which one?' Hughes asked, wondering which of the many offenders it could be. Many of the 'crooks' she dealt with had drug problems.

'Bloke by the name of Darren Fary. Overdosed on pills. We saw your name on some court papers we found at his flat.'

'Did he leave a suicide note?' asked Hughes.

'Yep. It says something about how he couldn't believe he had done what he had been accused of.'

Hughes thought the wording ambiguous. He hadn't denied what he'd done, but at the same time, it could be read that way. She thanked the detective for letting her know and slowly hung up the telephone. Her first thought about the suicide of Fary was that there were no winners in a case like this.

His death obviously spared Mrs Munroe's family the trauma of a trial and the subsequent media attention. Hughes had no doubt that because the attack on Mrs Munroe was everybody's worst nightmare, the media would have reported at length on the shocking nature of the case. But, in a strange way, Fary's death robbed those connected with the case of the proper closure.

Hughes rang Mrs Munroe's son. 'I don't know how you are going to feel about this,' she began, 'but the fellow who assaulted your mum has killed himself tonight.'

Again, she experienced a long silence before the son finally said, 'I don't know how I feel.'

A couple of years after the rape by Darren Fary, Sue Hughes remembered the case as the one in her long career in the police force that affected her the most – partly because of the horrific nature of an attack on one of society's most vulnerable, and partly because during this period, her own father lost his battle with cancer at the very same hospital.

Hughes's mum, sister and aunt were nurses – and she knew from her own experience that nurses were, by and large, wonderful people who do a hard job under often difficult circumstances. The fact that Fary was also a nurse, and had people's trust and then abused it, was a travesty.

She feels, in hindsight, that she was denied her own day in court. She wanted to prove the Rape Squad detective who'd said she had little chance of a conviction wrong. She wanted the wheels of justice to turn in the way they should, and send a rapist to jail.

Fary not only raped a dying patient, but traumatised her grief-stricken family. In the end, everybody lost. Darren Fary's family lost a son, and Mrs Munroe's family lost the only opportunity they ever had to support their mother gently along her journey to the hereafter.

Chapter Four

THE SEARCH FOR COMMISSIONER O'SHEA

Commissioner Jim O'Shea left his home in an inner-Melbourne suburb on Tuesday 20 April 1993 for a spot of bushwalking. His destination was the Buckland Valley, a drive of around three and a half hours north-east of Melbourne. He intended to walk the bushland Alpine Walking Track in the famed Banjo Paterson high country. Jim would have taken his youngest son, Tom, with him, but the boy had joined a new football team. His first game was coming up and he needed to attend training. Jim went alone, intending to take a couple of days and return Friday.

Jim enjoyed communing with nature and had been bushwalking for as long as he could remember. He had walked much of Victoria and knew some of the more popular walking tracks like the back of his hand. With a two-week break ahead of him from his job at the Industrial Relations Tribunal where he worked on the thirty-fifth floor of the Collins Street building, Jim couldn't wait to hit the bush. He was always conscious of 'sick building syndrome' – in his mind high-rise offices with windows that couldn't be opened, and thousands of workers breathing artificial air from giant air-conditioning units, just wasn't natural. He never felt completely well working in such environments. To add to the stresses of his job as Commissioner, all day, every day, he sat in judgement between arguing parties of unions, workers and bosses.

Yes, the peace and quiet of the bush was always a welcome change in the life of Commissioner Jim O'Shea.

It was the school holidays and Jim's wife, Rosie, was taking their daughter, Libby, away to Anglesea for a few days. Jim was looking forward to a couple of days to himself in the Victorian high country. In fine weather, there was nothing like a mountain view, spotting native birds, and challenging himself physically. Bushwalking elevated Jim O'Shea's spirits. If the truth be told, Jim was the only one of his family who yearned for the bush. When his children were younger, he'd tried to take them camping a couple of times, but they didn't take to it like he did. Sometimes he walked with friends. Often he went alone.

Leaving on the Tuesday, Jim drove to Bright and stopped for fuel and supplies. From Bright, he drove to the Buckland Valley. He had been to this area dozens of times and drove the winding road to his favourite camping place off the dirt road about 150 metres and pulled his four-wheel drive into a small clearing near a river of rushing water. He planned to spend the first day in the valley exploring and taking photographs. On Thursday, he planned a walk, and then he'd drive home on Friday. Rosie and the kids were expecting him. This trip was probably the last time he would be able to come up this way for some months. It was mid-autumn and come winter, many areas in the high country would be inaccessible or closed to the public.

After pitching a tent by the river, Jim collected a bundle of firewood and built a fire to cook sausages for dinner. As the dusk settled into night, Jim sat back, watched the sunset, and became reflective as the stars came out against a backdrop of inky black. Life didn't get any better than this. Every now and then, he heard the distant howls of dingoes, and occasionally, the splashing of a platypus near the riverbank. The campsite was isolated but that was what Jim craved – the peace of the bush.

The campfire crackled and Jim kept it built up. Nights get cold in the high country.

The walk Jim planned for Thursday 22 April was, by his reckoning, around twenty-eight kilometres. He would drive to the walking track that would take him to The Twins – two jagged outcrops above the tree line. Normally when he was bushwalking, Jim would photocopy the relevant maps, mark his course, and then carry the map in his pocket. But because this was a walk that he could comfortably manage in a day, he didn't do it this time. The quiet of the night was broken by the occasional rustling of a nocturnal creature nearby.

Jim was up with the sparrows on the Thursday morning. Kookaburras sang in a chorus with magpies and parrots. The mountain air was clean and crisp as the sun rose over a nearby hill. He cooked a breakfast of bacon and eggs and freshly brewed billy tea. After this, he had a wash in the river. He looked for a platypus, but the water was rushing too quickly for the little creatures and he didn't see any. Jim packed a bag with the supplies he would need for the day: a soft-drink bottle filled with water, a box of matches, a torch, some lollies, a couple of last night's sausages, and a banana. It was a lovely autumn day and Jim dressed in a T-shirt and shorts.

Around 8 am, Jim left his campsite and began the hour-long drive down Selwyn Creek Road heading towards the Alpine Walking Track. Other times when Jim had visited this region, he had met rangers and other bushwalking enthusiasts, but on this trip – between Easter and the snow season – there wasn't another soul around.

Jim parked his vehicle in the spot where the Alpine Walking Track met the four-wheel drive track. He loaded up supplies for his walk. Jim had a jumper with him but figured that if he wore it, he would get too warm, so he left it in the car. He locked his four-wheel drive and pocketed the keys.

When Jim walked in the bush, he focused his mind totally on his surroundings and got immeasurable pleasure out of everything – the smells, the sights and just being in his beloved bush. Jim set off walking at a brisk pace on this challenging hike. In the distance he could see The Twins and Mount Saint Bernard.

After Jim had been walking for a few hours, the landscape in the high country altered.

Initially, the vegetation was mainly gum trees and small shrubs growing densely on both sides of the walking track. Further on, at higher altitudes, the heavy bush gave way to ghost gums. Then finally, Jim found himself walking above the snow line, surrounded by hardy little plants that could survive and regenerate after the winter snow melted. At one point, he rounded a bend and stopped to take in the breathtaking view – it seemed that the whole of the Australian Alps was laid out before him for his enjoyment alone.

Once he reached The Twins, Jim stopped and had lunch –

sausages, a banana, and a generous swig of his water to sustain him for the long walk back to his car. Jim packed up his kit bag and began his return journey. Once he hit the dense bush beneath the snow line, Jim noticed that the sun was dipping rather low in the sky and he realised that he had badly underestimated the time it would take him to get back to his car. He quickened his pace, but to his dismay, late afternoon was upon him and he could tell from the terrain that he was still a long way from his car.

Dusk fell and Jim realised suddenly that he'd lost the ridge line – all along, he'd been on the walking track that followed a ridge line up and down the mountain. Now, he could see that he was on a track, but there was no ridge line. This could only mean that in the fading light, he'd inadvertently left the main track for another. He hadn't realised until it was too late and, by then, it was too dark to turn back and try to retrace his steps. Looking upwards in the darkening bush, he thought he could make out the ridge line above him.

The predicament that he found himself in was worrying, but Jim was more irritated than anything else. He knew that he would have to camp out for the night and find the track in the morning. He quickly gathered some wood to make a fire to protect himself against the cold. He had finished his water over the course of his long walk, and he knew that having no water presented him with a further problem. After walking over twenty kilometres in the sun, he was dehydrated and would need to find water as soon as possible. But at these altitudes, he knew finding water was impossible. He would have to do that first thing the next morning.

While he was confident he would find the track in the morning, Jim was momentarily afraid. He was also incredibly thirsty and worried about his dehydrated state. With his bare hands, he scraped out a hole in the ground and gathered some leaves to keep him warm. He spent an uncomfortable night curled up on leaves in a hollow of dirt on the hard ground and didn't sleep much at all.

When Jim woke the next morning, he was thirsty rather than hungry. He sorted out his remaining provisions – a few lollies and part of a bar of chocolate. In the dark, he inadvertently dropped some of the lollies at his campsite. At first light, he was surrounded by fog and mist and he found it impossible to distinguish any features of the landscape that surrounded him. He was below the ridge line but could make out none of the mountains he knew. He waited for as long as he could, but the mist didn't really clear.

Jim knew he needed water before he could even consider searching for the track. He also knew very well that creeks and rivers run down the mountains, so he decided to battle his way downwards through the thick bush to try to find water. Later, he could climb back up to the ridge line in search of the track.

There was no track in sight and Jim began his battle with the bush. Particularly destructive were the native nettles that looked like any other small knee-high bushes, but when you forced your way through them, they sliced at your legs. Jim was conscious of the scratches and cuts he was getting but that wasn't foremost in his mind. Most of all he needed water, but he did allow himself to think: *How silly am I to get lost out here?*

After a long and arduous descent, Jim could finally make out the sounds of running water. The hill he was climbing down was so steep he ended up sliding mainly in a sitting position, edging down gingerly with his feet to stop himself from tumbling down it.

All of a sudden, he lost his footing and started to slide.

The last thing he remembered was sliding down about ten metres and smashing the back of his head against a rock ...

When he regained consciousness, Jim opened his eyes and stared up at the sky and tried to focus. His vision was blurred and he realised that he had lost his glasses in the fall. He tried to move but he was paralysed and lay still where he had landed. It seemed like ages before he began to get some feeling back in his body and it was then that the terrible pain hit him. He lifted his head and felt underneath it. When he removed his hand, it was soaked in blood. Jim realised then that he was in deep trouble. His glasses were gone and without them he could hardly see, and now he imagined he was concussed as well. His first thought was that he had to find his glasses. Painfully, he rolled over so that he was on his hands and knees. He crawled a little way upwards and found his glasses. One of the lenses was missing and the other one was badly cracked and almost impossible to see through.

Jim crawled back down towards the waters of the Wongungarra River. He drank from the river and filled his water bottle. By now, the back of his head seemed to have stopped bleeding, but he could feel a substantial gash.

Ever the practical man, Jim's thoughts were: *What's the best thing I can do now to improve my situation?* He knew that the track was on higher ground but with concussion and no proper vision, he knew he would never find his way out unaided. On a practical level, he knew it was Friday and he wasn't due home till the afternoon. He also knew that his wife wouldn't start to worry till Saturday and possibly not even report him missing until Sunday so it was pointless trying to reach the higher ground when no-one would be looking for him for a day or two. He was stuck.

Jim had a dawning realisation that in his current predicament, he could conceivably vanish off the face of the earth and no-one would ever know what had happened to him. Caught in the bush with only light clothing, a head injury and no chance that anyone was looking for him yet, Jim worried that he might never see his family again.

For most of the day, he rested and tried to stay focused on what he could do to improve his situation. When Jim began to feel better, he decided to try to climb to higher ground just in case there were others in the bush who could rescue him. He lit a signal fire around midday. He wandered back and forth along a ridge and then made the slow arduous ascent until he reached a small plateau where he spent his second night in the elements. He used his matches to start a campfire to keep warm.

Saturday 24 April

Saturday morning came and Jim woke up sore, hungry and thirsty. He was a day overdue at home, and he thought that Rosie would report him missing either today or tomorrow. Just in case anyone was out looking for him at this early stage, Jim decided to enlarge his campfire. The wind sprang up and the fire quickly burnt away from him. Guessing that the fire was travelling west, he walked behind the fire figuring someone might spot it and him too. As he walked,

Jim tried to locate Mount Murray because he knew it by sight and if he found it, he would be able to get his bearings. The trouble was that without his glasses his eyesight was so limited, he didn't know whether he couldn't see Mount Murray because it wasn't there, or whether it was right in front of him and he simply couldn't see it.

Parts of the fire that Jim was following burnt out around midday, so Jim made his way back to the river to refill his water bottle. He climbed slowly back up the hill to the top of the spur where he figured his chances of being sighted were better.

With lots of time and little else, Jim decided to divide the days into blocks of twelve hours to better keep track of time. He spent the rest of the day resting and trying to figure out where searchers might begin looking for him. The trouble was, Jim had no idea where he was.

Sunday 25 April

On Sunday, when he made the descent back down to the Wongungarra River, Jim knew that he wouldn't have the strength to return to the higher ground. He found himself a sturdy stick for support and decided to follow the river. He knew from his study of maps of the region that the rivers ran like veins through much of the high country and often crossed roads or tracks. He figured that searchers would imagine he'd stay near a water supply. No food for several days and a head injury meant Jim was in no condition for a long hike. His legs were becoming infected after being scratched by the nettles and his whole body was a mass of bruises and cuts.

Along the Wongungarra River, Jim found a knoll that was elevated enough in the mountainous region to be clearly visible from the air and he set up camp there. The knoll was sunny and warm during the day so Jim decided that he should try to sleep during the day and have his waking hours at night where he could light a fire and keep it going for warmth. During the long nights, Jim's confidence in being found waned. He felt bad that he'd let his family down. Two of his children had left school and two were still at school. He knew there was only one person to blame for the mess he was in, and that was himself. The guilt was awful. Jim had no strong spiritual thoughts even though he now believed that there was a likely chance he would not make it through this ordeal. Once he'd come to this realisation, a peace descended on him.

So this is it, he thought.

He was sorry he wouldn't get to say goodbye to his family.

After arriving home from the couple of days away with her daughter, Rosie felt uneasy about Jim's continued absence. On Saturday, she did nothing about it because it felt like admitting out loud that something was wrong. But by Sunday, when Jim hadn't returned home to watch their son play for his new football team, her fears got the better of her and she telephoned the Bright police and reported him missing.

With any missing person, there is a graded scale to aid police to provide an appropriate response. Using the answers to a series of questions based around the age of the missing person, whether they were alone, their medical condition, any equipment and experience they might have, and several other factors, police give points: eight to twelve points denote an emergency, thirteen to eighteen points calls for a measured response, and nineteen to twenty-four points call for an evaluated response; any higher isn't regarded as needing a response. This scale, though originally used by Search and Rescue, had now gained a wider usage.

Local police and D24 took the initial reports and then passed the information along to Sergeant Barry Gibson at the Search and Rescue Squad at 2.30 pm on the Sunday afternoon. Given the time of day and the distance involved, Gibson was unable to provide a Search and Rescue Squad crew until the next day. He did, however, alert and dispatch a police helicopter to search the area.

While he briefed troops and organised equipment for the following day, Barry Gibson also knew it was important to speak to the missing man's wife. Second- and third-hand information wasn't as good as getting it directly from the source. Asking Rosie the emergency response questions, Gibson calculated Jim at fifteen points – a measured response. Jim was experienced, well equipped and in good health. What was tipping him into the emergency criteria was that he was now forty-one hours overdue.

A measured response in this case meant that police from Bright had driven up to the area where Rosie told them that her husband usually camped. They had located his empty camp but found no sign of the missing man. The police helicopter crew reached the scene around 5 pm and did an aerial sweep.

Meanwhile, local police found Jim's car at Mount Selwyn on the Alpine Walking Track.

Monday 26 April

A full search for Commissioner Jim O'Shea was activated on Monday 26 April. A convoy of vehicles from the Search and Rescue Squad left in the small hours of Monday morning for the five-hour drive to the Alpine National Park. Six Search and Rescue police, six local police, four special solo bike police, together with field catering, twenty-five volunteers, ten SES volunteers and fourteen Federation of Victoria Walking Club members made up the initial search contingent. The search was coordinated by Sergeant Barry Gibson from the bonnet of a Search and Rescue four-wheel drive and later from a command post caravan. While Gibson coordinated the search, his inspector, John King, monitored the proceedings. The searchers and coordinators were all fed regularly from the field catering truck.

Gibson knew that – despite early reports about a 'missing fisherman' – Jim O'Shea was not a fisherman and was more likely to be bushwalking. This meant that the search should concentrate on the walking tracks rather than fishing spots. The position of the parked car near the beginning of one of the walking tracks supported this theory. Gibson knew from Rosie and her oldest son, who had come to the search area hoping for news, that Jim had sturdy hiking boots and they thought he would probably have been wearing a jumper and jeans.

Gibson identified and allocated search areas to teams who were briefed and dispatched into the rugged bush. Finally, when all search teams had been dispatched and the search base was relatively quiet, Gibson inspected Jim's four-wheel drive. In the car, Gibson found a book of huts of the Alpine Region and he knew that if the missing man was interested in them, then the searchers needed to locate them too just in case that was where O'Shea was headed. In the car was an open newspaper. Coincidentally, the paper was opened to an article about suicide. The thought crossed Gibson's mind that Jim could have committed suicide and he couldn't rule this out. Gibson also knew that Jim had locked the car when he left it, something a suicidal person might not necessarily have done. Everything was conjecture at this stage.

One of the first things Gibson did as search coordinator was fly around the area in the police helicopter so that he could get as clear a picture as he could of the task ahead. In a situation like this, anything could have happened: the missing man might have met with foul play, might have fallen and injured himself, or he might have taken his own life. At this early stage, it was anyone's guess and all bases had to be covered.

Gibson flew along the ridge line of the Alpine Walking track. From his vantage point, leaning out of the door of the helicopter, he thought he spotted a gold mining pan on the ground below. Over the communication microphone, he arranged for the helicopter to drop him at the nearest clearing, which was about 500 metres from where he saw the pan. Gibson thought that perhaps O'Shea might have been doing a spot of prospecting.

Gibson made his way in the direction he'd seen the pan. Despite a search, he didn't find any sign of it, but he did stumble across a recent campsite. Scattered around were a few lollies. Gibson gathered them up and put them safely in his pocket. Having spent years in the Search and Rescue Squad and knowing a lot about survival in the bush, Gibson knew it was definitely strange that O'Shea – if indeed this camp had been his – would leave such a valuable commodity as lollies behind. It made him wonder if O'Shea might be disoriented in some way.

He then radioed for the helicopter to come and get him and take him back to search command. Once there, Gibson got some men from his crew to take the lollies down to O'Shea's original campsite and see if they matched ones found in the tent. The officers radioed back to say the lollies were a match.

By 10.15 am, the police air crew radioed in that they could see a small spot fire. The helicopter also located two Alpine huts and Gibson dispatched crews on foot to locate them and search the surrounding

areas. Searchers had also located the remnants of a campfire near where the spot fires had broken out.

At the command post, Gibson sectored off the region into easy and difficult terrain. The Walking Club volunteers walked the tracks blowing whistles. A lost person might hear the whistles and move towards the sound, so the tracks had to be walked several times just in case. Police on trail bikes rode along other paths that were less easy to walk. None found any sign of the missing man.

That night, the search management team met in Bright to debrief and discuss search strategies for the following day. Most stayed at local hotels or pubs and got a good night's sleep to be ready for day two of the search.

Tuesday 27 April

Jim O'Shea had climbed to a rocky outcrop near the river the day before and realised he was too weak to go much further. At exactly 12.57 pm the previous day, he had heard the helicopter fly overhead the first time. The outcrop he'd headed to had two large gum trees on top of it and Jim felt that the helicopter might be using this outcrop as a reference point. Every time the helicopter flew overhead, he would wave and shout, but no-one spotted him.

Jim had spent an uncomfortable night there and tried again to sleep during the warmth of the day. The nights were far too cold to sleep and Jim had run out of matches; he tried to rub two sticks together but that didn't work. It was comforting to know that there were people out there looking from him, but frustrating to not be able to make himself seen.

By Tuesday, the search numbers had increased to around seventy people with the police, more volunteers from the Federation of Victorian Walking Clubs, and the SES. Time was of the essence because a new computer program employed by Search and Rescue calculated that Jim O'Shea's 'survival time' was around thirteen hours if he was mobile, and around thirty-five hours if he was stationary. Depending on his condition, the missing man's survival time calculated on current weather conditions was only another day or so. While the days were quite warm, temperatures at night were getting down to single digits.

Things weren't looking good and time was of the essence.

Wednesday 28 April

By Wednesday, the number of searchers had increased to 114. The good news was that the searchers had covered nearly the entire area where they thought it likely Jim would be; the bad news – Jim was seriously running out of time.

Each search day started off positive – *today we'll find him* – then finished on a sombre note when they didn't. Rosie and her son were taken aside and gently told that because so much time had elapsed, the chances of finding Jim alive were growing slimmer with each passing hour.

In his weakened state, Jim decided that his outcrop theory wasn't working so when he made his way down the steep incline to the river to replenish his water bottle, he decided to follow the stream. Several times he saw the helicopter fly overhead, but it didn't see him. Even though he knew that the helicopter and possibly many others were searching for him, he also knew that they may not find him in time. On his backpack, he scratched the words: *Lost. Concussed. Love Rosie and the kids* – just in case his bag was the only thing left at the end of this.

At the evening debriefing, after consulting the complex Alpine region maps, it was clear that search groups would begin to converge the next day. It was also clear that searchers couldn't search under every single tree and fern or they would make no progress at all, so there was always the possibility that searchers had walked straight past an unconscious or dead man.

Thursday 29 April

For Senior Constable Don McConnell, the police helicopter, while sometimes useful to the Search and Rescue Squad, was overrated. It is extremely difficult to spot missing people from the air in the kind of terrain in which people usually get lost. For the Search and Rescue officers, riding shotgun in the helicopter was one of their least favourite things. It was okay if you sat securely strapped on a seat and looked out the window, but that wasn't how searches were conducted from the air.

McConnell strapped on a harness and attached himself to a hook on the helicopter's inside wall for safety. He positioned himself on the floor in the open doorway with his legs dangling out the door. He hung on as it lurched itself into the air. The best way to see below the craft is to hang out the door, and even if you are wearing thermal gear, the downdraft from the rotors means there's a constant powerful stream of air guaranteed to send anyone exposed to it into paroxysms of cold. Another difficulty is that the helicopter observer has to scan the landscape intensely for hours at a stretch. Eyestrain becomes a real problem and bloodshot eyes are often the observer's lot.

Height in the helicopter is deceptive. From the air, it looks to the observer like the land isn't that far away. It isn't until one of the ground searchers becomes visible in their bright orange search gear, and they look like ants, that the observer realises that spotting the missing person is nigh on impossible. McConnell constantly had to be aware of the height so that he could adjust his scanning to the size that O'Shea might be if he was spotted.

It had been a week since Jim O'Shea had lost his way on the Alpine Walking Track. He was weak and running out of energy. He lay on the ground and could hear the helicopter above, but he'd heard it constantly for the last five days and knew that while he could see it, they couldn't see him. This time, though, was different. The helicopter seemed lower and Jim waved with all the strength he could muster and made his way over to the river. With a long stick that he'd used to support himself, he banged it against a frond of a nearby fern.

The helicopter was low on fuel and darkness wasn't far away. Doing a final sweep down the Wongungarra River, McConnell thought he saw something – a fern frond was moving in a huge fern that was otherwise still. It could have been an animal, but the frond moved in a steady rhythm.

'What's that at one o'clock?' he said through the microphone attached to his helmet.

'Yep, I see it,' replied the pilot who banked the helicopter around for a closer sweep. The downdraft from the rotors swept the fronds apart and those on board could see a man below. He was slowly making his way out into the open near the creek.

They had found him.

When the helicopter swept down out of the sky, a feeling of relief overwhelmed Jim. He knew that he'd been found and was no longer alone.

Don McConnell checked with the pilot. Although fuel was low and the light was fading, it was decided that McConnell would be winched down to check on Jim O'Shea. McConnell connected himself to the winch and with the help of colleagues on board, he jumped out of the helicopter and made the swift descent to the ground.

When McConnell landed, it was immediately obvious to him that Jim had experienced a very rough time. What remained of his shorts and T-shirt were rags, and his legs were covered in deep, infected cuts and bruises. He also had a head injury. The first thing McConnell did was remove his heavy police-issue leather jacket and helped Jim put it on.

Until Jim felt the warmth of the jacket, he hadn't realised just how cold he was.

McConnell made a quick decision. They couldn't afford to wait for ground crews and paramedics to get to the scene and check Jim before moving him. It was now or never. McConnell suspected the Commissioner wouldn't last another night out in this weather and he knew that because it was nearly dusk, the ground crew wouldn't get to him until morning.

McConnell signalled the helicopter, which had moved off so the police officer could examine O'Shea away from the downdraft and the roaring engines. He explained to the Commissioner that they would be winched up together and all he had to do was hold his arms by his sides. When the winch cable came back down, McConnell attached O'Shea to a loop connected to his winch harness. Giving the thumbs up to the winch operator, the two men began their ascent.

'Just hang your arms by your side,' McConnell shouted.

'Yep, sure,' Jim replied while holding onto McConnell like grim death. Even though he knew he should let go, his arms simply would not obey. He hung on tightly all the way up to the safety of the helicopter.

Once they were on board, the crew wrapped Jim in warm clothing, and relief flooded into the rescued man's mind – only minutes ago, he was lost and on his own, and now he was being flown to safety. When he settled into his seat, he turned to one of the Air Wing's crew.

'How lucky am I?' he said happily. To his surprise, the police officer turned away without saying anything. At first Jim thought the man didn't hear him, but then he realised he must have look so emaciated, tattered and torn that his comment must have seemed ironic – how can a man so near to death call himself lucky?

The helicopter flew straight to the Bright Hospital, landing right outside, and Jim was admitted into intensive care. He had lost a lot of weight and the cuts on his legs were badly infected. He was also suffering some frostbite.

Just as hope he would be found alive had almost faded, Rosie heard over the radio at the command post that her husband had been found. She and her son went straight to the hospital to see him.

Aside from his joy at seeing his family again, one of Jim's predominant memories is of being in a warm bed. He remembers it feeling incredible. Inspector John King visited the Commissioner in hospital and took a statement of sorts. Jim told him how he had fallen and hit his head and broken his glasses. The statement, including the rescue, read like a lucky escape.

❖ ❖ ❖

It took Jim several months to recover from his ordeal. He stayed in hospital for two weeks after his rescue, while his legs slowly healed and he regained some of the weight he'd lost. For a long time afterwards, friends suggested Rosie attach a ball and chain to her husband to stop him from wandering off again.

As soon as he was well enough, Jim O'Shea wrote a letter of thanks to the then Chief Commissioner, Neil Comrie. He thanked Inspector John King who had attended the search from the beginning and visited him in hospital as soon as he was found.

> First and foremost, my family and I would like to record our appreciation of the role of the Police Search and Rescue Unit, headed by Inspector John King. My comments here cover two separate aspects: firstly the highly professional job of the coordination of diverse groups and resources within the time pressures involved was quite remarkable; secondly, at the human level, Inspector King was still able to find the time to give members of my family reassurance and support when it was most needed. I can do no more than express my thanks to Inspector King and his people for their outstanding contribution.
>
> Thank you again to the Victoria Police. My family and I owe your officers a debt we can only acknowledge: it is simply too big to ever repay ...

A year later, Jim received a letter from a member of the SES. The letter requested that Jim speak to a group of SES volunteers about what he went through to help with their training. Jim was glad to help, considering all that the SES had done for him and his family.

As the date of the talk grew closer, Jim got more nervous. One day, while he was watching a footy match, the mere thought of talking about what he had gone through made him break into a cold sweat. When he got home, he rang the SES member and explained that he couldn't do it – not because he didn't want to, but because he couldn't have spoken to them and remained objective. There was nothing objective about what he had gone through.

The SES letter wasn't the only one Jim received. People from all over the country who had been lost and then found wrote to him and told him that they were so glad he'd been found; reading newspaper accounts of him being lost in the bush had brought back their own lost memories. He wasn't alone.

What does a man learn from such a near-death experience?

'These days are bonuses,' Jim O'Shea said from the comfort of his suburban home a decade after his ordeal in the bush. Getting lost in the bush was a factor in his decision to take early retirement. 'I didn't want to spend the rest of my life going to and from work. Life is precious and I want to enjoy and appreciate it.'

Chapter Five

LOST
AT SEA

The year: 1981. The scene: a press conference at a beach at Point Lonsdale, near the Port Phillip Heads in Victoria.

A young senior constable called Barry Gibson stood near his boss, Inspector Bill Brand, who was one of the founding members of the Victoria Police Search and Rescue Squad in 1957. Brand was being interviewed by reporters. In a sombre voice, he described a recent diving fatality and explained the rescue operation to the media. While exploring the wreck of a scuttled submarine lying outside the heads in forty metres of water, a diver had gone missing, presumed drowned. The inspector explained to the media that his squad would comb the beaches and search the shallows in the hope the body of the diver would surface. When asked if his divers would search the scuttled sub, known as the J2 or 'the broken sub' because it had cracked in half when it was scuttled, the inspector had to admit that his divers weren't trained to dive below twenty metres.

Barry Gibson remained silent. He was only a reserve member of the squad but he couldn't help but feel frustrated. *We're supposed to be the Search and Rescue Squad and all we can do is scour the beaches*, he thought wryly. The sensibilities of the squad were further tested when members had to stand back and watch a team of part-time military divers dive the J2, but even they couldn't enter the sub.

Two subsequent underwater searches were conducted about a month later, but even then, the military divers only searched outside the sub. An internal search conducted months later by a RAN clearance diving team from Sydney found no trace of the missing diver.

Gibson had completed the squad training course the previous year and was working Search and Rescue on a two-month secondment. These secondments were standard so cops who were interested in this line of work could see whether the work actually suited them and, more importantly, the squad could see whether the trainees suited the work before offering them a permanent position.

Search and Rescue cops are specially prepared for rescues in extreme conditions – they are trained to abseil down cliff faces and to be winched from beneath the police helicopter to execute dangerous rescues. For cops of this calibre, having to watch others dive the wreck, then walk the beaches along the coast closest to the wreck hoping that the body would float to them, was an insult to their squad.

To add insult to injury, the diver's body was never recovered.

Members of the public constantly invent new and improved ways to put themselves in dangerous situations. Search and Rescue always needed to stay a step ahead. When caving became popular, the squad had to learn how to rescue cavers who got themselves stuck in obscure subterranean nooks. And when suicides from heights became more common, Search and Rescue learnt to manage recovery and investigation. The more people skied, the more the squad had to study ski and avalanche rescue at alpine heights. In other words, the Search and Rescue Squad had to continually evolve around the needs of members of the community and their leisure-time activities. In the 1980s, recreation diving was growing in popularity and many recreational divers were diving to depths beyond the capability of the police divers.

Barry Gibson became a full-time member of Search and Rescue in 1982 and then left on promotion in 1987. The following year, a position came up at the squad and Gibson applied for it. The position was for a sergeant in charge of the squad's dive portfolio. In his application, Gibson listed his vision that the squad be accredited as a diver training establishment and conduct deep-water diving operations. Gibson got the promotion, but the wheels of change are often slow to turn, and it wasn't until December 1990 that a coronial finding allowed him to pursue his dream of putting his team of divers into the best-of-the-best category.

Deputy State Coroner Wendy Wilmoth had investigated the deaths of a number of divers and in December 1990 handed down her list of recommendations – among them was the following:

> A related matter of importance is the current prohibition on police rescue divers diving beyond a depth of 20 metres. From evidence I have heard, it would seem reasonable to alter this prohibition to a depth of 50 metres, in order to enable rescue divers to affect the rescue or recovery of divers, bodies, or evidence at that maximum depth. It is my recommendation that this alteration be made.

With this coronial imprimatur, Gibson was given the green light to pursue the advanced training. In any given year, around half of the squad's jobs involve underwater operations so the update in skills was timely.

To the non–diving enthusiast, the difference between diving to twenty metres or fifty metres wouldn't mean much, but below twenty metres, diving conditions alter inexorably. On the surface, and in shallow diving, the air we breathe is around eighty per cent nitrogen and twenty per cent oxygen. As you dive deeper, the oxygen and nitrogen are compressed and so while the diver breathes the same volume of air, they are in fact taking in five times as much oxygen and nitrogen. Higher levels of the two chemicals are absorbed into the body. The diver doesn't notice any physical difference – it is only when they begin to surface and the water pressure decreases that the gases begin to slowly expand and diffuse from the system. If a diver from depths below twenty metres surfaces too quickly, nitrogen forms bubbles in the bloodstream and body tissue. This condition is known as decompression illness or 'the bends' – and can be fatal.

Another difficulty with deep diving is that divers can experience a condition known as nitrogen narcosis. The elevated levels of nitrogen can have the same effect on some divers as alcohol; it is well documented that nitrogen narcosis can seriously impair a diver's judgement and behaviour.

In April 1991, having located a group that could train his divers, Barry Gibson and four colleagues – Bob Manks, Don McConnell, Adrian Johnson and Michael Wright – went to Sydney to train with the NSW Police Diving Unit for seven weeks. One week was spent training in underwater cutting and welding. The other six weeks were spent diving in dams, Sydney Harbour, and the ocean – all at depths up to fifty metres.

Bob Manks found deep diving for the sake of it rather cold and uncomfortable. He was used to task-oriented diving where he would go down, follow instructions and then resurface. The movement kept him warm and focused. Simply sinking to great depths and waiting there gaining bottom time was, in Manks's opinion, tedious and cold.

One particular dive stands out in Manks's memory. The trainees had to do a penetration dive inside some huge square concrete outlets through which water flowed from a disused power station to the ocean. The divers had to penetrate the tunnels, which were full of water. Manks says that a diver feels safer if he or she has immediate access to the surface. When a diver doesn't have immediate surface access – such as in a deep water-filled tunnel – it can make for certain levels of psychological discomfort. To make matters worse, on this particular dive, the divers wore older helmets that kept filling with water. Rather than having a side valve that a diver can turn with his or her hand to increase the air levels in the helmets to push out rising water, the older helmets had a button on the inside back of the helmet. When the helmets began to fill with water, the divers had to bang their heads back to hit the valve. Having to do this regularly and cope with being in the huge tunnels was taxing to say the least.

During many of the dives, the five Search and Rescue members kitted themselves out in wetsuits and Kirby-Morgan 17B diving helmets reminiscent of old-fashioned diving helmets. These modern versions allowed the diver to speak to other divers and the surface team via radio. The helmets also allowed surface-air dives, which meant that the divers were connected to an unlimited supply of surface air via a breathing tube connected to the dive boat.

A week of training dives took place at the Avon Dam, south of Sydney. Stepping off the high wall into thin air, the police divers landed in the dam water and let themselves sink to depths greater than they'd ever experienced. They practised diving and measuring the required periods of decompression, to let the elevated nitrogen levels in their blood lower naturally.

Gibson remembers his first experience of deep diving. 'You become very aware of the mechanics of your breathing,' he says. He was also surprised that the increased pressure conditions made people speak like Donald Duck. A combination of Donald Duck–speak and the occasional episode of nitrogen narcosis on dives meant that one of the police divers became rather well known for singing the theme song to TV's *Beverley Hillbillies* in a Donald Duck voice with only a minimum of encouragement.

The training was often gruelling. Some days, the divers had to do 500 push-ups. All through it, Gibson kept saying to his colleagues, 'The benefits will come ...' This became their training mantra.

At the end of the seven weeks of training, the Search and Rescue police divers returned with certificates of diving competency to fifty metres. It was an achievement to be proud of for Gibson and his fellow officers. Never again would they have to stand on the sidelines and watch other divers do their job for them.

It would take a further five years for history to repeat itself.

A group of qualified recreational divers left the wharf at Queenscliff a little before 8 am on Friday 10 January 1997 aboard a charter dive boat called the *Corsair*. Ironically, the *Corsair* had been used in the search for the missing diver back in 1981. There were twelve divers and two crew members aboard the well-equipped dive boat. Julia and her husband Glen, both aged twenty-eight, were among the divers headed out to dive the wreck of the *Courier*, which was scuttled in 1928 in the ship graveyard. The *Courier* lay in around forty metres of water just outside the Port Phillip Heads, close to shipping lanes. On the way to the *Courier*, the dive group received radio information that there was a tanker in the shipping lane so they decided to dive the J2 submarine instead.

The J2 sub was one of six J-class submarines donated to Australia by the British in 1919, after the First World War had begun. Because of huge running costs and a decrease in the defence budget after the war, the subs proved too costly for the Australian government to run so three of them were scuttled in 1924. The salvage company who scrapped the subs had to sink them in deep waters. The J1, J2 and J5 were sunk outside a three-mile radius beyond the Port Phillip Heads.

When the J2 was scuttled, it was blown open in front of the coning tower, about halfway along its length. The break in the hull of the broken sub proved a popular entry point for recreational divers over the years. The sub's depth varied according to the tide, and since it was eighty-four metres long, the bow lay around forty-two metres deep while the stern was around thirty-four metres below the surface.

Julia and Glen had been diving together since 1992. Both were competent divers. Glen had completed several hundred dives, Julia, eighty-three dives – eight of those had been at depths greater than thirty metres. They both had deep-diving training and qualifications.

On this warm, overcast summer's day, the *Corsair* made its way through slightly choppy seas to the site of the J2 sub. A shot line with a weight on the end was released to indicate the site of the wreck. On the surface, the shot line was marked with an orange buoy with a dive flag on top. Another line was sunk carrying a spare tank of air at the nine-metre mark in case any of the divers needed spare air to decompress on the way up.

The dive master on this trip, an experienced diver called Geoff, briefed the group on the required safety considerations. Because the J2 was so deep, maximum bottom time was only seven minutes. If any diver exceeded seven minutes on the bottom, they would have to stop at the nine-metre mark for several minutes to let the nitrogen levels in their system subside.

Glen and Julia were first in. They had checked each other's equipment and dived downwards to have a look at the J2. Beneath the surface, they could see about three metres in front of them. Visibility reduced on descent to about one and a half metres. Once Glen and Julia reached the bottom and found the sub, they communicated by hand signals. Glen pointed to the top of the sub and both divers entered it via an open hatchway. The space inside the hull was high enough for them both to stand upright. Via hand signals, Glen asked Julia if she wanted to explore inside the sub. She gave the okay signal. The two carefully swam along the rusting corridors, Glen in front, Julia following behind. The divers had to be careful to avoid twisted bits of metal jutting from the walls. Twice, Glen stopped and turned back to see that his wife was okay. She was.

They swam towards the broken midsection and decided to keep going. Two other divers passed them going in the opposite direction. Glen intended to swim five or six metres further into the hull, then turn around and leave the sub, but the movement of the divers they'd just passed had disturbed the silt lying on the bottom of the sub, swishing and swirling it around them, reducing visibility to zero.

Glen and Julia became disoriented. Glen stopped and tried to feel his way along the sub's walls. His wife was still with him. When they were trying to feel their way out of the wreck, Glen's dive alarm sounded. He knew they had to get out quickly – they had exceeded their bottom time of seven minutes. Things were now getting dangerous. Glen reached out and grabbed Julia's hand and put it on his tank valve. He squeezed her hand indicating for her to hang on to him. He felt his way along the wall and came to a section he thought he'd passed already. By this time the silt and the walls seemed to blend in front of him and it was hard to tell which was which. He changed direction and continued to follow another wall. He finally made it to the first bulkhead and could see some light ahead. As soon as he reached the break in the sub, he turned to check on his wife, but she wasn't behind him.

Desperate, Glen swam back into the hull to the second bulkhead searching for Julia but he could see no sign of her. He turned off his torch to see if in the blackness that surrounded him he could see his wife's torch beam, but he couldn't. In his panic, Glen collided with something protruding from the wall of the sub, which knocked his mask off and his breathing regulator out of his mouth. Grasping for his secondary regulator, he cleared his mask and put it back on. He was dangerously low on air. He swam back to the break in the sub and had one last look for his wife. He was no longer certain whether she was still in the sub. She might have gotten out ahead of him. Glen made the choice to swim for the surface. He didn't stop for decompression – he didn't have enough air for that. He had spent seventeen minutes on the bottom, which required twenty-seven minutes of decompression on the way up. Glen hit the surface after a two-minute ascent with dangerous levels of nitrogen in his system.

When he surfaced, Glen signalled to the boat, which immediately came over to pick him up.

'She's in the sub!' he yelled. 'I can't find her! She's in the sub! Can somebody go back down and try and find her?'

Geoff, the dive master, radioed for other divers to assist. As he was on the radio, one of the crew yelled that he thought he saw a diver on the surface. Everyone looked over the side but no-one could see anything. Dismayed, they agreed it must have been a seal.

Glen was extremely distressed. He knew Julia would have been low on air but she could have been on the shot line. One by one, other divers began surfacing. Each diver was asked the same question: *Did you see Julia?* It was difficult because visibility was limited under water and of course, divers covered in wetsuits, wearing masks and regulators all looked alike in the dim, murky environment.

Two divers aboard the *Corsair* attempted a rescue. They were both experienced deep-divers but they had limited air in their tanks. They too had dived the wreck and knew the dangers of a second dive. The residual nitrogen from their first dive elevated their risk of decompression illness. However, two brave men, Alan and Paul, risked their lives to try to find Julia. As Alan climbed up the ladder of the *Corsair* after his dive, he could hear Glen's chilling message: *she's in the sub ... can somebody go back down and try and find her ...*

Alan pictured finding Julia and bringing her alive to the surface, and that image overrode his terror at the thought of running out of air. Alan used half his air on the descent to the sub. Visibility at the bottom was grainy and dark. He could feel his tank running out of air. By the time he made it to the sub wall, his air had run out and he made his way back to the shot line where he had attached a second regulator. He knew the second small 'pony' bottle wouldn't last and he had to ascend. Halfway up, the pony bottle began to run out and his dive computer beeped decompression warnings. He tried to slow down but air was dangerously low. He thought he was going to drown but then he saw the hang tank at the nine-metre mark. Alan remained at the hang tank breathing from the spare air supply until his dive computer indicated that he was out of decompression mode. Nonetheless, the two dives had put Alan at great risk. He was put on pure oxygen as soon as he resurfaced.

The other diver, Paul, also heard Glen asking if anyone had seen his wife. Paul also thought Julia might be on the shot line but as divers surfaced from the shot line, it became apparent that Julia wasn't among them. He asked Glen where he'd last seen his wife and it wasn't until Glen replied, 'In the sub,' that Paul realised that Julia was in grave danger. He tried to pin Glen down to an exact location. Glen explained that he and Julia had entered the sub at a hatch close to the shot line. They had gone through the wreck, out through the break and into the second half, and that was where they had become separated.

Paul swapped air tanks with someone who had more air left and dropped back into the water to make his way back down to the J2. He made it to the sub with enough air in his tank and was able to swim along the top of the sub, looking down through any openings. At the break in the sub, Paul swam inside a couple of metres but visibility was poor. By then, he too was critically short of air. He then saw a dim light through one of the openings and he made his way through it looking for tell-tale signs of bubbles that would show him a live diver was there. He saw none.

Racing for the surface, Paul wasn't near the hang tank and resurfaced quickly because he was running out of air. He tried to slow his descent at the three-metre mark but his air finally ran out. On the deck of the *Corsair*, Paul apologised to Glen: 'I'm sorry I couldn't find Julia.'

Paul felt light-headed and was given pure oxygen. He was later sent to the Geelong Hospital to be checked out. He was fine, but the other two divers weren't so lucky. Both Glen and Alan were rushed by air ambulance to the Alfred Hospital's hyperbaric chamber. Alan was severely affected. His decompression illness meant two weeks off work and ten subsequent sessions in the decompression chamber.

The harsh reality of the rescue attempts was that there was little chance of finding Julia alive. If her husband had run out of air on the way up, she too would have run out of air around the same time.

The Water Police and the Air Wing were dispatched immediately to do a surface search for Julia's body.

The evening of the tragedy, Senior Constable Greg Paul from Search and Rescue interviewed Glen after he came out of the hyperbaric unit at the Alfred Hospital. The other divers and crew from the ill-fated expedition had been interviewed at the Queenscliff police station. All of the dive equipment, bottom timers and dive computers had been collected for examination for the inevitable inquest brief. Greg Paul had spent most of the day at the scene and told the distressed husband that despite the huge police response to his wife's drowning, conditions were too rough for them to attempt a recovery operation. Rescue officers also didn't have access to a boat big enough and stable enough to cart their equipment and to support their surface-supplied air apparatus, but they had organised access to one for the next day.

Glen was distressed that Search and Rescue was unable to recover his wife's body. He urged the police officer to let members of his dive club find her. Greg told him firmly that it was the responsibility of Search and Rescue to conduct the recovery. He didn't need to remind Glen that of the experienced divers he'd been with that day, one had perished, one had ended up at Geelong Hospital, and two, him included, had ended up with dangerous decompression illness.

Despite the fact that Glen had just lost his wife in shocking circumstances, it was Greg's job to get as much information from the bereft husband as he could to narrow down the search area for the body retrieval. Diving the sub was dangerous, and the more information police divers had, the less time they might have to spend inside it.

Glen drew a rough outline of the sub and marked the spot where he had last seen his wife.

On 10 January 1997, Barry Gibson was enjoying a Christmas holiday break with his family when he got a phone call from work. He was due to start back again on the following Monday, but search and rescue jobs showed no respect for days off.

'We've got a job in the ship graveyard,' one of his colleagues told him. 'It's a body retrieval and it's over forty metres so it's yours.'

One of the deep-trained divers was interstate and therefore unavailable, and the remaining four were all required on deck.

The crew met at 4 am the following morning. They packed

equipment ready for the deep dive and loaded police vehicles with helmets, lines, and the squad's decompression chamber. They drove in convoy to the launching point.

On the dock in Queenscliff, loading their equipment onto the Ports Harbour survey boat, the *Shearwater*, Gibson didn't miss the irony. In 1981 a diver was lost diving the J2, and now the police divers were heading out to the exact same location.

Last time, they couldn't dive; this time, they could.

Normally, Water Police boats were used for dives but because it was a surface-supplied air dive and a decompression chamber was required on site, a larger and very stable vessel was required. If the divers were connected to a boat that was supplying their air, and the boat was tossed around in extreme weather conditions, the air-supply tubes could disconnect – and that would be dangerous for the divers. A Water Police boat followed the *Shearwater*.

On the way out to the J2 site, Barry Gibson, as the senior dive supervisor, felt a bit like a football coach. 'This is what we've trained for,' he told his team of divers.

Aboard the *Shearwater*, the weather began to turn squally. A search hadn't been possible the previous day because of strong winds and waves of up to four metres. The Air Wing and the Water Police had both attended as soon as the dive company had alerted them that Julia was missing, but the weather was so bad, the search had to be postponed till the following day. On Saturday 11 January, the weather looked like turning as bad as it had been the day before. Strong winds blew and the waves were barrelling around three metres. So fierce was the squall, some members of the rescue team suffered seasickness and vomited over the side of the *Shearwater*. Conditions were so rough that the annual Pier to Pub ocean swim classic at Lorne was cancelled.

Nonetheless, Gibson tried his best to keep morale up. He knew the importance of body retrieval in a situation such as this. On several occasions during his time at Search and Rescue, Gibson and his colleagues had had to admit defeat in their search for missing people. The one that stood out most in his mind was that of a teenager who'd gone missing a couple of years earlier on Lake Eildon after a boating accident. His body hadn't been found at the time and Search and Rescue returned regularly to the spot to search – usually a couple of times a year. Finally, in a drought, the water levels at the site of the boy's disappearance dropped by thirty metres, and Search and Rescue returned to do a land search. Walking over cracked mud left by the receding waters, Greg Paul had made his way to a shallow creek then waded across it. Wearing wetsuit booties, Greg had trodden on what might have been a stick. Bending over, he'd inspected the 'stick', which on closer examination proved to be a human femur. They'd finally found the boy.

To the police, an unrecovered body meant that the officers would keep returning to the scene of the accident. But for families, an unrecovered body meant no proper funeral, and no closure.

Aboard the *Shearwater* were four officers who were trained for the deep dive. Barry Gibson would buddy-dive with Bob Manks, while Don McConnell would buddy-dive with Adrian Johnson. Greg Paul, who had interviewed the grieving husband the night before, had joined the crew and briefed them on the possible location of the body within the submarine.

For Bob Manks, a body retrieval was one of the most important parts of his job – he regarded it as a great privilege. In a convoluted way, dealing with the dead on a regular basis forced Manks to think about life and its preciousness. With the majority of the bodies he retrieved, he knew most of them had left their homes for the final time having no idea of their date with destiny and mortality. If these people could be robbed prematurely of life, then so could he – or any of them, for that matter. Manks was widely travelled and he had seen death treated differently in other countries – open caskets, vigils with the dead – people treated death more naturally. In Australia with its closed caskets, he felt death was locked away, not spoken of and unseen. But for police officers like Bob Manks, death was often at the other end of a phone call.

The dive team planned and organised the complex diving operation on the way out to the sub. Manks offered to enter the sub – he had always preferred the action to the waiting. At the wreck site, conditions aboard the *Shearwater* worsened. The sonar told them that they were above the J2, and one of the crew fed out a shot line to mark the location. The *Shearwater* dropped three anchors in three different directions to try to stabilise the position of the boat. The first two divers, McConnell and Johnson, kitted up, tested their equipment and prepared to dive while Gibson briefed the team on the dive plan, including search techniques, hazards, decompression stops and emergency procedures. Each member of the team had a very specific and important role to fill.

Attached to the *Shearwater* by umbilicals and their surface-air breathing apparatus, the divers dropped over the edge to descend into the murky depths in search of Julia's body. The dive was perilous because even though the *Shearwater* had been chosen for her size and stability, the divers were still at the mercy of the rough seas that had the potential to toss them around. They also had to carefully measure their bottom time and decompress accordingly.

When McConnell and Johnson hit the bottom, they searched in the near pitch black for the sub. They couldn't find it. Communicating their frustration via the microphones in their helmets, the divers on the surface realised that the rough swell had pushed the *Shearwater* clear of the sub's location. The divers had to resurface – and because they had spent long minutes searching for the wreck, they were now 'burnt out' as far as any further deep diving was concerned. Even with adequate stops on the way up to decompress, the levels of nitrogen in their systems made a further dive as dangerous for them as it had been for Alan, the rescuer who had ended up with severe decompression illness from his repeat dive the day before.

'Are you happy to stay on site?' Barry Gibson asked the skipper of the *Shearwater*. The conditions were less than favourable and the considerable drift in the rough weather had sent them off-course.

'It's borderline,' said the skipper, realigning the boat and finding the sub again with the sonar.

It was now up to Gibson and Manks to find the drowned woman. Gibson sent two fresh divers, Greg Paul and Kent Clifton-Blight, down to do a bounce-dive, which meant that the divers were kitted out with scuba equipment to descend, confirm the location of the wreck, then come straight back up to the surface. A bounce-dive meant that the divers wouldn't need decompression, only a quick safety stop at three metres. When the two divers resurfaced, they were able to confirm that the *Shearwater* was now over the J2 sub.

Gibson and Manks kitted up. This was Search and Rescue's last chance on this expedition to find the body. Don McConnell would supervise the dive and operate the panel supplying air and communicating with the divers – having just dived himself, he knew exactly what Manks and Gibson were in for.

Manks would enter the sub and Gibson would feed in the umbilical line so that he could find his way out again. The two divers splashed over the side of the *Shearwater*. They only needed to swim down using fins for the first ten metres or so, and then the water pressure increased, pushing the air out of their wetsuits and making them sink. They descended the shot line to the sub. Once there, they located the broken section.

'Diver one at task,' said Gibson when they'd reached the sub.

'Diver two at task,' said Manks.

'Divers, commence your task,' said McConnell from the *Shearwater*.

'Entering the sub at the break,' said Manks. This communication and reiteration of tasks was absolutely necessary for deep dives. If either of the divers were affected by nitrogen narcosis, it would become obvious as soon as one of their frequent communications became slurred or incoherent.

Manks and Gibson swam in through the break and immediately stirred up the silt.

'Diver two to topside; it's silted up in here. Visibility zero.' For Manks, it had become a black dive.

Manks moved through the sub away from the stirred silt. As long as he kept moving forward, the silt would stir behind him. If he stopped, the silt would stir in front of him and he would be unable to see anything. Swimming through the sub was eerie and dangerous. Manks could see that the whole structure was slowly decaying and huge metal beams had collapsed and littered the pathway through the sub. Huge bulkheads were rusted and dangerous. And to make matters worse, bits of metal jutted out everywhere, snagging his wetsuit. For a moment, Manks realised that this site could be deadly for him – if the *Shearwater* moved and dragged him with it, he would be keel-hauled. He pushed the thought from his mind.

Inside the sub was dark, but Manks had a light in his helmet which allowed him to see fairly well. Swimming down corridors and passageways, he used common sense; when he came to a fork in the way, he simply chose the biggest opening to follow, reasoning that Julia wouldn't have had the time nor the inclination to squeeze herself through the smaller of two alternative openings.

His hunch would quickly prove to be correct.

Back at the break in the sub, Gibson fed out the umbilical cord to his dive-buddy. He was concerned that the 100-metre umbilical might not be long enough. The descent had taken forty metres, and he had fed out a further thirty to Manks inside the sub and they still hadn't found the body. As the cord reached thirty-five metres, Gibson heard his partner's voice over the radio.

'Diver two to topside. Got her!'

Manks had swum up a passageway and he could see that the way was blocked by a huge metal wall – he was coming to a dead end. And then he swam over something. It wasn't until he was almost on top of the sunken body that he realised he'd just found Julia. The last thing he noticed was her brightly coloured fins before the water silted up completely.

Oh God, in here, like this, he thought. Manks could appreciate the absolute horror of Julia's final moments. Her body was face-down; Manks reached around to feel her face and a quick inspection told him that her mask was still on and her equipment was all in place. It looked like she had swum away from the break until she had come to the dead end and then run out of air. Her air tank registered empty and there was not even a puff of air left to inflate her buoyancy vest. She would have to be carried out. Manks awkwardly arranged himself so that he could turn her around in the tight space. It was most important for him to secure her head so that she suffered no facial injuries that would be distressing to her family. Holding her close with one arm, he used his other arm to feel for anything in the corridor that he could grab hold of to pull himself and Julia's body along. In zero visibility, the task was exhausting and difficult. Manks lost count of the number of times his helmet collided with some hard metal part of the decaying sub, or of how many times sharp metal tore at his wetsuit, ripping holes through the thick rubber. On the other end of the umbilical, Barry Gibson kept taking up the slack, guiding Manks out.

After many long minutes, Manks appeared in the break. Gibson helped him get the body through the gap and both divers swam to the bottom of the shot line. There was no way that the exhausted divers could surface with the body because they had chalked up a full twenty-four minutes of bottom time, which required thirty-seven minutes of decompression stops along the way. They couldn't hold on to her for that long. Gibson fastened the body to the bottom of the shot line and began the slow ascent with Manks.

They had to stop at nine metres, again at six metres, then again at three metres to diffuse the excess nitrogen from their systems. The decompression stops were hampered by the tossing of the *Shearwater* on the surface; every time a wave lurched the boat up and down, the divers attached to it were tossed up and down like tea bags. It was impossible to maintain a nine-metre decompression depth when every wave dunked them violently up and down. Because of this and the long bottom time, the minute the divers hit the surface and were helped back aboard the *Shearwater*, they were given pure oxygen to help their systems stabilise.

The *Shearwater* was joined by the Water Police boat, and the body was finally brought to the surface with the shot line. Manks was glad he'd found Julia. He'd been on so many searches where the missing person wasn't found – this was a good result for all of them.

On the way back to the wharf, Gibson felt elated. He and his men had done what they'd trained to do and had done it well. He couldn't help but remember back fifteen years, to that day on the beach when he and his fellow Search and Rescue officers had to stand by and watch others do their job for them. But not today. For the football enthusiast in Gibson, this recovery was the equivalent of kicking the winning goal at a Grand Final. The irony didn't escape him, however, that a successful deep-dive body retrieval for the squad was still an utter tragedy for Julia's family.

It was the job of the Search and Rescue Squad to put together the inquest brief for the coroner. Because Senior Constable Greg Paul was relatively new to the squad and hadn't run a diving inquest brief before, it was decided that the experience would be good for him.

He had initially interviewed Glen and taken his statement. He had also taken and examined all the equipment associated with Julia, Glen, Alan and Greg. With the records of interview from every member aboard the ill-fated *Corsair*, Greg put together charts plotting everyone's movements. Interestingly, all the divers aboard the *Corsair* who had a lot of diving experience – some over twenty years – had decided not to penetrate the J2 sub. The divers who did enter it all had five years' experience or less.

When the investigation was completed, Greg identified a number of factors contributing to what happened to Julia. He compiled all these for the coronial inquest. He knew his research and preparation for the case were vital. Every time the coroner examines a case, the finding attempts to suggest improvements to the system – just like when Wendy Wilmoth suggested police divers should train to depths of fifty metres. In previous years, an examination of boat drownings led to the mandatory carrying of lifejackets in boats. Similarly, road accident deaths led to the introduction of seatbelt laws.

Coroner Max Beck, who held Julia's inquest around six months after her death, praised the work of the Search and Rescue Squad: 'It is not widely recognised, that men of such courage, confidence, and specialised skill are part of the Victoria Police Force. They are to be commended for the endurance, skill and professionalism.'

Coroner Beck examined each piece of evidence from Greg Paul's brief and concluded that Julia, Glen and the dive master on the charter boat all contributed to Julia's death – the dive master because he hadn't warned divers not to penetrate the wreck in his pre-dive briefing; Glen because he had more experience than his wife and shouldn't have suggested entering the wreck while the dive was in progress; and finally Julia herself, because the coroner felt that she 'should have had sufficient knowledge to know that it was not good sense to have attempted a penetration dive into the bow section of the J2'.

Interestingly, Coroner Beck, an enthusiastic recreational diver himself, said that it wasn't uncommon for charter dive boats to take divers to explore the wrecks in the ship graveyard and that many divers had successfully penetrated the wreck and come out safely.

'The anecdotal evidence, however,' he wrote in his findings, 'is that many of them have also got into trouble. Records reveal that in 1981, there was a fatality at the J2 sub when a diver "went missing". Some years ago, another diver "disappeared" while diving at thirty-eight metres at the "New Deep Sub" [the J1]. Julia … is the third diving fatality and it is fortunate that there have not been more.'

Coroner Beck concluded his findings with a suggestion: 'Finally, as a safety measure, it would be desirable to place a plaque on the entrance to the bow section of the J2 sub, perhaps along the following lines: *In memory of Julia … who died while diving this wreck. Divers are warned not to penetrate the hull due to dangerous silt conditions causing zero visibility.*'

Chapter Six

NOT JUST
A BURG

From 1964 to 1977, an iconic cop show called *Homicide* graced Australian TV screens. Little kids sat glued to the screens – in the days before programs had warnings or age-of-viewer recommendations. Everyone's mum had a favourite detective. Leonard Teale with his deep, cultured voice played detective 'Mac' Mackay, a tough cop with high ideals about justice. Or George Mallaby, who played bachelor detective Peter Barnes. The opening sequence was unforgettable with its dramatic music and the band of Homicide detectives walking up the steps into the Russell Street police headquarters with a view of the old Melbourne Magistrates' Court in the background. Actors like Charles 'Bud' Tingwell, Norman Yemm and John Stanton would appear on Australian TV for many years and become household names after their roles in *Homicide*.

The detectives in *Homicide* became role models for many an Aussie youngster with a yearning to carry a gun and catch bad guys.

David Noonan was such a lad.

His desire to be a detective sprang from evenings watching *Homicide*. As a young boy, David was fascinated with the way those TV cops in black-and-white, wearing their old-fashioned hats, solved cases and spoke in deep authoritative voices about who was guilty and why.

David Noonan was so keen to become a police officer, he signed on for the police cadets when he was just sixteen years old. He studied English, sociology and law at the cadet training school in the old Savoy Tavern in Spencer Street in Melbourne.

Growing up in a regular middle-class family and attending a Catholic boys' college did little to prepare Noonan for the big wide world facing a young police cadet. One of his earliest policing memories was working security for the Melbourne Cup in the bad old days when attendees could bring in their own alcohol.

Noonan, along with other cadets and fully fledged cops, worked the lawn area and watched the thronging crowds getting drunker and drunker. Inevitably a fight broke out. One drunk had fallen across another drunk's polystyrene esky and smashed it – and it was on for young and old. Booze-fuelled fights were nothing new for young Noonan, but what *was* new was the dawning realisation of two things: there were a lot of people out there who hated coppers, and there were a lot of people who would stop at nothing in a fight.

The most disturbing thing Noonan saw that day was a police colleague on the ground with a drunken fighter on top of him trying to gouge his eyes out by pressing his thumbs in the cop's eye sockets. Luckily for the downed cop, his colleagues are trained to aid an officer first and foremost, and the offender was dragged off him before any lasting damage was done. As the brawl died down, disgruntled drunks threw insults instead of punches, and swore and spat at the cops. It was all so different from Noonan's own experience with police. In his upbringing, police were to be respected – and slightly feared – not spat at and eye gouged. The drunks in the Cup Day brawl had behaved like a pack of animals. Noonan wondered how people could stoop so low. The young cadet found himself on a steep learning curve.

At Noonan's first police station as an eighteen-year-old constable in the peninsula suburb of Frankston, he found the same lack of respect for police. Just prior to his arrival in the early 1980s, a bunch of drunken thugs had marched on the old police station in Davey Street to protest against the arrest of another bunch of drunks. So bad was the situation that a Justice of the Peace was called in to literally read them the Riot Act.

Even so, it was an exciting place for a young constable to begin his policing career. Seasoned cops would point out offenders on patrol and Noonan soon came to know crooks by sight too. And because of the close proximity of four pubs in the main street of Frankston, Saturday nights around 2 am became a regular mass brawl as drunks were ejected at closing time. Divisional vans were filled, and so were the lock-up cells back at the old police station. It would be over a decade before the new police station was built with state-of-the-art lock-up facilities with video monitoring of prisoners. In the 1980s, a drunken brawler could look forward to a stay of several hours in one of the 1950s police cells known as the drunk tanks.

While general duties policing was exciting, Noonan still wanted to pursue his dream to work as a detective. When his time at Frankston was over, he was seconded back to the city to work security at his original stomping ground, the cadet training school. After the obligatory six months in the city, Noonan was so desperate for action, he sent out over forty applications to everywhere he could think of. Finally, he was accepted at the St Kilda police station, which at the time dealt a lot with sex workers, drug addicts and gutter crawlers. In the mid-eighties, sex work was illegal. The girls came from all walks of life. There were drug-addicted women working to fill their veins with heroin, and some managed to stay off drugs and make money from the profession. Noonan remembers one young woman made over a thousand dollars a day – it was hard to suggest an alternative day-job where she would make a fraction of that kind of money.

After a few years in uniform on the beat, Noonan finally achieved his ultimate goal – he became a detective at the St Kilda Criminal Investigation Branch (CIB). And within a few months, he had his first homicide, but it wasn't quite like the TV show from all those years ago. A homeless woman cooking a barbeque at one of the local St Kilda parks had stabbed a vagrant through the heart and killed him after he pinched one of her sausages. Hardly worthy of Leonard Teale's character, Senior Detective Mac Mackay, from *Homicide*. However, Senior Detective David Noonan from St Kilda took the case with gusto. The killer and others caught up in the ensuing knife fight over barbeque sausages had all fled the scene, straight to the nearest pub for a quick beer, then to a local chemist to buy bandages for their respective wounds. Left a trail a mile wide. Not like TV at all.

But Noonan's next murder investigation would make national headlines.

On 29 June 1991, six-year-old Sheree Beasley went missing in Rosebud. She had ridden her bike to the local milk bar and vanished. Her parents learnt of her disappearance when a neighbour reported finding Sheree's abandoned bike. In the beginning, police and neighbours all hoped Sheree had simply wandered off to play with friends. But it wasn't to be. Later, several witnesses came forward to report seeing a distressed child being driven away by a middle-aged man in a blue Toyota hatchback.

And after those sightings, she vanished without a trace.

When a police search failed to find the missing girl – and everything pointed to an abduction – a taskforce called Operation Zenith was launched. David Noonan was seconded to the taskforce. All owners of the make and model of the car sighted at the time of the abduction were located, interviewed and given a questionnaire. While Robert Arthur Selby Lowe initially didn't stand out from all the other middle-aged men, police checked his responses to the questionnaire and found him to be less than honest. He said he wasn't in Rosebud on the day of the abduction, but friends at his church informed investigators that Lowe had indeed been in Rosebud that weekend. Lowe said he had no prior criminal convictions, but an easy police check revealed fourteen convictions.

When it became obvious Lowe fit the bill as a likely suspect, police watched him around the clock. Noonan formed part of this shadow detail and was appalled by what he saw; Robert Lowe stalked children constantly. Detectives would see him make a beeline for a group of children playing at a park or on a school excursion. Lowe would walk directly into the crowd and brush up against unsuspecting kids. It was sickening. Lowe was also a chronic shoplifter, stealing whenever he had the chance.

The articulate, church-going man interviewed by police certainly proved to be less-than-holy when he thought he was away from prying eyes. Unfortunately for Lowe, there were eyes everywhere. Not only were police tailing Lowe's every move, but surveillance cameras inside his Rosebud holiday house gave detectives further insight into their suspect, who would parade naked around his unit acting nothing like the church elder he was in another life.

When Lowe was finally arrested, and Sheree's body located and laid to rest, Noonan could breathe a sigh of relief. With a life sentence, he knew Robert Lowe would be off the streets forever, but only he and a select few who had followed him for months knew just how dangerous a predator to all children Lowe had been.

Noonan's next opportunity as a detective was a stint in the Homicide Squad, something he'd wanted to do since he was a young boy. But like many boyhood dreams, the reality was very different. At the Homicide Squad, David Noonan realised that the variety of work that the CIBs offered was missing. In reality, Homicide was death and paperwork – and because detectives worked in squads of six, there was also the loss of freedom and independence that Noonan thrived on. In the CIB, detectives often worked alone and called the shots, so inevitably, the Homicide Squad was not for Noonan and he soon returned to his job of choice – suburban CIB work. After a few moves, he ended up in Brighton in 1997.

One of his early cases was a schoolgirl from a nearby Catholic girls' school who reported being flashed at. The offender had escaped and there was little the cops could do with no more than the girl's description of him. Not long after the incident, the girl rushed into the CIB offices and told Noonan that she had seen the flasher at the local shops and had followed him home. She knew where he lived.

'Well, where does he live?' asked Noonan, surprised and a little worried at the risk she'd taken.

'Right over there,' said the girl, pointing to a house across the road from the police station.

Instead of simply walking across the street to apprehend the flasher, Noonan put on a show. He hopped into a marked police car, turned on the lights and sirens, and drove across the road to make the arrest. If the neighbours all wondered what the man had done wrong – well, that would just be a bonus.

Geographically, much of the CIB division curves for several kilometres around Port Phillip Bay. The Brighton CIB covered a number of surrounding suburbs: Elsternwick, Hampton, Moorabbin, Sandringham and parts of Cheltenham. The district has one of the highest concentrations of sporting clubs in Melbourne. So prevalent are some clubs that their names leave little to distinguish them from each other – Hampton had the Hampton Central Cricket Club, the Hampton East Cricket Club and of course the plain old Hampton Cricket Club. And so when these clubs began to become targets for midnight raids by thieves, detectives at Brighton CIB had their work cut out for them.

Social clubs are traditionally soft targets; often they don't have alarms, and often they are deserted, and only open when there is a function on. Mostly, the clubs are run by people in the community who want to provide a service and raise a bit of money to support their club. Thousands benefit from the abundance of clubs around Melbourne that provide a social gathering place, and a place where people can play sport.

One of the first clubs to be hit in the Brighton CIB district was the Moorabbin Baseball Club. Distressed club officials reported the break-in to police and the local uniform cops took the initial report. Once the report was passed on to the Brighton CIB, detectives attended the scene, took photographs, dusted for fingerprints, and looked for any evidence to suggest who was responsible. Seasoned detectives could read a crime scene and to them, it looked like kids had been responsible. An older crook would have just taken beer and money, but the Moorabbin Baseball Club offenders had helped themselves not only to beer and money, but also to mixed drinks and confectionery. Also missing was a rubbish bin – probably used to cart away the haul.

And that was just the beginning. Before long, it seemed every shift hand-over conversation started with: 'I went to another one of those sports club jobs ...' They were all the same: slabs of beer and mixed drinks taken along with cash and lollies, and always, the stolen rubbish bin to cart it all away in.

Early in the investigation, experts from the Fingerprint Branch notified detectives at the CIB that fingerprints lifted from several jobs matched; police were looking for the same offenders. All the cases investigated were sent to the police analyst, who prepared a report including maps, dates and times of the burglaries and information from witnesses. An analysis of the robberies showed they usually occurred on a Friday night when the clubs were closed but stocked up for Saturday-night functions. The analyst also linked burglaries in other policing districts spanning from Brighton right down the peninsula to Mount Martha. Figures suggested that the thieves were becoming more brazen by striking more often; some clubs had been hit five times.

An untold part of the investigation is the fact that almost daily, David Noonan and his colleagues received phone calls from the people affected. It wasn't just that they'd lost uninsured goods worth thousands of dollars; it was the fact that clubs operated largely on a trusting community basis. Each time a club was burgled – and on quite a few occasions, the thieves gained access with keys – members of the clubs began looking at each other suspiciously. The spate of robberies sparked off a lot of ill-feeling between people.

By mid-October, the sports club burglaries had been occurring for six months and had escalated to over twenty a month. Then detectives got what could have been a big break. Would-be thieves had tried to break into a sports pavilion in Hampton East. The front door was damaged – it looked like the offenders had tried to kick it in – and more importantly for the detectives, one of the thieves had left his wallet behind, complete with student ID. Nothing had been stolen but there was several hundred dollars' damage to the front door.

A couple of teenagers called Daniel and Sean were brought into the Brighton CIB for questioning. According to Noonan, both boys were scared and nervous. Neither had been in trouble before, and their fingerprints, which had been lifted at the scene from an abandoned can of bourbon and coke, didn't match the prints found at the other burglaries. The two boys told detectives they'd been drunk and tried to break into the pavilion in the hope of finding money or alcohol. Their modus operandi didn't fit either. The series of robberies were committed by thieves using tools like jemmy bars – these kids had tried to *kick* the door in. Noonan and his colleagues also thought these young lads weren't organised enough to be the offenders they were seeking. Nonetheless, the boys were kept under occasional surveillance just in case, which revealed that they were so spooked by being interviewed by police that they didn't go out at all, except to visit each other.

By the end of November, a task force had been set up to catch the thieves. By this time, eighty-six sports clubs had been hit. To say that the cops were frustrated would be putting it mildly. Detectives chose Friday 21 November for a big operation. The following day was the Rugby World Cup and the thieves would know that most clubs would be stocked up for the game. Groups of three detectives sat in unmarked cars outside a number of selected clubs. Noonan and his colleagues chose to sit off the Hampton Central Cricket Club because it had been robbed the previous week, and keys to the premises had been stolen. With these thieves, lightning did strike twice, and sometimes four or five times, in the same spot.

Sitting in their unmarked Commodore parked under low-hanging tree branches, out of sight of the road, Noonan and fellow detectives Mick Grumley and Chris Von Tunk discussed their own theories about the robberies.

'I reckon they'll hit here around midnight,' predicted Noonan.

'Yeah, it's a good night for it,' said Von Tunk.

During the stakeout, several people walked through the car park. Each time, the three officers hunched down in their seats and watched them like hawks.

After several hours in the cramped car, midnight struck and Noonan wondered if his guess would be right. In one of those air-punching moments, the three detectives saw a red Toyota four-wheel drive pull into the club driveway at 12.05 am. From their vantage point, they could see the Toyota drive slowly up to the front door, curve around the driveway and then turn back. And then, the headlights of the four-wheel drive swept around and illuminated the unmarked police car with the three officers inside. Instead of stopping, the Toyota headed straight for the driveway. And the police car followed.

Within metres of the driveway, the detectives attached their magnetic blue light to the roof of their car and pulled over the Toyota.

Detective Sergeant Mick Grumley went to the driver's side door and Noonan went to the passenger side in a classic divide-and-conquer manoeuvre. Inside the Toyota were two young men, the driver, Mark, aged nineteen, and the passenger, Trent, aged twenty-two.

'What were you doing in there?' Grumley asked Mark.

'Um ... we were ... er ... looking for a toilet,' he replied nervously.

'Mind if we take a look at your vehicle?'

Meanwhile, Noonan asked Trent to step outside. He led him away from the four-wheel drive over to the back of the police Commodore and asked him to turn out his pockets. Trent, a large young man, turned out his pockets nervously. Noonan noticed a walkie-talkie clipped to his belt. Trent was wearing a jacket with zippers and pockets everywhere. Noonan indicated a pocket at the shoulder of his right sleeve. Trent unzipped it and a set of keys dropped out and landed with a clink on the boot of the police car. Unbelievably, the tag was printed with 'Hampton Central Cricket Club' and underneath was a little logo – two crossed cricket bats. As both men stared at the keys, Trent's eyes rolled heavenward.

He knew the game was up.

'We got 'em!' murmured Noonan to himself. It was hard to remain professional when you feel like doing a car-ad jump into the air.

While Noonan and Grumley talked to the suspects, Chris Von Tunk checked out the back section of the Toyota. It was lined with what can only be described as a break-and-enter kit. There was every tool imaginable all laid out like in an operating theatre. Among the tools were balaclavas and gardening gloves.

While Trent was fairly matter of fact, his fellow thief, Mark, burst into tears. It was as if the danger of what they had been doing and the reality of getting caught finally hit. After the detectives called for backup, Trent was taken away in another car, and it was left to Noonan to try to calm Mark down.

'It's not the end of the world,' he said soothingly, but it was like a floodgate had opened. By the time they got back to the CIB office, Mark had confessed to around thirty burglaries and was singing like a canary.

Mark and Trent were interviewed and processed and then the detectives set off to the house they shared in Frankston. It wasn't until they went inside the rented white weatherboard that the cops could fully appreciate the magnitude of the operation. Inside the house were over eighty rubbish bins – all stolen from clubs. The house stank of rotting food and some of the bins had been re-used as receptacles for junk-food wrappers. Both young men were quite overweight and they confessed to detectives that they'd used the proceeds from their robberies to live the high life – which when you're nineteen and twenty-two means daily KFC and Pizza Hut takeaway. Scattered among the bins were also wrappers from dozens of Mars Bars and other confectionery stolen from the clubs. While robbery wasn't good for the waistline, it was good for the bottom line and the boys had made a fortune. Their scam was to re-sell the stolen alcohol at a thirty per cent discount, and they had gotten so good at their job that they were now taking orders. Empty boxes littering the house marked 'Bob – beer' or 'Kelly – mixed' were waiting to be filled with loot from the next robbery.

The young men had established quite a network of clients in their steal-to-order business. They were charged with eighty-six burglaries, seventy-two thefts and five counts of criminal damage because, inexplicably, at five of the clubs, the thieves had squirted fire extinguishers or tomato sauce around. This horseplay had caused thousands of dollars of damage. Trent and Mark pleaded guilty to all charges. Both were sentenced to two years in prison. On appeal, the judge reduced the sentences to good behaviour bonds.

In the aftermath of the spate of robberies on sporting venues and in the lead-up to the court date, David Noonan still received calls from clubs. Mostly club members had questions: *Do you think they'll get jail?* or the more poignant: *Why did they target us?* Others simply said in frustration: *I'd like five minutes alone with those two …*

Noonan says that you can't underestimate the damage these offenders did. Many of the clubs were hit multiple times and lost goods to the value of thousands of dollars. Few could afford insurance premiums that cut into their meagre profits. Sadly, some clubs had to close because they simply couldn't recover from the financial loss. Other clubs were infected with suspicion against the kids they were trying to help. So many people were affected in the wider community – all so that two young men could fund their lifestyle of junk food and shopping sprees.

No, these were not just burgs …

Chapter Seven

HANGAR 104

Nestled within the Essendon Airport lies Hangar 104 – home of the Victoria Police Air Wing. An airy reception room connected to offices and a lunchroom bordered a cavernous hangar housing the Air Wing's four helicopters and maintenance equipment.

Two of the helicopters were N3 Dauphin craft and one was the older style Dauphin craft C model. The fourth helicopter was a single engine Squirrel used mostly for aerial surveillance. At any given time, one of the four helicopters received extensive maintenance by specially trained police engineers, leaving the remaining three machines operational and ready to attend jobs at two minutes' notice.

Workers at Hangar 104 fall into several categories including pilots, observers, paramedics and ground crew. Most police in the Air Wing wore navy blue flight suits, which were better suited to the work they do. When members wore traditional police uniforms, they had a special badge sewn onto their shirts that incorporated the Victoria Police emblem with a wing attached to it.

Talking about his job on the helicopters in 1994, Senior Constable John Williamson of the Victoria Police Air Wing says that in many ways, the helicopters were 'basically flying police cars'.

Williamson explained the duties of the police helicopters using the acronym ASTRO – Aerial Support to Routine Operations. The helicopters assisted police in normal day-to-day work, surveillance, search and rescue operations, and spotting drug crops from the air, the latter being the primary domain of the Squirrel.

Officers attached to the Air Wing are highly trained operatives. Some pilots were lateral-entry officers, which meant they didn't enter through the police academy as new recruits, but rather they were ex-military or ex-general aviation experts recruited to the police force for their expertise. This form of recruitment was seen by police command as a more cost-effective way of providing the necessary level of flying experience.

Senior Constable John Williamson, at thirty-three, was a typical member of the Air Wing: tall, trim and articulate, with a firm handshake. His neatly pressed blue shirt was adorned with the customary winged emblem. As a member of the Air Wing, Williamson had successfully combined his love of police work with his love of aviation. It takes little stretch of the imagination to picture him suspended thirty metres underneath a helicopter from a winch over the rough seas of Bass Strait in a daring rescue bid – which is exactly what his job required him to do.

Williamson had been attached to the Police Air Wing for five years and worked, as did his colleagues, on board both police and ambulance helicopters. In 1986, the Victorian Health Department supplied funding for the Police Air Wing to purchase the air ambulance with the agreement that the police force lease it to the ambulance service. A condition of the funding and the lease was that the Police Air Wing provided the crew, maintenance and storage of the helicopter while the ambulance service provided Mobile Intensive Care Ambulance (MICA) paramedics to fly with the crew.

The agreement made good sense because many ambulance jobs required support from both ground police and ground medical teams so as a result, the operations ran more smoothly. In addition to the support, the Police Air Wing had extensive facilities for the maintenance-intensive machines.

One call typified the coordination required for the air ambulance helicopter to be effective. Williamson was working a day shift when the Air Wing received a call requiring the attendance of the helicopter at a child drowning in Werribee. Calls were received on a special telephone at the Air Wing hangar and the sound of the ringing echoing via an intercom through the space told officers their services were required even before they answered the phone. On this particular day, officers were given a street name, a house number and a description of the job. A four-year-old boy had fallen into an unfenced backyard swimming pool and needed urgent transportation to the Royal Children's Hospital.

Within two minutes, the helicopter's rotor shuddered to life, lifting the machine into the air. Williamson's job on this occasion was as the pilot's observer. It was his responsibility to guide the pilot to the scene and to be his second pair of eyes. With the assistance of a street directory and his considerable knowledge of Melbourne from the air, Williamson guided the pilot to the street in Werribee. Communicating through headphones with a microphone attached, the crew were in constant radio contact with D24, ground police and paramedics at the scene.

Three houses down from their target was a vacant block and Williamson and the pilot decided to bring the helicopter down there. Williamson radioed uniform police already at the scene to block off surrounding streets and to keep the swell of spectators as far back from the helicopter as possible.

The biggest risks to the helicopter at these kinds of jobs were power poles and electrical wires. Williamson vigilantly checked all directions and carefully guided the pilot down towards the confined spaces of the vacant block.

'Tail's clear.'

'Roger that.'

'Three metres to the left. Looks good.'

The long green grass in the paddock bent flat in a sweeping circle as the huge gusts of wind from the powerful rotor sent dirt and stones flying. The force of air from the rotor blades wasn't just confined to the vacant block. Williamson could see washing flying off clotheslines in neighbouring backyards. The helicopter landed and he was assaulted by the thundering noise as he opened the door of the machine. Williamson covered the short distance between the helicopter and the tiny child who was dwarfed on an adult-sized stretcher. Ambulance officers were already wheeling him down the middle of the street towards the helicopter.

Ground paramedics signalled to Williamson that this was a 'hot load'. The police officer in turn gave the thumbs up signal to the pilot to keep the helicopter rotor spinning ready for an immediate take-off. The deafening roar of the rotor meant that Williamson's impression of the scene was purely visual. The unconscious child was surrounded by paramedics, police, and his distraught mother saying things that the noise of the helicopter stopped Williamson from hearing.

Working so closely with ground paramedics at many such cases makes verbal communication between the two parties largely superfluous – updates on the child's condition had already been radioed through to the helicopter paramedic and all that remained was to load the child onto the air ambulance with the least possible delay.

Another strong visual image was the crowd, of what Williamson estimates to have been about 150 people, gathered on the other side of the street watching. Their presence gave the tragic scene what Williamson described as a 'sort of macabre human street theatre'. Onlookers were dressed in typical weekend clothes; kids were on roller skates and BMX bikes – all pressing forward. Police urged them back. Later when Williamson had time to reflect, he felt sorry for the crowd. He wondered if their life experiences were so limited that they could find the drowning of a four-year-old child fascinating enough to stand watching for twenty minutes. He simply can't comprehend their interest. But in the heat of the moment, Williamson didn't have the luxury of time for such reflections – the young boy wasn't breathing and his pupils were fixed and dilated.

John Williamson spoke with great respect for the paramedics with whom he works. They are experts with thousands of such operations under their belts and the paramedic working on this job was no exception. He quickly went to work on the young child, attaching a drip and trying his best to revive the tiny boy. After clearing the pilot for take-off and guiding the shaking, screaming craft upwards, Williamson assisted the paramedic in the back of the helicopter, leaving the pilot alone to fly to the Royal Children's Hospital.

Despite requests from ground police to move away from the helicopter, onlookers had been reluctant to relinquish their front-row positions at the unfolding drama. The surge of air from the take-off sprayed them with dirt and stones.

People bowed their heads and covered their eyes.

John Williamson explained that in a job such as this, officers always hope they can make a difference and that the child will live, but the reality is that victims such as the small child with the damp blond hair lying before them usually didn't make it. Indeed, Williamson has never been to a child drowning where the child has been successfully revived and consequently survived. He said, 'You hope within yourself that it's going to be all right, but you've got a gut feeling that it's going to be like all the others.'

The helicopter flew vertically upwards and those on board felt the powerful surge when the machine hit an altitude of forty metres and went from hover to forward motion. The pilot radioed through a 'Med 1' priority and was cleared immediately for a direct flight path to the Royal Children's Hospital. Landing at the hospital, Williamson again felt a rush of annoyance at the lack of adequate accommodation for helicopter landings. The Royal Children's Hospital didn't have a helipad like the Alfred Hospital. Scant provision was made in the form of a small mowed patch of grass marked with a white H in Royal Park behind the hospital. When the helicopter radioed through details of the emergency, an ambulance had driven around from casualty, down Gatehouse Street, stopped to unlock the park gate and reversed up to await the landing. The child, once loaded, was taken back to casualty along the same lengthy route. Williamson estimates the ambulance transportation after landing can add around ten minutes to the journey – ten minutes that some critically ill patients just don't have.

After dropping off patients, Air Wing crew fly off to the next job and often don't hear the outcome. But in this case, he did. Two days later, John Williamson was at work and asked the paramedic who worked on the young child, 'How's the kid?'

'He died,' replied his colleague.

Such tragedies are part of the job. Williamson thought for a minute before articulating his reaction to such events.

'A couple of times a year there will be a job that follows me around for a couple of days. You think about how the parents are handling it more than anything. It's a feeling of utter helplessness. What can you do? It's so avoidable – it angers you and you think if only they had brought in a pool fencing law eighteen months earlier, maybe this wouldn't have happened.'

Another case that took Senior Constable Williamson a few days to shake was when he was part of the crew that transported to hospital a three-year-old boy who had been accidentally run over by his mother. She had been backing out of her driveway and drove over her tiny son, snapping his spine at the base of the neck. The mother was distraught and the boy died. Memories of the tiny scratched body, marked black from the car's axle, were more resilient than most and Williamson had to try constantly to push them from his mind.

On a blustery winter's day, John Williamson performed one of his most daring rescues. He was working in the operations room when a call came through requiring the police helicopter to airlift an injured man from a container ship in Bass Strait. The seas were too rough for the huge vessel to enter Port Phillip Bay through the Heads; wind was gusting at forty knots and conditions for a rescue could hardly have been worse.

The police helicopter was on patrol and Sergeant Andrew Tait was acting as an observer. Tait radioed the office and told John Williamson and paramedic Alan Scott to be ready for a 'wet winch' when the machine landed. The two men donned wetsuits, grabbed medical equipment and the harnesses necessary for the airlift, then clambered into the helicopter, which lifted into the air straightaway.

The powerful machine flew over Port Phillip Bay towards Bass Strait and those on board kept a close eye on the weather conditions. The wind was howling as Williamson and Scott squatted down at the rear of the helicopter, checking their harnesses and preparing the gear needed for the rescue. The task was made more difficult owing to the considerable air turbulence buffeting the helicopter en route. The two men had to constantly steady themselves by grabbing the rear bulkhead.

Due to the appalling weather conditions, Scott would follow Williamson down on the winch only if absolutely necessary. He would give medical advice over the radio once Williamson landed on the container ship.

Williamson strapped a collapsible stretcher known as a Paraguard to his back as the container ship came into sight. He took one look at the huge vessel pitching violently in the choppy seas and nervously murmured to himself, 'This should be interesting!'

Waves were breaking over the bow section of the huge container ship and the helicopter crew decided to winch Williamson onto the stern section. The container ship was colossal. Ocean waves pounded the seagoing vessel, pitching it in slow motion. It reminded John Williamson of a huge whale lurching in and out of the water.

A rush of cold air hit Williamson as Andrew Tait opened the helicopter door. Tait made one last check of his harness and gave his crewmate the nod. Williamson nodded back. Tait let out the winch a couple of metres and attached it to the front clip of Williamson's harness. The two men worked together as Tait wound in the winch, sliding Williamson across the floor of the helicopter towards the door. The mechanical whirring of the winch device couldn't be heard above the roar of the twin-engine helicopter but Williamson was left in no doubt of the job he was about to perform once Tait helped him jump down onto the rail outside the sliding door. It took around fifteen seconds from the time Williamson was suspended outside the helicopter before Tait guided the pilot over the intercom until they were hovering directly above the container ship.

Williamson described the environment outside the helicopter in mid-air as 'totally alien'. He could see the pilot through the front window working to steady the huge machine. Turning his head towards the rear of the helicopter, he could see the tail shaft vibrating madly through the heat haze of the jet-turbine exhaust.

The two men nodded to each other and Tait released the winch.

Slowly Williamson was lowered, keeping his feet on the rail until he was almost upside down. If he had taken his feet from the rail any earlier, he would have swung headfirst into the side of the helicopter. Using his legs to push himself away from the helicopter, he went sailing downwards. He was now completely at the mercy of the winch operator.

In order to mimic the container ship's pitching motion, Tait guided the pilot up and down. The pilot, unable to see over to the left-hand side of the machine, was virtually flying blind, relying completely on Tait's instructions from the opposite side of the aircraft. Williamson continued to plummet downwards as Tait let out the winch via a hand-held control. It seemed to Williamson as if the helicopter suddenly rose above him, but in fact the helicopter remained steady as he plunged down towards the ship below. The last thing he noticed as he dropped was the oil stains on the bottom on the helicopter.

The winds were so strong that it was nearly impossible to maintain a perfect hover and Williamson found out later that the pilot had to draw upon every bit of his experience and expertise to keep the helicopter relatively steady.

Williamson swung towards the ship, hearing little besides the roar of the engines above and the roar of the sea below. He began to swing violently back and forth. This was known as the pendulum effect, and there was nothing he could do to right himself and stop the swinging. As Williamson neared the deck, still swinging, he saw a guard-rail approaching fast. He quickly swung himself around and smashed back-first into the rail. Luckily, the bulky Paraguard strapped to his back prevented injury but it didn't stop the impact from knocking the wind out of him.

Finally, Tait and the pilot had negotiated Williamson to the slippery decks. His feet had just touched firm ground when it disappeared beneath him as the ocean swell pitched the ship downwards. The brief feeling of relative safety dissipated as Williamson saw the deck drop away and was left dangling ten metres in the air. Tait saw what happened and attempted to match the drop by letting the winch out further.

The combination of the extra line being fed down and the ship righting itself by rising rapidly up out of its plunge sent Williamson crashing to the deck. He again landed on his back, protected by the Paraguard but winded a second time.

Greek seamen rushed over and helped Williamson to his feet. He quickly detached himself from the winch, wary of becoming airborne again if he didn't. An odour of floor polish and disinfectant assaulted his senses as sailors led him through a labyrinth of spotlessly clean corridors into the bowels of the huge seagoing vessel. Nobody spoke English and Williamson didn't speak Greek, so communication was done through impromptu sign language. The young police officer grappled for words to request they turn up the lighting in the musty, dark cabin they had entered so he could see to assess the sick man.

Via portable radio, Williamson explained to the paramedic that the man was in considerable pain breathing. The police officer suspected broken ribs – nothing life threatening, but certainly painful for the patient. Soon the captain arrived in the tiny room and was able to communicate in broken English. Williamson explained that they would have to airlift the injured man to hospital.

Over-enthusiastic Greek seamen tried to help the police officer assemble the Paraguard stretcher. Williamson shook his head as five burly sailors each grabbed sections of the disassembled stretcher, trying desperately to follow his instructions as to which part went where. They laughed and congratulated themselves in Greek when one of them fitted a pole correctly or unwound parts of the complex harness system. They were only trying to help and Williamson didn't have the heart or the language to explain to his enthusiastic assistants that he could have done it quicker himself.

Williamson strapped the man in securely and crew members helped carry the stretcher back through what seemed like kilometres of corridors and up stairways.

Once they appeared on deck, the helicopter that had been hovering above the container ship repositioned itself back over the deck and lowered the winch cable. Williamson and his patient would go up together, the patient lying on his stretcher in front of the police officer. Williamson harnessed himself and his patient and both men rose into the air. He laughed as he recalled the look of 'sheer terror like I've never seen before' on the man's face.

Williamson looked up towards the hovering machine and saw the silhouette of Tait's head looking out through the doorway. When the winch brought them past the oil stains and level with the helicopter, Tait helped Williamson to swing both the stretcher and himself into the machine, which took off immediately on the twenty-minute journey to the Frankston Hospital.

Still wearing his harness, Williamson clambered over into the front left seat next to the pilot, leaving Tait and Scott to work on the patient in the confined space at the back of the helicopter. The patient was sweating and exhausted. Looking back as the pitching container ship faded behind them in the distance, he said quietly to himself, 'Thank God that's over!'

Winch rescues are used only if there are no rescue alternatives. Senior Constable Williamson was part of a crew that assisted in the rescue of a young man who had been diving in Port Phillip Bay and had been dragged by strong currents out through the Heads into the treacherous waters of Bass Strait.

The diver had swum towards a container ship that failed to spot him and he had to swim quickly out of the way to avoid being hit. In total darkness, the diver used a flashing torch to get the attention of the captain aboard the *Abel Tasman*. The captain continued on his course but radioed Search and Rescue to pick up the diver. The police helicopter was used in the rescue to locate and illuminate the diver, who was keeping himself afloat by treading water in the rough seas.

As Williamson and his crew hovered over the diver, the general consensus was: *You lucky bastard. It doesn't come any closer than this!* The experienced officers knew that if the diver had not been spotted, he would have been washed out to sea and his remains probably would never have been found. Winching the diver to safety was unnecessary because a pilot boat was only minutes away. The crew of the police helicopter watched as the man was dragged aboard the rescue boat and they all headed for Queenscliff.

The helicopter landed ahead of the pilot boat. Williamson described the memory of the diver being brought in as 'surreal'. He said the diver alighted from the rescue boat and simply walked off down the pier still wearing his wetsuit, flippers and goggles. He simply turned and said, 'Thanks mate,' to his rescuers. It was obvious to the rescuers that the seriousness of his situation had yet to sink in. He didn't understand – or perhaps didn't want to acknowledge – just how close his brush with death had been.

Some helicopter rescues weren't as dramatic as this. Williamson and his crew had to airlift twenty Girl Guides out of a flooded valley after they became stranded while camping. The helicopter acted as a bus ferrying them out, four at a time. Another bush rescue had the crew airlift a youth with a suspected broken leg that turned out to be nothing more severe than a sprained ankle.

The capabilities of helicopters to hover at low altitudes and to land in areas that are otherwise inaccessible make them ideal for rescues in difficult areas. In 1991, John Williamson was involved in a search and rescue operation at Mount Macedon when a Japanese pilot had crashed her light aircraft into the side of the mountain in the middle of winter. An extensive land and air search had failed to find her or the wreckage, largely because of low cloud and difficult weather conditions. At first light the following morning, around fifteen hours after her plane went down, the wreckage was finally spotted. Remains from the aircraft were strewn across the mountain. Unbelievably, the pilot had survived and Williamson had the job of winching her to safety.

The woman had crawled from the wreckage of her aircraft and had covered herself with navigation charts to guard against the freezing night-time weather. Ground searchers had found her injured but alive. As the police helicopter approached the scene of the crash, Williamson could see other aircraft that had joined the search. He saw volunteers on the ground in their bright orange suits and he directed the pilot to the exact location. Seeing the wreckage, Williamson marvelled at the fact the woman had survived.

Two paramedics were winched to the crash site and gently secured the injured woman onto a stretcher. The patient presented symptoms of a spinal injury and once she was aboard the helicopter, the paramedics administered medical aid. Williamson noticed her filthy clothes and her hands, mottled from lying on the damp mountain all night. The grateful woman spoke little English but kept repeating, 'Thank you very much,' over and over again.

Months later the Air Wing received a letter in Japanese from the woman thanking them for rescuing her. She and her family visited the Air Wing in late 1993 to present them with a gift.

Providing aerial support to routine police operations ensures members of the Air Wing have a huge variety of jobs and working conditions. On a typical nightshift, a crew will cruise the skies establishing a police presence; the whine of the Dauphin's engine is familiar to the citizens of Melbourne. The Air Wing may receive any number of calls through D24 – a man thinks someone is walking across the roof of his house, a factory alarm has been activated, a fire at a park in Keilor, pursuit of a stolen car or a pub brawl. In many of these jobs, offenders are only apprehended because of support from the Air Wing, and pub brawls quickly dissipate when illuminated by the helicopter's powerful NiteSun searchlight.

On one nightshift, Senior Constable Tim Morgan piloted the police helicopter over the skies of Melbourne to an inner-city suburb where a ground pursuit was in progress. A stolen late-model red Mazda was being chased by a marked police car whose blue and red flashing lights were easy to spot from the air. D24 called for other police vehicles to assist in the chase.

'We've lost him,' came a voice over the radio.

From the air, the flight crew scrutinised the surrounding network of back streets and alleyways and spotted a shadowy vehicle – only visible when the red brake lights flashed on and off as it wound its way through unlit side streets.

'We've got him!' radioed Senior Constable Cameron Hardiman, who was acting as the pilot's observer. He gave D24 the car's location as Senior Constable Roger Puehl shone the powerful NiteSun on the car. From the air, the crew saw the car turn into an alleyway and suddenly, both the passenger's and driver's side opened simultaneously and two men jumped from the moving vehicle, which continued to roll out onto a main road, narrowly missing an oncoming bus. It lost speed as it crossed the road, and came to a halt when it crashed into a parked car on the opposite side of the road. Puehl kept the NiteSun trained on one of the men as he ran into the driveway of a block of flats and seemed to disappear under a tree. The helicopter crew radioed his location and he was quickly apprehended by ground crews. Without the helicopter and its bird's-eye view, the offenders in this case would have gotten away.

John Williamson sees the Victoria Police Air Wing as an essential police service. The Air Wing finds drug crops, and does aerial speed detection blitzes to catch speeding drivers. They assist in Search and Rescue operations and winch around a hundred people to safety each year – and it is this life-saving service that can't be measured. The Air Wing is also a preventative policing tool, flying over schools and factories at night, deterring crime. While public encounters with police helicopters are mainly confined to hearing the loud whirring overhead at night, the Air Wing's results speak for themselves.

Chapter Eight

THE CHAIRLIFT COLLAPSE

Cameron Hardiman had always wanted to join the Police Air Wing. As a young boy growing up on a military base where his dad was stationed, he once saw an RAAF Iroquois helicopter fly low over their house. Cam had never forgotten one of the crew leaning out the big side door and waving at him.

The spell was cast.

He grew up and joined the police force.

Before applying to join the Air Wing, Cam's experience of the elite squad was what he saw as a uniform cop. He would hear them on the radio all the time, helping ground crews with searches, giving a bird's-eye view of a car chase, or looking for dumped cars after armed robberies. It was a popular thing in the 1980s and 1990s — robbers would steal a car, hit a bank, then dump the getaway car a couple of streets away and swap it for a different one. The helicopter was a good way of spotting cars from the air.

The first time Cam got close to an actual Air Wing crew was at an armed robbery in 1992 at Melbourne Airport. Armed robber Normie Lee, long suspected of being part of the gang who did the Great Bookie Robbery, had planned a million-dollar heist at the Ansett freight terminal. The cops got the heads-up and had staked out the airport. As well as the police helicopter watching from above, the place was surrounded by police: the Special Operations Group, the Armed Robbery Squad, and National Crime Authority members. The cops closed in as Lee and his accomplice loaded stolen money bags into the back of the getaway vehicle.

The war cry sounded. 'Police! Don't move! Police! Don't move!' All of a sudden, an army of cops raced towards the getaway vehicle.

In a burst of panic the driver sped off but, in a deadly miscalculation, Lee and his accomplice fell out the back. They scrambled to their feet and Lee chased the van screaming for it to stop. When it didn't, he turned and raised his gun at the police. So did his accomplice. SOG members took no chances and shot both men. Lee, fatally.

Cam was on the periphery with the other uniform cops. He busied himself trying to dodge CIB detectives, thinking they might make him take statements or do paperwork. But he forgot all about hiding when he saw three Air Wing guys walk up to the police van. They seemed taller than everybody else. Their uniforms were different too; they were wearing the police flight suits and the enviable leather jackets, all branded with the coveted wings.

The Air Wing guys had been circling the airport in the helicopter, waiting for the robbery to go down. They'd had a front-row seat to the shootout and had landed the helicopter to come over and check out the scene. Cam listened, fascinated. He was also impressed that once they decided to leave, they walked off towards their helicopter and flew away. No paperwork at all.

From that moment on, Cam had vowed to do his best to realise his childhood dream. After spending eight years as a general-duties uniform cop, his chance finally came. The Air Wing advertised three jobs – an almost unheard-of intake. Of the eighty who applied, Cam got shortlisted, did a physical, got an interview, and found himself with a badge of police wings to add to his newly minted flight suit.

Once he was accepted to the crew, Cam found out that the Air Wing also ran the air ambulance. It had come about when the ambulance service had wanted a helicopter but couldn't afford one. The story went that the legendary Chief Commissioner Mick Miller said that he was going to buy a helicopter anyway so he did a deal with the Ambulance Service that if he bought two new helicopters, one could be dedicated to the ambulance, crewed by both police and a paramedic. They would only pay for what they used. The bonus for Victoria Police was that they would have a second helicopter to support police operations, twenty-four hours a day.

To be able to crew the air ambulance as well as the police helicopter, Cam did a three-day course at the Ambulance Service headquarters in Doncaster. He then spent three shifts with a MICA ambulance as an observer. One of the cases was a drug dealer in Glenroy who'd overdosed. The MICA paramedic asked Cam to get a 14-gauge Jelco needle. From his training, he knew that 16-gauge was the normal size.

'Gee, that looks big,' Cam said, handing him the large hypodermic needle.

'He's used to it,' the ambo said dryly.

That was the moment Cam realised paramedics and cops had a similar sense of humour.

Riding with the ambulance necessitated a switch from cop mode to paramedic mode. As the MICA paramedic was helping the drug dealer, Cam fought the urge to snap the handcuffs on him and lock him up. Providing medical attention and care was very different from the cops' job of getting dealers and druggies off the street. Over time, Cam learnt to see them as people who needed medical help, and not always a set of handcuffs.

Cam's first flight as a new crew member at the Air Wing was in the front passenger seat of the helicopter. He'd had a ride in the back before he applied, just to get a feel for flying. But it was in the front seat, as the impressive Dauphin helicopter rose skyward, that Cam realised policing in the air from a helicopter was a whole different world.

But he didn't always stay in the helicopter.

Cam was trained in winch work. When the situation presented itself, he would be hooked to a winch and head out the door of the helicopter. One job was over Port Phillip Bay. An old motor yacht had sent out a mayday signal – they were taking on water.

A tractor pulled the helicopter out of the hangar at Essendon Airport and the flight crew climbed on board. A couple of minutes later, the whine of the Dauphin's engine reached fever pitch as the helicopter rose into the air. It took around twelve minutes to get to the bay and locate the motor yacht. From the air, it looked like an old restored wooden boat – it reminded Cam of the SS *Minnow* from the TV show 'Gilligan's Island'.

While the boat looked okay from the air, once Cam went down on the winch and landed on the deck, he could see the area below deck was full of water and floating debris. A man and a woman were in the slightly elevated cabin area, trying to steer the doomed vessel.

They had been coming back from Queenscliff after picking up their newly repaired boat when she started taking on water.

Cam quickly located two life jackets floating in the swamped cabin.

'Better put these on,' he said, tossing them to the couple, who perhaps should have thought to do that already.

Over the radio, he could hear the Water Police boat was on its way. They wanted Cam in position to connect a tow rope between the floundering vessel and the police boat so they could tow it in. But there was a necessary stipulation – if the boat started sinking, they would cut the rope. A sinking boat would pull theirs down.

Overhead, the helicopter circled like a buzzard.

When the police boat pulled alongside the stricken boat, they threw Cam the rope. He tied it to the cleats on the front of the yacht. As he secured the tow line, he did not hold out any hope that the operation would be a success. There was just too much water inside the boat, and wherever it was coming in from, it would continue to come in.

Once the ropes were connected, Cam's job was done. He bid goodbye to the yachting couple and wished them luck. Cam radioed the waiting helicopter that he was good to go, then climbed onto the roof of the motorised yacht. As the two boats moved through the water, one towing the other, the helicopter winch operator sent the winch flying down towards Cam. He grabbed it and connected it, and was swept up into the air.

It took six minutes to get back to Essendon Airport. By the time they landed, the yacht had sunk. Over the radio, Cam heard that the couple had to jump overboard in the final moments and then had to be pulled out of the bay by the Water Police crew.

Cam had been in the Air Wing for eleven years when he got called to a job that was one out of the box. He was working an air ambulance shift, which meant that the crew consisted of himself, the pilot and a paramedic called Steve Grove, or Grover. On this particular day in

January 2003, they were joined by a new operative called Rachel O'Brien. She had been rostered on with Cam's crew for a couple of shifts before being signed off as proficient on the air ambulance, marking the completion of her air observer training.

While crews always hoped for a big job in these circumstances so Rachel could cut her teeth in the high drama of the Air Wing, it was Murphy's Law – sometimes big jobs were nowhere to be seen when you really wanted them.

This wasn't one of those times.

At 2.30 pm, a call came through the Ambulance Service – the chairlift at Arthurs Seat had collapsed mid-ride. People were injured; many were trapped in mid-air.

The chairlift was a Melbourne icon. Cam had been up to Arthurs Seat himself, but he had never been on it.

The flight to Arthurs Seat took seventeen minutes.

En route, updates came over the radio from ambulance ground crews. A pylon had collapsed. People were stuck in chairs in the air. A number of chairs had fallen. From those early accounts, a lot of people had been injured.

Working the shift with paramedic Grover was always a laugh. Cam reckoned Grover was in the wrong job – he should have been a cop. He had that wicked sense of humour, perfect for the job. While Cam sat up the front with the pilot, the paramedic sat right up the back so conversation was over radio comms, and Cam reckoned Grover was like the voice in the back of his head. Grover liked to keep things light, no matter what the job. It was like his superpower.

Rachel sat up the back with Grover. As an eleven-year veteran, Cam was used to carnage and could only imagine what was going through her mind. A collapsed chairlift and people dropping from great heights was a nightmare. But she had done the hard yards in uniform, so Cam guessed she had seen it all before too – just not from the air.

As the helicopter approached in that summer afternoon of 3 January 2003, the first thing Cam saw was the chairlift cable running across the top of the massive steel pylons, from the top of Arthurs Seat down towards the lower lift station. He could see a line of chairs dangling in the sky, not moving. Some people were suspended in their chairs above the tree line. Cam traced the cable line down the hill, where it disappeared into the trees.

The local State Emergency Services (SES), all dressed in their bright-orange overalls, were already there and ambulance crews were treating passengers who had hit the ground close to the lift station. The helicopter flew over the top and then turned, entering a right-hand orbit, looking for a landing site as close as possible to the worst damage.

There were cables snaking across the road, and Cam saw a dark-blue car on the road with a huge pylon smashed across its bonnet.

'Geez, how lucky were they?' he said. Half a metre further on, the pylon would have landed on the cabin of the car; looking at the damage to the front, it would have annihilated the people inside.

The lucky escape for the car occupants was also lucky for the air ambulance. The pylon and the smashed vehicle had blocked the road in front of the lift station and created an area big enough for the helicopter to land on. The pilot manoeuvred the helicopter around powerlines on one side of the road and trees on the other, then touched down in the middle of the road, near the chairlift station.

Cam could see at least three or four chairs from the chairlift smashed on the ground. When the pylon had come down, they'd come down with it. The collapsed pylon had dragged the cable down between itself and its adjoining pylons and halted the rest of the chairlift. That meant sixty-five people were stuck in the air. The unlucky ones who had hit the ground needed urgent medical treatment; they had fallen nine or ten metres.

The scene was littered with paramedics, police, and emergency services workers.

Grover walked up to the closest paramedics and asked, 'Who's the worst?'

'We've got two in chairs here who've hit the ground,' said one of the paramedics.

Cam followed Grover, ready to take direction from him. Grover moved smoothly from being the joker on the flight to the professional on the ground. While he examined the woman closest to him, he pointed to the next chair up the hill.

'Go check her out, Cam.'

Cam left the two cases of equipment with Grover and made his way up the incline to the woman on the next chair. She was surrounded by paramedics who had removed her from the chair and laid her flat on the ground. She was conscious, speaking in a thick European accent and moaning in pain.

'She was in that chair.' One of the paramedics nodded to the nearby chair. Broken and shattered on the ground, they looked so flimsy. Cam imagined she would have landed on her backside and done untold damage to her back, spine, legs and God knows what else.

'Can you wriggle your toes?' Cam asked, kneeling next to the fallen woman.

She was wearing sandals. He watched her toes. Nothing.

'Try and wriggle them,' Cam said again. He watched her face grimace in concentration. Again, nothing.

'She has no feeling in her legs,' the paramedic said in a low voice. That meant he'd done the pain test – if a patient didn't respond to or couldn't feel a scratch on the leg with the end of a pen, that wasn't a good sign. Cam knew what that could mean. Some sort of nerve damage – if not a spinal injury.

Cam looked down at the woman. 'Does she need to go with us, or can she be transported by road?'

He nodded. 'She needs to go by air.'

In other words, her condition may deteriorate during a long road trip.

Even though the ground crew ambo had already checked, Cam felt the woman's head for head injuries.

'Do you remember what happened?' Cam asked her.

'The chairlift fell and I hit the ground,' the woman told him through groans. In halting English, she described the sound coming from the chairlift pylon as it groaned and collapsed behind her, then the sensation of falling and the shock to her back when she hit the ground.

'Did you lose consciousness?'

'No.'

Cam couldn't find any bumps on her head. There was no blood and the woman wasn't slurring. But while she probably hadn't hit her head, her level of pain didn't rule out a neck injury.

Grover appeared over Cam's shoulder. 'How's she doing?'

'She's in a lot of pain. Can't move her feet. The road crew wants us to take her.'

'Can we take two passengers?' Grover asked.

Cam knew from the question that Grover's patient was in a similar condition to his. Or worse.

In his eleven years in the Air Wing, Cam had only seen the air ambulance take two patients at once a couple of times — usually at really bad car accidents where two patients were at risk of dying. Cam knew that a ride in a ground ambulance from Arthurs Seat would take too long for these badly injured women. By helicopter, they were seventeen minutes away from the Alfred Hospital.

Cam had no idea how much fuel they'd had onboard when they left Essendon Airport. He called the pilot over to see if they could handle the additional weight of a second patient.

The pilot did the calculations and agreed. But if they took two patients, they'd have to leave Rachel behind. Considering the breadth of destruction and mayhem at the scene, Rachel was happy to stay on scene and help. She could catch a ride back to Essendon Airport in a police car later.

Cam returned to his patient. Grover spent the next few minutes inserting an intravenous cannula into Cam's patient's arm, allowing the administration of fluids and, more importantly, pain relief, before returning to his own patient.

Cam's patient was still groaning loudly with pain. In contrast, he could see Grover's patient was worryingly quiet. Conscious but quiet. That wasn't good.

Despite Cam's patient's limited English, she knew enough to answer basic questions. Luckily it sufficed and he began to assess her injuries. Spinal and internal injuries were a sure bet. From the chair smashed on the ground next to her, Cam looked upwards and estimated the drop would have been like falling from a three-storey building strapped to a garden chair. She would have had several seconds to realise what was happening while she waited for impact.

Cam's patient complained of severe back pain. He again asked her to try to move her fingers and toes. Again, he could see the amount of effort she was putting in to moving, grimacing in pain. Her fingers barely moved, and her toes didn't move at all.

Rachel went down the slope to the equipment box and grabbed a cervical collar while Cam kept talking to his patient, engaging her in conversation. When Rachel returned with the cervical collar, she

Danger and death on the frontline
Chris Glasl in his SOG uniform.

The stairs of Sharpie's flat. It was here that Sharpie realised he'd been stabbed.

The scene of the siege in Wandin. In the foreground lies the burnt-out car.

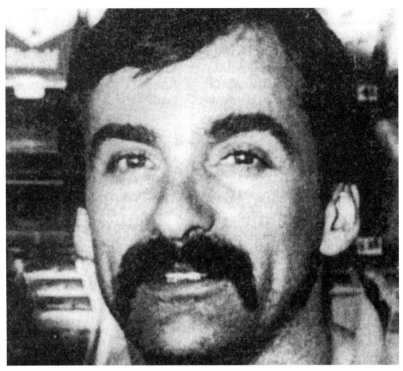

The Black Widow
Gina Agostinelli told police that her husband Angelo had disappeared after an argument.

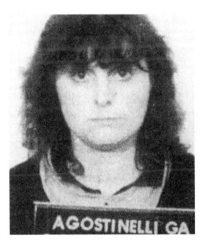

Police mugshot of Gina Agostinelli, who, with her husband, ran a caravan park and deli at Millicent, on the Victoria–South Australia border.

Neighbour Gary Lewis was one of the last people to see Angelo alive. Lewis was working as a butcher at the time.

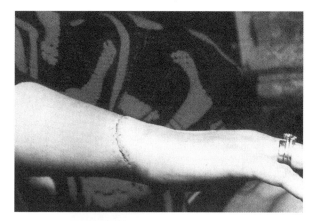

Gina claimed Angelo had inflicted this deep cut to her arm.

The cramped interior of the Agostinellis' caravan.

Police sensed that neighbour Helen Miller knew more than she was admitting to.

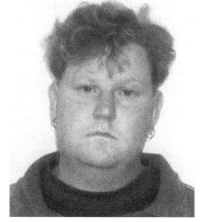

Helen Miller's son Adrian had also been drawn into the drama.

A police officer stands on the bush road at the spot where Angelo Agostinelli's remains were found.

Detective Ron Hope.

Detective Alan Rodda.

Lost at sea
The *Shearwater*, fully laden with search and rescue equipment, including the Duocom decompression chamber.

Barry Gibson, who 'buddy-dived' with Bob Manks, exhausted after the body retrieval. He breathes pure oxygen to help rid his system of dangerous levels of nitrogen.

Bob Manks (foreground) on oxygen after successfully retrieving the body of a woman diver from the wreck of a submarine outside Port Phillip Heads.

Searching for Sarah MacDiarmid

Sarah MacDiarmid disappeared from the Kananook railway station on 11 July 1990. Her car was found in the car park. No trace of Sarah has ever been found.

In early 1990, Sarah MacDiarmid bought her first car. She planned to use it to get to the Kananook railway station each day. She also planned a trip away with a friend later in the year. She vanished before this could happen.

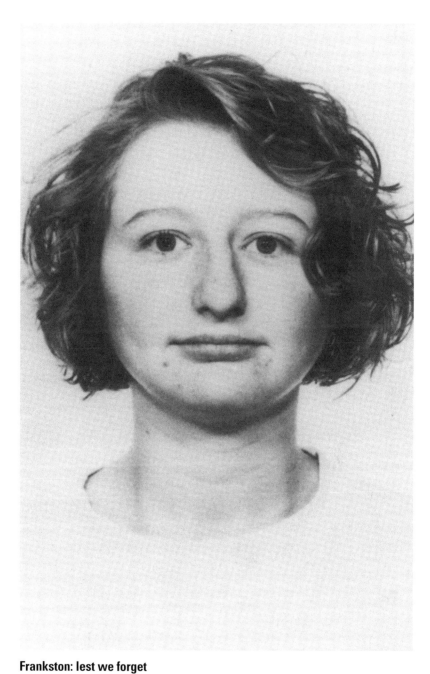

Frankston: lest we forget
Elizabeth Stevens, Paul Denyer's first victim, was partially hidden in a reserve in Langwarrin.

Denyer targeted Debbie Fream when she went to the milk bar to buy milk.

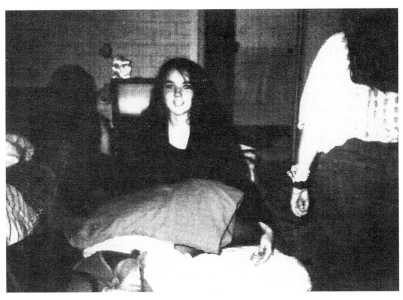

Denyer murdered his third and final victim, Natalie Russell, on her way home from school.

Denyer's car, parked by the bike track where he killed Natalie Russell, was checked by police.

Denyer was canny enough to burn the soles of his shoes so they couldn't be matched to any crime scene footprints.

Paul Charles Denyer after his arrest.

Fingerprints
Senior Sergeant Jim Falloon's vital fingerprint evidence helped solve a
particularly gruesome murder.

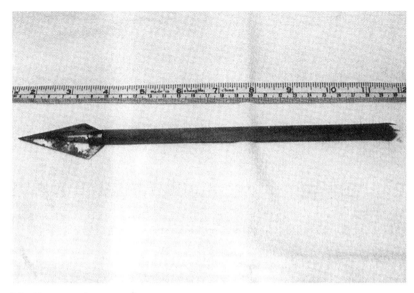

The Rye crossbow murder
The broken arrow retrieved from Jimmy Pinakos's chest wound during the post-mortem examination.

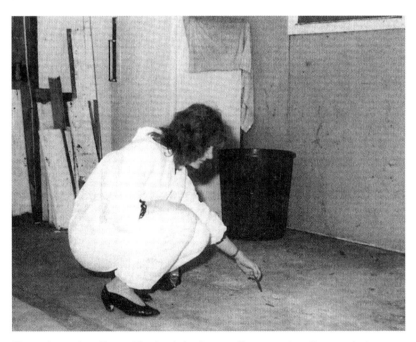

Three days after Jimmy Pinakos's body was discovered, police carried out an exhaustive search at Ron Lucas's home. Here, biologist Jane Taplin examines bloodstains on his garage floor.

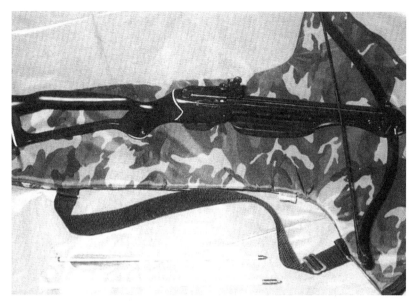

The murder weapon and its camouflage carry-case, which had been stored by one of Lucas's neighbours.

Two faces of Ron Lucas. He tried to alter his appearance while on the run.

Forensic evidence provided by crime scene examiner Sergeant Brian Gamble and a team of forensic science experts proved vital for Lucas's conviction.

fitted it around the woman's neck, careful not to cause any more damage. Grover was using all the monitoring equipment on his patient, so all Rachel and Cam could do for theirs was to get her ready for transport. After Rachel assembled a stretcher, and Cam got the spinal board ready, they ever-so-carefully rolled their patient to one side in a slow continuous movement. Rachel supported her head and neck, keeping it aligned with her spine while Cam slid the spinal board underneath her. Then they rolled her back. Gently, gently.

The stretcher straps were fitted across and around her feet in a figure eight pattern, two across her legs and two across her abdomen and arms. They rolled two ambulance towels and set one on either side of her head, then fitted the last strap across her forehead, securing her head onto the stretcher. It was impossible for her to move – even if she could, which wasn't certain.

Once she was secure on the stretcher, Cam looked over at Grover. He had his patient all packaged up too and was about to head for the helicopter. Rachel and Cam followed him, lifting and carrying their patient over to the helicopter.

Glancing up, Cam noticed two people stranded in the air on the next chair along from the broken pylon. He reckoned they must've been counting their lucky stars as they watched the air ambulance crew load the two fallen passengers into the helicopter. Aside from the shock of what they had witnessed, the worst part of their day was going to be the long wait for rescue crews to get them down.

The helicopter had one standard stretcher and one winch stretcher. The former was a regular cushioned type, while the latter was little more than a piece of hard board. Cam's groaning patient was assessed as less severely injured than Grover's quiet one, so she got the soft stretcher while Cam's patient got the hard stretcher. Cam put her on the cabin floor, using straps to anchor the stretcher to fixed points on the floor to keep her in place. While it wouldn't have been the most comfortable position for her to be lying in, her back had the best support possible.

With four people in the back of the air ambulance, it was cramped. Grover sat in the ambo's seat along the back wall while Cam stood in a crouch, his back wedged up against the cabin ceiling, a harness belt around his waist connected by an extension strap to another hard point on the floor.

On the short flight to the Alfred Hospital Emergency and Trauma Centre, both patients lay on their stretchers, eyes open, staring at the roof. Cam could only imagine what was going through their minds. The memory of falling, the fear of permanent injury.

Once they were airborne, Cam fitted a small device to his patient's fingers and connected the other end to a pulse oximeter that monitored the percentage of oxygen in her blood and her heart rate. Every five minutes he scribbled the readings on a notepad attached to his knee board.

Just before they landed, Grover told Cam they would have to separate once they entered the hospital. He would go with his patient and Cam would take the woman he'd looked after. Cam had never done handover before. That was the realm of the paramedic, not the Police Air Wing observer. He had witnessed the rapid-fire medico handovers, experts talking to experts, and he had no idea if he could do it. For a moment, he thought it might be one of Grover's jokes, but a glance at his paramedic colleague dispelled that notion.

Cam got an immediate vision of every doctor and nurse in the trauma cubicle listening to him, focusing on every word, asking him important questions. He gulped.

The pilot guided the helicopter to the landing site at the Alfred Hospital and shut down the engine. There were two helipad teams waiting, both with trauma nurses and orderlies.

Cam spotted Judy, one of the trauma nurses he knew. He gave the thumbs up once the helicopter was safe to approach and they moved onto the landing site with stretchers. The teams separated into two groups, one on each side of the helicopter.

The roles had changed this time around. The nurse and orderly pushed the patient and stretcher into the trauma centre and into the cubicle, just like Cam normally would, while he followed them in like a paramedic would. Grover and his patient were close behind.

Cam recited the handover information silently to himself as many times as he could while waiting for a nod from the doctor to start.

Doctors and nurses crowded around the patient ready to get to work, and the orderly wedged a large flat slide underneath the patient. In one swift movement, they slid the woman over to the trauma bed. Gown-covered trauma staff all converged on the patient and Cam got the nod.

He took a deep breath and began his handover. 'The patient is a fifty-year-old female who was a passenger on the Arthurs Seat chairlift when it collapsed. The patient fell approximately nine metres, landing ...'

He rattled off the handover as if he'd done it a million times before.

Cam's nurse friend Judy looked over to Cam and gave him a thumbs up and a smile. He'd made it through without looking like he didn't know what he was doing.

After dropping their patients off, Cam and Grover climbed back into the helicopter, half wondering – half hoping – they might get called back to winch the trapped riders off the chairlift. Cam, the pilot and Grover discussed how they would do it. Grover wasn't a winch operator, which meant he would be the one going down the wire in an event of a call-back, while Cam would operate the winch from the helicopter.

'It'd be like a cliff rescue,' Cam said. 'Go down, put 'em in a strop, move away sideways clear of the cable, then winch 'em up.'

'Yeah, I'll give it a go,' said Grover.

But the helicopter wasn't called back.

It was just as well though. Instead, they got called to a serious car accident in Rosebud where a man was trapped in his car. Cam and Grover spent the rest of the shift trying to disassemble the dashboard with a spanner and screwdriver, trying to free the driver's trapped legs.

Later, as they flew overhead with the released driver, they could see Arthurs Seat and the rescue lights of the ground operation. The red and blue flashing lights of the police and ambos on the ground were beacons in the dark.

All up, eighteen people fell from the collapsing chairlift that day. They suffered neck, head and spinal injuries. Most were taken to the Frankston Hospital by ambulance. The rescue operation to get the sixty-five dangling people back on solid ground took six hours, using a combination of a cherry picker and people on ropes. Cam reckoned the helicopter and winch could have rescued each one in minutes. Rachel was picked up later by the police helicopter.

An investigation found the collapse was caused by corrosion and fatigue in two anchor bolts at the pylon base.

Cam and Grover didn't ever find out the fate of the two women they helped that day. That is the nature of the work of the police air ambulance. They swoop down out of the sky, scoop up the fallen, deliver them into the hands of the trauma surgeons, then fly away again to help the next person in the never-ending queue needing police help.

Chapter Nine

SEARCHING FOR SARAH MACDIARMID

The disappearance of Sarah MacDiarmid and the unimaginable grief that followed has been the burden of Peter and Sheila MacDiarmid and their son Alisdair. Sheila says, 'Everyone focuses on the parents when something like this happens, but Alisdair also lost a sister.' Alisdair was the one who drove to the Kananook railway station when his sister Sarah didn't come home. He was the one to wait for the last train, which came and went without any sign of her. He was the one who had to go home and tell his parents that Sarah wasn't there.

Even though she was twenty-three years old, Sarah MacDiarmid was the kind of daughter who always told her parents what time she would be home. She always took the time to ring so they wouldn't worry. Back then, there were no mobile phones; Sarah would ring from work or call from a public phone box.

On Wednesday 11 July 1990, Sarah left work in the city at around 5.10 pm. For the past couple of years, she had worked at CE Heath Underwriters in Collins Place in the Melbourne CBD. Sarah was sporty and four or five months earlier had started a weekly evening tennis game with some pals from work – Gavan, Dianne and Mike. On that day, Mike drove everyone in his car and they got to the National Tennis Centre at Flinders Park (now Melbourne Park) at 5.25 pm. They played for over an hour, and then had drinks and supper in the Tennis Centre lounge for the next two and a half hours.

From the Tennis Centre, Mike left in his car, while Gavan, Dianne and Sarah walked to the Richmond railway station and caught the

9.20 pm train from Richmond to Caulfield station. At Caulfield, they transferred to the Frankston line, catching the 9.39 pm train. There were three carriages on this train. The three friends hopped into the third carriage, which was the only one with its lights on; the first two were dark.

It was sixteen stops from Caulfield station to Bonbeach, where Gavan and Dianne got off the train. Sarah had two further stops – Carrum and Seaford – before reaching the Kananook railway station. When her family had moved to Skye Road, Frankston six months earlier, the woman they'd bought the house from advised the MacDiarmids that Kananook was a safer station to park at than Frankston. They had taken her advice and Sarah had purchased a car for the purpose of driving to the station to catch the train to her job in the city. The car was also part of a plan she had made with her friend Caroline, who was coming over from Scotland in October to visit. The two planned to do some road trips.

The train pulled in to Kananook railway station at 10.20 pm.

Sarah was seen by several witnesses walking towards the car park. A man observed her in the car park wearing a green tracksuit and carrying a bag and a tennis racquet. Another witness reported hearing a woman's voice say, 'Give me back my keys and stop fooling around!' Then a scream.

Several people would later report hearing screams coming from the direction of the car park.

And then Sarah MacDiarmid was gone.

By 11 pm, Peter and Sheila MacDiarmid were starting to worry. Sarah was such a creature of habit; they could almost set their clocks by her comings and goings. She was always home by 10.30 pm on tennis nights, 10.40 at the latest. To allay their own fears, they reasoned that maybe she missed the train and decided to stay with a friend – she was twenty-three, after all.

Even so, there was no rest that night for the MacDiarmids. They studied the train timetable, and Shelia asked Alisdair to drive to the Kananook railway station at 1 am and wait for the last Frankston-bound train of the night. Alisdair did as his mother asked and headed for the station. When he got there, he could see Sarah's car in the car park. He pulled up next to it and got out to look around. He checked the doors, the boot; both were locked. Then from the warmth of his car on the cold winter's night, he watched the last train pull into the station at 1.15 am.

When he returned home, Alisdair told his parents that Sarah's car was still in the car park but she didn't get off the last train. Even though it was most out of character, Sheila tried to convince herself that her daughter must've decided to stay with a friend and thought it too late to ring and let them know. By then, it was also too late to ring any of Sarah's friends to see if they knew where she was. The family discussed it and decided they would ring Sarah's work first thing in the morning. Because as Peter – who used to be a police officer – kept pointing out, Sarah was an adult. Even if they rang the police, no cop would take seriously a report of a 23-year-old woman, late home from a night out.

The MacDiarmids spent an uneasy night waiting for morning.

The next morning, Peter MacDiarmid left for work at 5.45 am, only after Sheila promised to let him know as soon as they heard from Sarah.

Sheila didn't even wait till 9 am to ring Sarah's work. Her first call was at 8.15 am. She spoke to a woman called Katrina, who told her Sarah wasn't in yet but promised to ask around to see if anyone knew where she was. She suggested Sheila wait till 9 am and ring back then. But Shelia couldn't wait. She made a call at 8.40, then a third phone call just before 9 am. This time when Sheila asked if her daughter had arrived at work yet, Sarah's boss came on the line.

'Hello, Mrs MacDiarmid, it's Mark here,' he said. 'No, Sarah's not here.' And then he said the words that would forever shatter the peaceful world of the MacDiarmid family. He said, 'But Di and Gavan are here, and they said they were on the train with her last night. They got off at Bonbeach.'

Sheila barely remembered dropping the phone. When Alisdair rang Peter at work to tell him, Peter could hear Sheila screaming in the background.

Two constables arrived at the MacDiarmids' home in Skye Road at 10 am and took the initial report. From there, the uniform cops drove to the Kananook railway station car park and located Sarah's car. It was covered in dew and didn't appear to have been used recently. From the railway station, they drove to the Frankston police station and rang Dianne and Gavan to verify their story about being on the train with Sarah.

Detective Inspector Laurie Ratz was the local crime coordinator; it was his responsibility to ensure the proper investigation of crime committed within the district. By 11 am, Ratz was notified of Sarah's disappearance. He was told how she had caught the train with friends, then failed to make it to her car parked at the station. Ratz immediately contacted the Frankston CIB and asked them to detail two detectives to start the inquiry. Detectives Colin Clark and Geoff Randall were put on the case. Ratz instructed them to have police crime scene examiners process her car.

By 2.30 pm, Sarah's car had been examined and a substance that appeared to be blood had been discovered by the driver's-side door of the car. Most worrying, investigators saw drag marks – like someone had been dragged by the shoulders, leaving heel marks on the ground – leading into a small area of trees and bushes on the border of the car park. There was more blood there, enough to suggest that the person whose blood it was may not have survived the attack. The amount of blood that had seeped into the soil suggested the person bleeding might have been there for some time. From the ground near the blood, police collected a green cigarette lighter. On it was the logo of the cafe downstairs from Sarah's work.

The Homicide Squad was called in.

When Detective Inspector Ratz went to the Kananook railway station car park and saw the scene near Sarah's car, he understood why detectives Colin Clark and Geoff Randall were so concerned. If the blood near the car belonged to Sarah, then it meant she had been targeted by someone between the station ramp and her car door, attacked at the car, then dragged into the bushes.

The offender – or offenders – had been very thorough in making sure there was no trace of Sarah left behind. They had removed her handbag, sports bag and tennis racquet. The only thing left behind was the little green lighter, easy to miss in the dark.

But why? Ratz wondered.

If she was attacked in a robbery-gone-wrong scenario, then why take *her* as well? And if it was a robbery gone wrong, why would a purse-snatcher escalate to murder? Or, if Sarah was attacked by a random knife-wielding assailant, why drag her to the bushes to conceal her, then come back later to move her? Could there have been DNA evidence that the offender wanted to conceal? Or was Sarah still alive when the offender took her?

As a detective, Laurie Ratz tried to keep an open mind about what might have happened to Sarah. In the beginning, the first and most urgent matter was finding her, but like all investigations, this one was hampered by timing. It's nobody's fault, it's just the way it is. By the time the MacDiarmids reported Sarah missing and the police checked out the car at the Kananook railway station, twelve hours had elapsed. By the time the detectives arrived at the car park, it was mid-afternoon, then by the time the forensic team set up, it was early evening. The investigation was in full swing by nightfall.

Brian McMannis, the person in charge of the Frankston SES, saw the police gathering in the car park at Kananook late Thursday afternoon and stopped to ask them how the SES could help. Their headquarters was about 300 metres from the station car park. McMannis got his team ready to help with the search for Sarah.

Police cordoned off the Kananook railway station car park and took the names of everyone alighting from the train to collect their cars. Each person was asked if they had been on the train the night before with Sarah. The media was also alerted and anyone with information was urged to come forward.

The forensic team finished their crime scene examination, finding no blood evidence outside of the area between the car and the bushes. If the blood was Sarah's – and the police had to work under the assumption that it was – it was unlikely she could have been physically carried away because there would have been a blood trail. And even if the offender had carried Sarah – she was of small build and 153 centimetres, or five feet, tall – they could hardly manage to carry her bag, backpack and tennis racquet as well. They would have been noticed by the many people in the area at the time. That left the possibility that Sarah was moved in a vehicle. Right from the start, the amount of blood in the bushes had suggested Sarah had been left there for some time, then moved. This meant that police had to consider the possibility that whoever attacked Sarah had been on foot and left her there to go and get a car. This could explain the length of time she was left in the bushes. Surely, someone with a car in the car park would have moved her straightaway rather than risk her being discovered.

If Sarah was collected by car, she could be anywhere. But if a car had been used just to move her from the immediate vicinity, the person responsible may have disposed of her locally. There was nothing to suggest whether either possibility was more likely.

The obvious question for the detectives was why an offender would go to get another vehicle when he – or she – could have just taken Sarah's car.

On Friday 13 July, the police Search and Rescue Squad launched an intense large-scale land, water and air search that would run for two months and involve over a hundred police and SES volunteers.

Once detectives began talking to the MacDiarmids and Sarah's friends, it quickly became obvious that Sarah MacDiarmid was a quiet young woman who didn't have a boyfriend, spent time socially with friends, but equally enjoyed staying home with her close-knit family. She had no enemies. There was nothing to connect her to anyone who might do this to her. Was this a case of her being in the wrong place at the wrong time?

The police put together a pamphlet detailing Sarah's disappearance and handed one to each of the 5000 motorists they stopped in the days after on Wells Road, near the Kananook station. They travelled on the train from the city to Kananook asking people if they'd seen Sarah on the night she vanished. In the first week, police also ran a re-enactment on the train with the help of Sarah's friends Gavan and Dianne, who had travelled with her on that final train journey. The two sat with a model dressed in the same clothes that Sarah had been wearing on the night, recreating their journey home, hoping to jog the memory of train travellers.

The Search and Rescue Squad and a band of SES and volunteers searched a one-kilometre radius out from the Kananook railway station. Every house was doorknocked, every bin and dumpster were checked, along with drains, creeks, pockets of bushland, tips, and along the freeway and the railway lines.

Bit by bit, detectives pieced together a picture of who had been on the train and who had seen Sarah in her final moments. They identified and interviewed as many people as they could, then released a statement calling for anyone else travelling on the same train as Sarah to come forward.

They also called for the people others had seen at the station to come forward. Almost all the witnesses had seen a man with a red jumper on who had a suitcase with him, pacing back and forth on the city side of the platform. Three women had been seen walking down the station ramp. Two of them went to a phone box and appeared to make a call, then a van arrived to collect all three women, driving off towards Frankston. A man wearing blue overalls was seen riding a bicycle north along the station side of Wells Road. He then rode up onto the footbridge and stood there looking down on the station.

The three women contacted police. They had been at a local bingo game and had called a family member from the phone box to come and collect them.

A man and his twelve-year-old daughter had walked their dogs to the station to wait for his wife. Her car had broken down the day before and she had arranged to walk home from work and her husband and daughter would meet her halfway – at the Kananook railway station.

The girl would later tell police:

> Only a couple of minutes after I saw these males, I heard what I thought
> was a female voice screaming loudly, immediately followed by more
> than one male voice. These males were screaming out loudly also.
> They weren't saying anything but just screams. These male and female
> screams came from the car park end of the railway station. I thought
> that the screams came from the middle of the car park. There was only
> one scream from a female. As I heard this so did the dogs because
> they started barking out and the one that I had hold of started pulling
> towards the car park way. I could not see who these persons were that
> were screaming. This screaming took place about three to five minutes
> after the Frankston-bound train pulled out of the station.

But that wasn't all the girl had to say. Once her mother arrived and the family began walking towards home, they saw a man.

> We were walking along the footpath past the car yard towards
> Melbourne way. Dad was in front with one of the dogs, Mum I think
> had the other. Dad was walking first, followed by Mum, and me last.
> We crossed over Bardia Avenue, which leads to the basketball court,
> and continued walking up the footpath onto the Klauer Street railway
> bridge. As we were about near the sign on the left going up the bridge,
> I saw a man walking towards us along the same footpath. I saw that
> he was walking very fast and he looked to be very worried. His facial
> expressions made him look worried, along with him walking very fast.
> He looked as though he was deliberately trying to keep his head down.
> I saw Dad pull the dog over and he walked past Dad and then Mum
> who was carrying the other dog. I got a very good look at this man's
> face as he came towards me and went past. There was a light shining
> in the area that lit us up. He then passed me and kept walking along the
> footpath towards Frankston. I remember turning around and looking at
> him walking away.

When the dad was questioned by police, he too described the screaming:

> I heard more than one male voice and one female voice. I couldn't
> hear what the voices were saying, it was more like they were yelling
> out loud noises, but not happy noises. I heard the female voice
> between the two male voices. The female was screaming. I think she
> screamed two times and then I heard the two male voices again. The
> yelling and screaming only lasted for about two minutes altogether. I
> thought it must have been naughty kids playing in the car park at the
> station. It sounded as if they were near the end of the car park towards
> Melbourne but not right at the end. I couldn't see them from where I
> was standing. I was looking to see where the voices were coming from.
> The dogs started barking straightaway. I didn't hear anything after that.

While the mother had arrived too late to hear the screams, she did see the man her daughter described. Here's what she told police:

> I was holding the terrier on the lead and ... I suddenly looked up and
> saw a man coming towards me. He was near me and he kept coming
> towards me so I stepped to my right onto the roadway. The man walked
> past me and kept going. He had a worried look on his face and he was

looking down all the time. He didn't look at me. I looked at his face as he was coming towards me.

While the girl and her dad described two male voices, another witness who got off the train Sarah was on heard it differently. She told police:

> As I reached the turnstiles everyone was ahead of me; I was the last person through ... I was walking slowly ... I reached the top of the ramp, to where it joins the bridge, and just started turning right when I heard a female voice say, 'Give me my car keys back and stop fooling around.' I could also hear other talking but I couldn't understand what was being said. It sounded muffled. The words I heard were in a firm but not a yelling-type voice. I couldn't see what was going on when I looked over the bridge as it was dark and obscured by bush. I continued walking along the bridge and also continued looking towards the car park. I saw a red-coloured car, a small car, which appeared in the first half of the car park. Within a few seconds of hearing the female voice, I heard a female scream. It was cut off after a very short time, for less than a second. I stopped and looked everywhere – the car park, the station and the railway line – but I couldn't see anyone. I stood there looking and waiting to hear something else for about three minutes. I didn't hear or see anything.

A lot of witnesses described the bad lighting in the car park. A few said that while they heard screams, they were fearful of investigating any further.

To the police hearing these accounts as they came forward, it seemed that so many people were in the vicinity, it was by sheer bad luck that whoever attacked Sarah had escaped detection.

Perhaps it was the number of people in the area that made the offender leave her in the bushes and return for her later, when no-one else was around.

An odd feature that emerged in the wake of Sarah's disappearance was that a few local wannabe thugs boasted to girls they wanted to impress that they were responsible for killing Sarah MacDiarmid. Instead of being impressed, the girls contacted police and more than one young man found himself sitting across from detectives explaining how he'd made it up to make himself 'a big man' and that he didn't have anything to do with Sarah's disappearance.

On 17 July – six days after Sarah vanished – Homicide detective Charlie Bezzina spoke to a woman who might hold the key. A friend of hers, a young woman with a troubled past called Jodie Jones, had confessed to her that she had been there when the 'girl at the Kananook railway station was murdered'. At twenty-five years of age, Jodie Anne Jones had fronted court seventeen times for forty-five offences including convictions for street offences, drugs, prostitution, burglary and manslaughter. Jodie was sentenced to twelve years' imprisonment in 1984 for the manslaughter charge, with a minimum of ten years. She was granted pre-release in August 1989. Her parole was revoked in October of 1989 and she was later released in February 1990.

Jodie had told a number of friends that she was involved somehow in the death of Sarah MacDiarmid. The problem the detectives faced was that her story was never consistent, and it usually ended with an appeal for money.

I killed her and now I have to skip town. Can you give me a hundred dollars?

Another problem with the Jodie-did-it stories was that she was supposed to have been with two men that no-one knew, though various names were thrown about. This was cause for suspicion among detectives because in Jodie's world, everyone knew everyone. They were all bound together because they had served time in prison or were drug users. For Jodie to have found two men who appeared with her at Kananook railway station, then disappeared off the radar, was unlikely. Any men who *were* mentioned regarding the attack on Sarah were interviewed and discounted.

Perhaps the biggest problem of all was that no-one could place Jodie Jones and her two mystery accomplices at Kananook railway station on the night Sarah disappeared.

On 23 July, Homicide detective Charlie Bezzina and Frankston CIB detective Colin Clark brought Jodie Jones in for questioning. They interviewed her at length. The young woman who had served serious prison time for killing a man by jumping on him with stilettos didn't necessarily look like a seasoned criminal. But she certainly knew how the system worked. She was cooperative up to a point, but she was not looking to help the police. She added no extra information, and in response to some of their questions gave a shrug or a shake of the head.

During the interview, Jodie Jones became belligerent, saying she had recently been raped and had overdosed. When the detectives pushed her on details, she began 'no commenting' all their questions. Then they read her a statement from a man she knew who claimed Jodie had told him that during the rape, Sarah MacDiarmid had 'helped tie her to the bed' while two men raped her and that Jodie had attacked Sarah in retaliation.

Jodie denied saying this.

'Why has he said that?' Bezzina asked.

'I wouldn't have a fuckin' clue,' she snapped.

Bezzina continued to read from the witness's statement. 'All right. It goes on: "I then put a newspaper article down in front of her about the girl, Sarah, and she said, 'I was there that night, there were police everywhere and I was pissed off.'" Did you in fact say that?'

'No.' Jodie went on to claim that the witness had only said these things to cooperate with police and curry favour in his own upcoming court appearances.

According to the friend Bezzina quoted from, Jodie had also told him that she and Sarah had gone to school together and that Jodie used to stay at her house. If Jodie's friends were speaking the truth and were not 'full of shit' as Jodie claimed, the narrative Jodie had spun around being friends with Sarah was clearly fanciful. The MacDiarmids had lived in Queensland, then moved back to Scotland for much of Sarah's schooling. They had returned to Melbourne in 1987 and had only lived in Frankston since January. Jodie had been in prison from 1984 until February 1990, which left no effective window for contact with Sarah.

After hearing Jodie's reference to being at the Kananook railway station with 'police everywhere', some investigators concluded that she may have gone past on the train on Thursday 12 July – the night *after* Sarah went missing, when there were indeed police everywhere.

By the end of the interview, Jodie Jones did admit to going past the Kananook railway station on the Thursday when the police were there.

When asked again about her whereabouts on the Wednesday, Jodie said she was staying with a friend in Mentone. The friend later corroborated this.

With no evidence aside from Jodie Jones telling everyone she knew a different version of being involved in the attack on Sarah, the police in the end had nothing to charge her with and had to let her go.

In January 1991, a detective sergeant from the Homicide Squad conducted a full review of the investigation into the disappearance of Sarah MacDiarmid. He concluded: 'Upon reviewing this investigation I assess the evidence and information implicating Jones to be tainted and I hold serious reservations concerning any comments made by Jones.'

On 24 September 1991, Jodie Jones died of a drug overdose.

Many detectives in the intervening years have looked into the case of Sarah MacDiarmid. Another possible suspect emerged in 1993 in the guise of Paul Denyer, who was arrested for murdering Elizabeth Stevens, Debbie Fream and Natalie Russell over a seven-week period in June and July 1993.

In his police interview, Homicide detective Rod Wilson asked Paul Denyer about Sarah MacDiarmid. Denyer denied having anything to do with her disappearance. The detectives figured that since Denyer was willing to talk at length about the three recent murders he'd committed, if he'd killed Sarah, surely he would have admitted to it.

Maybe. Or maybe not.

Sarah's body hadn't been found. Denyer knew the police had nothing to link him to the crime. He may have also suspected that his sentence would be greater if he were convicted of a fourth murder. Throughout his police interview, Denyer was cocky and self-assured, and it seemed he fancied himself better and cleverer than the police.

Some detectives felt that the modus operandi of Sarah's disappearance was different from that of the later three murders. But there were similarities too. The three Frankston victims were snatched off the street and taken elsewhere. So was Sarah. A knife was used in each Frankston case. There was enough blood at the scene of Sarah's disappearance to suggest a knife could have been used. Denyer concealed the Frankston victims up to a point. Could it be possible he concealed Sarah too well and made a point of not doing that with later victims?

Denyer was eighteen when Sarah disappeared. He was old enough to drive and transport her body somewhere. By his own admission, he had been stalking women for several years and he told detectives he had wanted to kill since he was seventeen.

Denyer: 'Yeah. I've been stalking women for a few years in Frankston.'

Wilson: 'How long do you think you have been doing that?'

Denyer: 'Three or four years, or since I was seventeen, I think. I've been following heaps of women around.'

Wilson: 'Just waiting for the opportunity?'

Denyer: 'Waiting for the sign.'

Could Paul Denyer have seen a sign that night in the car park when Sarah came down the ramp?

There's another moment in the interview when Rod Wilson mentions the case. 'So you are aware that there was a woman who was taken from the Kananook railway station in 1990?'

Without missing a beat, Paul Denyer replied, 'I didn't do that, not Sarah MacDiarmid.'

Denyer had no reason to remember the name of a woman who had disappeared three years earlier. Why would she be in his mind at this moment when he would presumably be concerned only with the predicament he was in?

The argument that Denyer confessed to the three Frankston murders so he would have confessed to Sarah's murder is flawed. Denyer spent many hours calmly denying everything. He only confessed to the three murders when the detectives took samples from him for DNA testing and he knew the game was up.

So perhaps Denyer shouldn't be ruled out just because he said he didn't do it.

The date 11 July 2020 marked the thirtieth anniversary of the disappearance of Sarah MacDiarmid. For thirty years, her family has hoped for a resolution. They just want to find Sarah's remains and put them in a place they can visit and pay their respects. Not knowing what happened to their precious daughter and sister is a fate you wouldn't wish on your worst enemy.

But for them, every day brings the possibility that someone who knows something might choose that day to come forward.

May their prayers be answered.

Chapter Ten

FRANKSTON: LEST WE FORGET

Bernadette Naughton suffered more than her fair share of grief in her life, yet she tried never to let it beat her. She became her family's spokesperson when Bernadette's niece, Natalie Russell, was murdered on her way home from school by a serial killer on Friday 30 July 1993.

Natalie, a Year 12 student, left school around 2.30 pm to walk home along a bike track off Skye Road in Frankston. The track was a shortcut between the two Frankston golf courses and kids used it all the time. Along the track, she was targeted by serial killer Paul Denyer and became his third and final victim. Her aunt Bernadette became a public figure. Whenever the media wanted a quote from the family, more often than not it would be Bernadette who would brave the reporters and the cameras and give a measured, dignified response.

While Bernadette hated what Denyer did, she was never bitter or vengeful. She didn't believe in capital punishment and just wanted Denyer to serve a life sentence to pay for what he did. She also felt sorry for Denyer's family because she could imagine their suffering was similar to that of her own family. Bernadette was an ex-nun and a practising nurse, and she had all of the finest qualities of both professions. She met with members of Denyer's family to reassure them that she didn't blame them for what Paul had done, and offered them the hand of friendship.

Bernadette regularly visited Natalie's grave at the new Cheltenham Cemetery to weed around it and lay fresh flowers. Natalie was buried with her grandparents and Bernadette chatted to her niece's grave, joking that she was buried with the 'oldies'. But the bereaved aunt took comfort in the fact that on one side of Natalie, a sixteen-year-old girl was buried and on the other side, a girl of seventeen. She thought it was nice that her niece also had some young girls for company. Nearby was the grave of a policeman, Albert Haag, who died in 1961 at the age of thirty-five. Bernadette often said, 'Nat, you have a nice policeman to protect you now.' She weeded his grave too.

More than anything, Bernadette wanted to be around for another thirty years so that when Denyer came up for parole, she could be the voice that reminded a forgetful public of what he did and what he took. Sadly, it wasn't to be. On Friday 13 August 1999, Bernadette Naughton died; she succumbed to cancer after a year-long battle. Her twin brother had died on their fiftieth birthday a couple of years earlier and Bernadette always said the stress of Natalie's murder contributed to his fatal heart attack – as no doubt it did to her own premature demise in her early fifties – six years after Natalie was murdered. Losing Bernadette is yet another chapter in the Frankston murders tragedy. She was a truly wonderful, dignified woman to the end. We can only hope that in death, she is reunited with her beloved Natalie.

Bernadette's fears that Denyer and his heinous crimes would be forgotten weren't unfounded. Paul Denyer's name was well known for a couple of years after the Frankston murders, but ten years later, many remembered the crimes, but not him. Back then, there were no true crime podcasts and once a prisoner went to prison, that was pretty much it.

But then, eleven years after the murders, Paul Denyer hit the headlines again. He wanted to become a woman.

On Monday 28 June 2004 a picture of Paul Denyer graced the cover of the Melbourne *Herald Sun*. Denyer, who had last been seen at his trial looking like a brutal thug with close-cropped hair, now sported two shoulder-length pigtails and sculpted eyebrows, and was posing like a model under the headline: 'NOW LOOK AT HIM'. For the man who became infamous when he killed three women over a period of seven weeks in Frankston in 1993, the attention was no doubt exciting.

In all the media coverage about the sex reassignment requested by the convicted murderer, his desire to wear make-up and his alleged sexual liaisons with other prisoners, the names and ages of his three victims were given but a sentence or two. Natalie Russell, seventeen, Elizabeth Stevens, eighteen, and Debbie Fream, twenty-two. The names of these young women, regardless of who they were in life, are now forever inexorably linked with the name Paul Charles Denyer and will appear whenever his name is mentioned. But while he moves forward, the girls are frozen in time and remembered in person by those who loved and lost them – and by name by people who read about their brutal deaths at the hands of a serial killer.

Before the sex reassignment request, Denyer had largely faded from public memory but a couple of timely reminders came in 2004 courtesy of two television shows on the case. Firstly, the premier episode of the television series *Forensic Investigators*, hosted by Lisa McCune, featured the Frankston murders and got the public talking once again about the brutality and callousness that Denyer had displayed consistently throughout the taped police interview, parts of which were shown on the program. The public watched Denyer reconstructing his crimes for the tape and showing no more emotion than if he were talking about the weather. About a month after *Forensic Investigators* began its successful run, another television program called *Sensing Murder* touched on the possibility that Denyer could have been involved in the disappearance of Sarah MacDiarmid in July 1990.

While it pains them, family members who lost loved ones know that while the public remember what he did, he is less likely to ever be released.

Lest we forget …

Late Saturday night to early Sunday morning, 1 August 1993

Homicide detective Senior Sergeant Rod Wilson sat opposite Paul Denyer. Detective Darren O'Loughlin sat to the side. The video camera taped the interview as Rod Wilson advised Paul Denyer once again of his rights.

The young man looked sullen.

During a break, after hours of interviewing during which Denyer had denied any involvement in the Frankston serial murders, the 21-year-old suspect took a shine to detective Darren O'Loughlin and had finally admitted he was the one police were looking for. The revelation – during a coffee break – took the young detective by surprise and Denyer was taken back into the interview room. After hours of stubborn denial, he had changed his mind. He was finally ready to talk.

Seated back in the interview room, cameras rolling, Rod Wilson asked Denyer to describe the murder of Elizabeth Stevens in his own words. After a day of studying at the Frankston Library, Elizabeth didn't return home on 11 June 1993 and her body was found the next day at Lloyd Park, Langwarrin. Her throat had been cut and a strange criss-cross pattern had been carved into her chest. Denyer stared downwards, then looked up at the camera, hesitating a full twenty seconds before beginning.

> I saw her get off the bus. I was walking across the road. Just something hit me straight in the head, you know, Go! – so I ran across the road in front of all these cars and got to the other side, where I followed her around the corner ...
>
> I walked up behind her and stuck my left hand around her head right here.' [Denyer indicated with his own big hand how he had grabbed Elizabeth Stevens.] And then I dragged her into the front lawn, told her to shut up, and she just agreed to my terms. And I said, 'Well, we're gonna take a walk.' So we walked down on the road. A couple of cars drove past us and I held her hand to make it look like, you know, a couple, I suppose ... so it wouldn't arouse any suspicion. Walked past two people on the footpath, a guy and a girl, and they just didn't take any notice.

Wilson asked if Elizabeth had screamed or cried out.

'No, I told her I'd kill her if she did,' he said. Rod Wilson nodded and Denyer added, a grin flashing across his face, 'With my fake gun.' Describing the gun, Denyer said it was a square bit of aluminium piping with a wooden handle and a rubber-glove finger taped to the end. Inside the glove finger, ball bearings were wedged in order to 'fire' it.

Darren O'Loughlin left the interview room to get a Melway street directory. Denyer lit a cigarette as the street directory was opened so he could show detectives the route he had taken from the bus stop to Lloyd Park with his captive. Denyer confidently traced the route with his finger, then began describing her murder. His account at times lacked continuity and would leave out some aspects. Those listening wondered if Denyer's memory was selective. They also wondered at the kind of person who could sit in front of them without any emotion and talk about taking the life of an eighteen-year-old woman.

> Walked in a bit of bushland beside the main track in Lloyd Park. Sat there, you know, stood in the bushes for a while just … I can't remember, just standing there I suppose. Held the gun to the back of her neck, walked across the track over towards the other small sand hill or something. And on the other side of that hill, she asked me if she could, you know, could go to the toilet or – so to speak – so I respected her privacy. So I turned around and everything while she did it and everything. When she finished, we just walked down towards where the goal posts are and we turned right and headed towards the area where she was found. Got to that area there and I started choking her with my hands and she passed out after a while. You know, the oxygen got cut off to her head and – and she just stopped. And then I pulled out the knife … and stabbed her many times in the throat.
>
> And she was still alive. And then she stood up and then we walked around and all that, just walked around a few steps, and then I threw her on the ground and stuck my foot over her neck.

Rod Wilson asked Denyer why he had stood on her neck.

'Oh, to finish her off,' Denyer replied casually – as if it should have been obvious. His lack of emotion and casual manner would be consistent throughout the entire confession.

He told the detectives that Elizabeth Stevens's body had begun shaking. He even demonstrated her final death shudders for the detectives and the video camera. Denyer described dragging the body of Elizabeth Stevens to the culvert where it was later found.

Before he confessed to the murders, Denyer had spent hours in the interview room discussing where he was and what he was doing at the time of each of the murders. Sergeant Wilson questioned Denyer on the first part of his statement, when he had said that he walked from his girlfriend Sharon's mother's house to his own mother's house.

Denyer said that he really had gone to his mother's house, and had killed Elizabeth Stevens after he saw her get off the bus on his way back to Sharon's mother's house. Denyer traced the route with his finger on the street directory. So well did he know the areas, he pointed to locations on the map with barely a glance.

Denyer described and sketched the knife and its dimensions for the detectives and told them he had worn a green army jacket, black pants and shoes, a blue jumper and a blue and white baseball cap.

Rod Wilson asked Denyer if he had ever met Elizabeth Stevens before he killed her. He said he hadn't.

The detective knew that the injuries to Elizabeth Stevens were more extensive than Denyer described.

Wilson asked: 'When the body of Elizabeth Stevens was found, it had a number of marks on the chest area and seven stab wounds around the breast. Do you know how they came to be there?'

Denyer shrugged. Said he couldn't remember.

'You don't remember? What do you mean by that? Could you have done this?'

'Possibly,' the young man conceded with a slight nod of his head.

If the criss-cross pattern was a signature of sorts, or had some meaning to Denyer, he wasn't letting on. This evasiveness would also become a pattern.

Wilson wanted to establish the reason for the killing of Elizabeth Stevens. So far Denyer seemed happy enough to talk about *what* he did, but the burning question was *why*.

'Can you tell me why you attacked her on that night? What led to it?'

'Just ... I just had ... just the feeling, that's all.'

'What sort of feeling? Can you possibly describe it – where you had this feeling?'

'Just wanted ... just wanted to kill.' Denyer looked down at the table in front of him. 'Just wanted to take a life because I felt my life had been taken many times.' Denyer's quiet voice became even softer and he looked downwards.

'By whom?' asked Wilson.

'David,' Denyer murmured.

'Who is David?'

'My eldest brother.'

'When did he … do you wish to say what he …?' Rod Wilson hesitated.

'No, no.'

'Was it of a sexual nature?'

'Yeah.'

'When you were younger?'

'Mm.'

'Abused you?'

'Mmm hmm.'

'And you felt cheated by that or something?'

'Yeah.'

Paul Denyer didn't want to expand upon what was obviously an uncomfortable subject for him. Wilson didn't push him further and led the questioning back to the night Elizabeth Stevens was murdered.

'Do you remember what Elizabeth Stevens was wearing?'

'Dark sweater with a hood, grey tracksuit pants. White socks with orange bands and …'

'How do you remember all that?' asked Wilson. 'Is it something you found out later in the newspapers, or can you remember?'

Denyer told him that he had seen the mannequin the police had prepared to help jog the public's memory of Elizabeth Stevens and her last movements.

'So you don't really remember what she was wearing?'

'No.'

Denyer said he had picked Elizabeth Stevens because she was the only one who got off the bus.

'When would you say that you first started feeling this aggression when you were walking around here? When did you first feel like you had to kill?'

'Somewhere between Sharon's mum's place and my mum's place – somewhere between.'

'And did Elizabeth Stevens offer any resistance to you at any stage?'

'A little bit … when we got to the park.'

'Was she frightened, do you think?'

'She didn't cry,' Denyer said as if he admired her bravery.

'Well, did she see you take the knife out of your pocket?'

'No, she would have blanked out or something.' He told them he had choked her before he took out his knife.

Wilson asked where the knife was and Denyer told him that he'd dumped it at the side of a road in Langwarrin. He explained that the blade had broken off and he had dumped the pieces together. Wilson asked him if he had broken the blade off himself and Denyer explained, 'Well, it bent when I was stabbing her. The blade went *zoop* and then I broke the rest of it off and then carried it in my pocket till I got to there when I dumped 'em.'

'When you said that you were stabbing her at this location back at Lloyd Park, what were you feeling at the time? For example, were you angry?'

Denyer reflected for a moment. 'Happy, sad, angry ... many things.'

Rod Wilson led the questioning around to evidence at the first crime scene. It was necessary for Paul Denyer to account for as much as possible. False confessions were not unheard of, and the detectives needed to make absolutely certain that the man sitting in front of them was indeed the killer.

Wilson asked him why he moved the body from the site of the murder and Denyer told him that it was in order to destroy evidence. He explained that he thought the rain would wash away footprints and blood, and that investigators would have difficulty finding the exact location of the murder. Denyer then described ripping a branch from a tree near the drain to conceal the body.

He told Wilson that Elizabeth had been carrying a bag when he had taken her to the park and said that he left the bag about ten metres from her body.

Wilson took Denyer over the details of the abduction and murder once again, covering everything in minute detail. Denyer admitted that he told Elizabeth Stevens that he would 'blow her head off' if she screamed and he also admitted telling her to kiss the end of the gun but she had refused.

Wilson asked Denyer if he had felt any sexual urges towards Elizabeth Stevens and he admitted that he had but that they had subsided immediately after he had grabbed her. He described his conversation in the bushes at Lloyd Park with the woman he was about to kill. He had asked her name and sounded indignant when he said, 'She said she was seventeen when she was eighteen.'

'I said to her, "Do you want a fuck?" and she said, "How do you do that?" And I said, "Are you a virgin?" She said yeah and I said, "Well, I won't rape you or anything."'

Rod Wilson could only imagine the young woman's terror and he was fully aware that he was only getting one side of the story. Paul Denyer almost made it sound like a casual conversation between friends – not between a killer and his victim.

'She had her top rolled up tightly. Do you know how that came ...?'

'Yeah, that happened when I was dragging her. It sort of got caught up on some blackberry bushes and pulled it all the way up.'

'But you can't remember inflicting those injuries?' asked Wilson, referring to the criss-cross markings on Elizabeth's chest.

'It's possible, but I don't remember.'

Denyer described strangling Elizabeth Stevens and showed the detectives how he had pushed his thumb into her throat and made a stabbing motion as he described stabbing and slashing her throat. He told them that Elizabeth Stevens had then got to her feet.

'Are you saying that she got up after that? Did that surprise you?'

'Yeah, it did in a way. She got up and walked. And she didn't cry. She was just normal.'

'So how far ... when you say she walked, how far did she actually walk?'

'Around in circles with me.'

'You were holding her still?'

'Yeah, just under one arm.'

'Why were you doing that? Did you help her up? Is that what you're indicating?'

'Yeah.'

'So what happened after she walked around in circles?'

'There was a puddle of like ... flooded area there. And I pushed her into there so she could wash her ... you know ... blood off her and all that. And then I dragged her across the water.'

'Well, when did you put your foot on her neck as you described before?'

'When she was lying on the side of the sort of flooded area with her legs in the water.'

'And why did you do that?'

'To kill her.'

'So you did that and then she went into a sort of spasm, you said before, or some sort of quivering?'

'Yes, her whole body just shook and everything ... and then she stopped.'

'Did you think she was dead?'

'No, she was still breathing ... from her neck ...'

'How did you know that?'

'I could hear it.'

'How long did that last for?'

'Five minutes.'

'Did you do anything more to her then to stop that ...?'

'No.'

'Did you ever strike her in any way, punch her, I mean?'

'I might have.'

Denyer told Wilson that he had first seen Elizabeth Stevens around 7.15 pm and the entire attack and hiding of the body had taken about half an hour. He described walking back to Sharon's mother's house and Sharon's mother had asked him where he had been. He told her that he had been to visit his mother but she hadn't been home. He explained to Wilson that he didn't have any blood on him, the rain had washed the blood from his hands, but he was drenched from being out for hours in the rain. Denyer told the detectives that he had eaten dinner – soup and a roast – and then waited for Sharon to come home from work.

When Rod Wilson was satisfied that he had covered the murder of Elizabeth Stevens in as much detail as he could for the time being, going over all the details at least three times, he moved on to the second murder. Denyer's knowledge of the crime scenes and the young woman's movements were something only the killer would know. The young man had displayed little emotion during the questioning, which had by now entered the early hours of Sunday morning.

Rod Wilson had put in a long day. He was called at 4 am on Saturday morning to the scene of Natalie Russell's murder, and found himself twenty-four hours later still only in the early stages of interviewing the self-confessed killer. The combined triumph and relief at catching

Denyer before he could claim any more lives well and truly made up for the gruelling pace. Darren O'Loughlin, too, had put in as many hours and it would probably be another twenty-four hours before any of the detectives would go home and catch some well-deserved and much-needed sleep.

The questioning moved on to the abduction of Roszsa Toth and the murder of Deborah Fream. Only hours before Debbie Fream disappeared, 41-year-old Roszsa Toth had been grabbed by Denyer as she walked home from the Seaford railway station.

Denyer told Wilson and O'Loughlin that he had seen Mrs Toth walking near the station and he described approaching her from behind and grabbing her with his left hand around her mouth, while sticking his fake gun to her head with his other hand. Denyer thought Mrs Toth was Spanish when she cried out in a language he didn't understand. She bit his finger and screamed. He showed the detectives the mark still visible on his finger from the bite.

'I wrestled with her. She ran out on the road but no-one stopped. And I grabbed her by the hair and dragged her back towards the park and I said, "Shut up or I'll blow your fucking head off." And she said, "Si, si," in Spanish or something. And then she stood up and then went against her word and ran out on the road again ...' Paul Denyer sounded indignant that the woman he tried to kill had lied to him and tried to get away – almost as if she owed him some kind of loyalty.

Denyer had run away when Roszsa Toth escaped the second time. When Wilson asked him what he had intended doing with her, he replied, 'I was just gonna drag her into the park and kill her, that's all.'

Wilson asked him if he had again felt the urge to kill, and Denyer tried to articulate the feeling building up inside him.

'Yeah, like every day it was just going up, boiling up ... till I got to that stage.' He raised his hand in front of him to simulate a rising temperature gauge.

Denyer described making the home-made knife that he'd carried during the attack. He had cut the aluminium at his old place of employment in Seaford, and had carried it most of the time in his sock.

After the attack on Roszsa Toth, Denyer had jumped on a Frankston-bound train that took him from Seaford to the next station down the line, Kananook. He got off the train and crossed the overpass. Thwarted in his bloodlust, he had gone in search of another victim and found Debbie Fream. As he was walking down McCulloch Avenue towards the milk bar on the corner, he had seen a woman pull up across the road in a grey Pulsar. He showed detectives on the Melway map.

'What caused you to select her at the time?' asked Wilson.

> Just that go feeling. While she was in the milk bar, I walked up to the car and checked the driver's door and it was unlocked, so I opened the door and put my hand through and unlocked the back door. I hopped in the car and crouched down behind the seat and pulled out a gun that I had. Then I looked up out of the car window and I saw her in the milk bar. I crouched down and I could hear her footsteps coming closer to the car. And then she opened the door. The interior light went on and then she hopped in the car. She didn't see me in the back. And then she closed the door, you know, the light went out and everything and it was dark. And I waited for her to start up the car so no-one could hear her scream or anything. And she put it into gear and she went to do a U-turn. And I startled her just as she was doing that turn and she kept going into the wall of the milk bar, which caused a dent on the bonnet.
>
> I told her to, you know, shut up or I'd blow her head off and all of that shit.

Denyer said he held the fake gun against Debbie Fream's side. Rod Wilson asked Denyer if he had noticed anything in the car when he had hopped in. Denyer told him that he had seen the baby capsule in the back seat. Even if Debbie Fream hadn't told him, Paul Denyer would have had a pretty good idea that he was killing the mother of a young baby.

Denyer said that he had instructed Debbie Fream to drive back up Kananook Avenue – ironically right past the house she shared with Garry and their newborn son, Jake. Denyer traced the journey on the map to Hartnett Drive in Seaford.

'I told her when we got there that if she gave any signals to anyone, I'd blow her head off; I'd decorate the car with her brains.'

Denyer was sitting upright directly behind the young mother as he directed her towards Taylors Road. Wilson asked if Denyer knew this area well.

'Yeah, I know it very well,' he replied. 'I used to sit down there in the car at night a couple of years ago and smoke marijuana.'

Denyer had directed Debbie Fream to stop the car near some

trees on Taylors Road. He told the detectives that she had told him to take her money and her car, and that he had told her he didn't want either. He then told her to get out of the car. Denyer had tucked the fake gun down the front of his tracksuit pants and pulled a cord from his pocket.

'I popped it over her eyes real quickly so she didn't see it ... coz I was gonna strangle her. But I didn't want her to see the cord first. I lifted the cord up and I said, "Can you see this?" And she just put her hand up to grab it to feel it and when she did that I just yanked on it real quickly round her neck. And then I was struggling with her for about five minutes.'

'She was struggling?' asked Wilson.

'Yeah, until she started to faint a bit. And then when she was, you know, like weaker, I pulled my knife out of my sock then ... and started stabbing her around the neck and the chest several ... several times.'

'You strangled her?' asked O'Loughlin. 'Is that the first thing that happened?'

'As she sort of weakened and fell onto the ground, that's when I stabbed her in the throat.'

'Once?'

'Many times and once in the stomach.'

'Where was she ...?' asked O'Loughlin.

'Lying on the ground.'

'Was she dead or alive when you stabbed her in the throat?'

'Almost dead.'

'So you stabbed her a number of times. And what happened then?' asked Rod Wilson

'She started breathing out of her neck, just like Elizabeth Stevens. I could just hear bubbling noises.'

'Did Debbie Fream put up any resistance?'

'Yeah, she put up quite a fight. And her white jumper was pulled off during that time as well. I just felt the same way I did when I killed Elizabeth Stevens.'

'What happened after you stabbed her round the throat and chest area?'

'I lifted up her top and then ploughed the knife into her gut.'

The detectives knew that the top had a hole in it corresponding with the stab wound. Denyer hadn't lifted the top until the young mother was dead.

Wilson asked Denyer why and he said he wasn't sure.

'You lifted the top to do that?' asked O'Loughlin.

'Yeah,' Denyer affirmed.

'Do you know why you lifted her top?'

'I wanted to see how big her boobs were,' said Denyer.

'Beg your pardon?' asked O'Loughlin, momentarily taken aback by the childish statement.

'I wanted to see how big her boobs were,' he repeated.

'Was that part of the fantasy?' pressed O'Loughlin, trying to keep a hint of disgust from creeping into his voice.

'I don't know.'

'You actually recall thinking that way?'

'Sort of,' Denyer replied, 'and I saw her bare stomach so I just lunged at her with the knife.'

Denyer couldn't explain the small pinpoint stab injuries Debbie Fream had suffered to her back. He described dragging Debbie about a metre away into a group of trees and leaving her lying against a fence. He broke off two branches from the nearest tree and threw them over her body. Denyer detailed the five-minute search for his knife, which he had dropped in the attack. He found it and put it in his pocket.

'I took off my jumper because it had blood stains all over it. And I had blood all over here, all over my hands, all up my arms, blood all over the place. And then hopped in her car.' Denyer explained that he had adjusted the seat 'to match my height coz she was a lot smaller than me'.

Denyer had wiped off most of the blood using his blue jumper, tossing it into the car, and Debbie's white windcheater into the bushes.

'I hopped back in the car again and then done a U-turn and headed back down Taylors Road. I pulled up outside the New Life Christian Centre. I grabbed my jumper and wiped my prints off the steering wheel. Wiped my prints off the transmission lever or gear stick. Off the handbrake, off the doorknobs on the inside. I got out of the car and just walked home.'

Wilson established the route Denyer had walked.

'Yeah, when I got back there, I took off all my clothes and washed 'em.' Denyer was home in time to telephone Sharon at work and arrange to meet her at Kananook railway station.

Incredibly, Denyer then admitted returning to the unlocked car the following morning after his girlfriend had gone to work. He told the detectives that he took the two cartons of milk and eggs out of the car along with a packet of cigarettes and a chocolate.

'Did you think that was a bit risky?'

'At first, yeah.'

'And you took her purse?'

'It had exactly twenty-two dollars in it.'

'What happened to the money?'

'Spent it or something. Can't remember.'

Denyer told the detectives that he had gone back for the purse to find out the name of the woman he had killed. Taking the groceries home with him, he emptied the milk down the sink, threw the eggs out the back and burnt the cartons, which he saw as evidence. Denyer took the purse and buried it at the golf course along the same track where he had killed Natalie Russell. After his busy morning, Denyer told the detectives, he 'just sat back and did nothing'.

'Did at any stage Debbie Fream mention anything about her personal life to you?'

'No.'

It was hard for the detectives to believe the new mother wouldn't have begged for her life for the sake of her baby. But again, Denyer was evasive when things got too personal.

'Why did you kill her?' Wilson asked.

'Same reason why I killed Elizabeth Stevens. I just wanted to.'

Denyer described dismantling his home-made knife and hiding the pieces in the air vent in the laundry at his flat.

'Why didn't you get rid of that? Why did you put it in the air vent?'

'Couldn't think of anywhere else to hide it.'

'Like you buried the purse ...'

'Well, I thought that I might have been under surveillance so if I took it anywhere and buried it I would've been seen doing it.'

'But you might have been seen burying the purse for that same reason, wouldn't you have thought?'

'Yeah, different time of day, different method of thinking,' Denyer said cryptically.

Denyer told Wilson that he had dug the hole with his hands to bury the purse. 'How would you be able to find the spot?'

'Oh, I'll find it. I know where it is.' His voice was confident.

Foremost in the minds of the detectives interviewing Paul Denyer was the murder of Year 12 student Natalie Russell less than two days earlier. The Sunday-morning sun had yet to rise, but birds were beginning to waken and sing while inside the Frankston police station, a young man began telling two tired detectives how he had cut the throat of a schoolgirl.

Ironically, as the Sunday newspapers arrived on doorsteps around Melbourne, Denyer was coming to the end of his extensive statement to police. Headlines in both the *Sunday Herald Sun* and the *Sunday Age* screamed, 'Killer Strikes Again' and both papers ran stories about how police were frantically hunting for the killer of Natalie Russell, 'convinced he would strike again'. The papers would have to wait until Monday to run their 'Man, 21, in Court' headlines, much to the relief of everyone in Melbourne – especially those living in Frankston and its surrounding suburbs.

Rod Wilson began the home stretch, almost forgetting that Saturday had turned into Sunday. 'The next incident occurred yesterday … sorry, it's now the day after, but on Friday. What can you tell me about that?'

Denyer told Wilson about his car overheating and having to stop at the Flora and Fauna Reserve and then on Skye Road opposite the entrance to the bike track.

'Well, you already knew the track existed because that's where you—'

'I went up there earlier that day and cut the holes in the fences.' Denyer explained that he had cut three holes in the cyclone-wire fences with a pair of pliers that he kept in the car. He had tested each hole for size by climbing through. Afterwards, he explained, he had visited his mother's partner, Jim, and then gone to hunt for car parts at a local wrecker's yard.

Denyer had driven back to Skye Road to wait for a victim.

'I sat in the car for twenty minutes till about quarter to three and then I saw the girl coming down the road.' Denyer explained that the girl he saw was wearing a blue school uniform and he had seen her coming out of the road where John Paul College was.

'When I saw her coming over the hill, I predicted straightaway where she'd be heading 'cause she crossed the road. She crossed the road onto the golf-course side. I knew exactly where she was heading.'

Strangely, Denyer denied feeling the urge to kill this time even though he had admitted cutting the holes in the fence earlier and then sitting in his car for twenty minutes waiting for a victim. He told Wilson that he had just decided to take a walk up the track. He also admitted being armed with a red-handled knife for his 'walk'. Denyer walked down the track ahead of Natalie Russell and climbed through one of the holes he had cut to wait for her.

Wilson asked him if he had any other weapons. Denyer replied, 'Oh, and the leather strap.'

'What was that? What sort of leather strap?'

'Just a thin ... you would have found it at the scene – in two pieces.'

'What was that used for?' asked Wilson.

'Strangling.'

Denyer described the murder of Natalie Russell. 'I saw her walk ... she was coming up the track and I saw her walk past, like, that way, and I ran out through the hole in the fence again and followed her.'

'Did she see you?'

'She turned around once and saw me. And I stuck about ten metres behind her until I got to the second hole ... and just when I got to that hole, I walked up behind her and stuck my left hand around her mouth and held the knife to her throat ... and that's where that cut happened.' Denyer indicated the cut on his thumb that he had earlier explained was due to sharpening a knife at home. 'I cut that on my own blade,' he admitted.

'Dragged her through the hole in the fence,' he continued.

'Was she struggling?'

'At first, but then she sort of stopped.'

'Why?'

'Because I told her I was gonna cut her throat … I said I was gonna, yeah, cut her throat. And I walked through the hole in the fence. I followed her through and I dragged her into the trees. Like she offered, she said, "Oh, you can have sex with me if you want." She goes, "You can have all my money, have sex with me," and things – just said disgusting things like that really.' Denyer shook his head.

It was the only time during the many hours of interviewing that he showed any emotion. His anger and disgust at Natalie Russell were obvious. It was equally obvious to the detectives that Denyer had no comprehension of the fact that Natalie Russell had been begging for her life. She must have realised she was in the hands of the serial killer the details of whose crimes had been splashed so extensively through the media and she had obviously been willing to do anything to save her life. Denyer completely failed to see that.

'And did that … did that upset you?' Wilson asked, surprised by his sudden outburst.

'In a way,' replied the killer, his anger quickly subsiding and his voice becoming even once again. 'And I got her to kneel down in front of me and I held the knife blade over her eye, really closely, and yeah, she had the same colour eyes as I have.'

'Why did you hold that knife so close to her eye for?'

'Just so she could see the blade.'

'And why was she kneeling?'

'No, she was lying on the ground at that stage and I was lying on top of her. I wasn't lying, I was kneeling on top of her. Just holding her by the throat and with the knife next to her eye. And she struggled and then the knife cut her on the face. And she was bleeding a bit then … Yeah, and then when she got up, she started to scream a bit. And I just said, "Shut up. Shut up. Shut up. Shut up." And, "I said if you don't shut up, I'll kill you. If you don't do this I'll kill you, if you don't do that." And she said, "What do you want from me?" I said, "All I want you to do is shut up." And so when she was kneeling on the ground, I put the strap around her neck to strangle her and it broke in half. And then she started violently struggling for about a minute until I pushed – got her onto her back again – and pushed her head back like this and cut her throat.'

Denyer mimicked Natalie Russell's last moments as he described his attack on her. But his description of what he then did to the dying schoolgirl made the detectives' stomachs turn.

'I cut a small cut at first and then she was bleeding. And then I stuck my fingers into her throat …'

'Mmm,' murmured Wilson.

'… and grabbed her cords and I twisted them.'

'Why'd you do that?'

'My whole fingers – like, that much of my hand was inside her throat,' Denyer indicated on his hand the depth it had penetrated his victim's neck.

'Do you know why you did that?' asked Wilson again.

'Stop her from breathing … and then she slowly stopped. She sort of started to faint and then when she was weak, a bit weaker, I grabbed the opportunity of throwing her head back and one big large cut, which sort of cut almost her whole head off. And then she slowly died.'

'Why did you want to kill her?' asked Wilson rubbing his forehead.

'Just same reason as before, just everything came back through my mind again. I kicked her before I left.'

'Why's that?'

'While she was dead, just booted her.'

'Why did you kick her after? Like she was obviously dead at that stage.'

'Make sure she was dead.'

'Kicking her, would that make sure she was dead?'

'Well, if she had've moved, I would've known.'

Denyer described walking back down the bike track and passing a young boy going the other way. The boy had looked at him as he passed.

Denyer stuck his bloodied hands in his pockets and walked to the end of the lane. Coming out onto Skye Road, he saw something that made him stop short – two uniformed police officers were walking around his car, writing down its details. Denyer told Wilson that he had merely ducked his head, turned right and walked down Skye Road towards home.

Wilson and O'Loughlin couldn't help being struck by the carelessness of Denyer during his final murder. They remembered his account of his frantic search for the knife with which he had killed Debbie Fream and now here he was telling them that not only had he left the leather strap at the scene, but he had bled at the scene too and left his car where it could be checked by police. Not only was there forensic evidence that could link him to the crime scene, but he had parked his car on Skye Road adjacent to the bike track and sat in the car for almost half an hour before the killing, in full view of passing traffic, not to mention other pedestrians – many of whom had already come forward to report seeing him. Ironically, one witness who knew Paul Denyer saw him as she was driving past. She had described seeing him sitting in his car smiling to himself and then his expression had changed when he caught sight of her. The two had made eye contact as she drove past. Yet Denyer had still followed Natalie Russell down the bike track. Wilson had the distinct impression that Denyer had become cocky. He had got away with two murders and thought he could now kill in broad daylight and get away with it.

Denyer told the detectives that he had gone home to change, washed his clothes in the bath and then walked back to collect his car, by which time the police were gone. Denyer had thrown the knife in a drum in his backyard and then gone to pick up Sharon from work. That evening, he explained, he and Sharon went to her mother's and he had thrown his wet clothing into her washing machine.

Wilson asked Denyer if there was anything else he would like to talk to them about.

'Yeah, I slashed her across the face.'

'Who's that?' asked Wilson.

'The last victim.'

'What do you mean you slashed her across the face?'

'After she was dead.'

'After she was dead?'

'Yeah, I just cut her straight down this side of her face.'

'Why was that?' asked Wilson.

'Don't know,' he replied, shrugging.

❖❖❖

Coming to the end of Denyer's account of the three murders and the attempted abduction of Roszsa Toth, Rod Wilson asked, 'Anything you haven't told us?' Denyer thought for a moment and then began explaining about the knife he had used to kill Elizabeth Stevens. He had bought it a while back from the Big W store at Karingal Hub.

'I walked into the store one night and went to the sporting department and I grabbed a fishing knife. And I grabbed one of the female shop assistants there in the toy department and held it to her throat and said I was gonna cut her to pieces.' Denyer couldn't remember exactly when the incident had occurred, and he said he hadn't physically hurt the shop assistant and that the knife was still in its packet.

Rod Wilson asked Paul Denyer when he had first begun to 'feel the urges' to kill. Denyer told him that he had wanted to kill since he was about fourteen. Wilson wanted to know why it had taken Denyer so long if the urges had been with him for the last seven years.

'I don't know,' Denyer replied. 'Just waiting for the right time, waiting for that small silent alarm to trigger me off.'

'And the incident you spoke about at Karingal Hub in the Big W, was that the first time you felt you were progressing into something …?'

'Yeah. I've been stalking women for a few years in Frankston.'

'How long do you think you have been doing that?'

'Three or four years, or since I was seventeen, I think. I've been following heaps of women around.'

'Just waiting for the opportunity?'

Denyer nodded. 'Waiting for the sign.'

Rod Wilson questioned Denyer about the unsolved murders of Sarah MacDiarmid and Michelle Brown. MacDiarmid disappeared from the Kananook railway station in July 1990 and Michelle, two years later. Denyer denied knowledge about the two murders apart, he said, from what he'd heard on the news.

Denyer had told detectives that while he was still at the flat, a friend had heard his name mentioned over the police radio scanner on Friday when his car was checked as a suspicious vehicle on Skye Road. Wilson brought this up again. When Wilson asked who owned the scanner, the question solved another crime on the books of the Frankston CIB. The scanner, Denyer told them, belonged to a friend of Donna Vanes. Donna was the sister of Denyer's neighbour Tricia.

'That was the girl I went to Claude Street for that night.'

Wilson and O'Loughlin didn't understand what Denyer was talking about.

'She used to live there. She moved out of Claude Street because I broke into her place and killed all of her cats.'

Darren O'Loughlin, a local detective, knew of the incident.

'When did you do that?' asked Wilson.

'Earlier this year.'

'What did you do that for?'

'I went there to kill her but she wasn't home.'

'Did you prepare yourself for that?' asked O'Loughlin.

'Yeah, I had a large knife on me.'

'Where did that come from?'

'Well, I bought that for about seven dollars fifty from Aussie Disposals in Frankston, Beach Street.'

'Was there any other preparation?'

'I had gloves,' Denyer volunteered, 'so I wouldn't leave any prints. I don't think I did leave any prints, no.'

'When did you put the gloves on?'

'Just as I walked up to the front door. I knocked on the door first to see if there was anyone there, but there was no-one there so I walked around the back and climbed through the window. Cut a hole through the fly screen and sort of wedged myself through.'

'Was the window open?'

'Yeah, wide open.'

'What did you want to kill her for? You knew her, didn't you? Isn't she –?'

'Vaguely,' interrupted Denyer.

'Tricia who lives in flat 3. Isn't it her sister? What had she done wrong? Or had she done anything wrong?'

'Didn't like her sister.'

'Trish?'

'No, didn't like Trish at all,' Denyer said shaking his head.

'So what did that have to do with Donna?'

'Well, I knew she was home by herself most of the time.'

'Donna was? Did you dislike Donna for any reason?'

'Never really liked her, no.'

Denyer and the detectives established that the cats had been killed in February and Denyer volunteered that he thought it was 28 February. It was in fact 19 February.

'And you went to Donna's flat in Claude Street to kill her?'

'Yeah.'

'And she wasn't home?'

'No, she wasn't home.'

'So you broke in and what did you do?'

'I killed her cats.'

'How many?'

'Three.'

'How did you kill her cats?'

'Stabbed 'em all.' Considering the carnage witnessed by investigators in Donna Vanes's flat, Denyer had done a lot more than just stab them. O'Loughlin asked exactly what had happened when Denyer had first entered the flat.

'I walked slowly into the lounge room 'cause the lights were all on, just 'cause I thought somebody was there. And then I just went into a blind rage and just killed anything that was alive in the house.'

'What would have happened if Donna was there?' asked O'Loughlin, knowing the answer.

'I would've cut her throat,' Denyer said casually.

'Can you explain what happened to the cats? Where were they?'

'In the lounge room. A mother and her two kittens.'

'And what happened to the cats?'

'Well, the mother cat ran into the laundry and I chased after it. It lunged at me and I just stabbed it in the side and it died straightaway.'

'And what happened to the others?'

'I slit their throats and threw 'em in the bathtub.' Denyer didn't mention disembowelling the mother cat and he didn't mention placing a picture of a bikini-clad model cut out of a magazine on its stomach, writing on the wall or slashing Donna's baby's clothes.

Denyer told Wilson and O'Loughlin that Donna had reported the break-in to police. 'It was on the news,' he said, sounding proud. 'Everybody knew about it.'

Apart from the incident at Karingal Hub and the killing of the cats, Wilson asked Denyer if he had anything else he wished to tell them.

'No, that was about it,' Denyer replied. Rod Wilson decided to try one last time to get to the bottom of Denyer's motives for the killing spree. He asked the young man what his general attitude towards women was.

'Just don't like some of them,' Denyer explained.

'Obviously you're in love with – or, I'll assume that you're fond of Sharon.'

'Sharon's not like anyone else I know,' Denyer said earnestly, looking straight at Wilson.

'Well, you wouldn't think of hurting her?'

'Never,' replied the killer of three young women. 'No, I'd never hurt her. She's a kindred spirit.'

Responding to questions that would help explain forensic evidence, Denyer described wearing his black runners while committing each murder. He had, he explained, put them on the stove at his flat to melt the soles so the pattern on his shoes could never be linked to shoe impressions at the crime scenes, because the pattern no longer existed. Although the detectives didn't consider Denyer particularly bright, they gave him credit for a degree of animal cunning.

Exhausted of questions, Rod Wilson turned to Darren O'Loughlin and asked him if he had any matters he wished to raise. O'Loughlin, who had been sitting silent for most of the lengthy interview, asked the question that was foremost in his mind.

'You mentioned David, your brother … was the cause. Is that correct?' he asked, referring to the earlier mention of sexual abuse.

'Some of it,' replied Denyer.

'Some of it,' repeated O'Loughlin. 'If that's the cause, then why have women been the victims?'

'I've only ever had two relationships and Sharon was the third. And the first two ones were older women with kids. And one of them was using me for something … yeah.'

'Can you explain why we have women victims?' O'Loughlin persisted.

'I just hate 'em.'

'I beg your pardon?' said O'Loughlin.

'I just hate 'em,' Denyer repeated.

'Those particular girls,' asked O'Loughlin, referring to Denyer's three victims, 'or women in general?'

'General.'

'You told Detective Senior Sergeant Wilson that you stabbed them in the throat. Is there any particular reason why there?'

'Well, it looked like the most vulnerable spot.'

'Did each girl get stabbed in the throat?'

'All of 'em ... I saw it in a movie once and it just looked effective.'

'What movie was that?' asked O'Loughlin.

'It was called *The Stepfather*. And a guy stabbed a guy in the neck with a broken glass and, yeah, just looked effective.'

Denyer went on to deny memory of any of the vicious marks and cuts he had inflicted on his victims, although he conceded he must have done them. O'Loughlin asked if he was in a habit of forgetting things. Denyer said he wasn't.

'How did you feel afterwards?' asked O'Loughlin, trying to get a picture of what was going through the killer's mind.

'Like the temperature gauge was coming down.'

'What do you mean?' O'Loughlin asked him.

'Well, it was going up to boiling point, then afterwards it just came down till it stopped at a level and then climbed up again.'

'You're referring to what type of feeling?'

'Hate, anger.'

'Is this something that you plan?'

'No, I would just go to a certain area and then pick targets around, just, you know, anyone you see walking around is ... anyone, women, woman by herself. So I'd just wait for them. No, it wasn't premeditated in that way.'

'Wait for the right opportunity to come along. Is that fair to say?'

'Yeah, just sort of go to the area and hope for the best.'

Denyer discussed his weapons with the detectives. The cord he used, he told them, had come from around the waist of his tracksuit pants. It had come off and he had kept it to strangle someone with, and the fake gun, he told O'Loughlin, was on a shelf in the spare room at his flat.

Placing a scrapbook that had been taken by police from Denyer's flat on the table, Rod Wilson asked Denyer if it was his. Denyer told Wilson that it was and explained that he had been practising drawing. There was a sketch of one person pointing a gun at another. It was labelled 'The Last Great Act of Defiance'. Denyer admitted drawing it. There were other pictures – a gun as well as old sketches of scrub and bushes that Denyer said he had done from sites around the Flora and Fauna Reserve where he had stopped on Friday before going to the bike track on Skye Road.

With no further questions for the time being, Rod Wilson checked his watch. It was 6.05 am on Sunday morning. The interview had lasted all night. In order to prevent future possible allegations of maltreatment of the murderer, Wilson mentioned on video tape that Denyer had been supplied with a hamburger and a few cups of coffee.

'Yeah, I was well looked after,' Denyer agreed politely.

Wilson told Denyer that he would make arrangements to go to the areas mentioned in the statement. First port of call would be where Denyer had buried Debbie Fream's purse.

'Do you have any objections to that?'

'No,' replied the confessed killer.

Rod Wilson suspended the interview.

It is always worth remembering just how callous Paul Denyer was in his dispensing of women, and how selective his memory was in the recounting. He remembered what he had for dinner on the night he killed Elizabeth, but not painstakingly carving the pattern into her torso. To him, women existed as objects of his rage and he killed with no remorse. The only emotion he showed throughout the whole interview was when he recounted the women fighting for their lives saying something he didn't like. Elizabeth lied about her age – perhaps thinking seventeen sounded younger than eighteen and that her attacker might find mercy for someone under eighteen, a child. Roszsa Toth went against her word when she said she wouldn't try to escape. And Natalie – he had reserved his most brutal attack for the girl willing to bargain anything for her life.

Natalie's mum Carmel received untold comfort when she visited a psychic who told her that Natalie came through and said, 'Don't worry, Mum. When he started doing those things to me, I was gone. I floated up and could see it, but I didn't feel it.'

Messages like that help a mother sleep at night.

Had she survived, one wonders what Natalie's aunt, Bernadette Naughton, would have made of Paul Denyer's bid to become a woman. A part of her would perhaps be glad that 'Paula' was seeking out the limelight. It would help people remember what he did during his seven-week reign of terror, and that was Bernadette's goal – that people didn't forget the brutality and the loss her family and all the other families suffered. Since she is no longer alive and has no chance of carrying the torch of justice, one can only hope that stories of Denyer's brutality keep circulating in books, articles and podcasts. Male or female, Paul or Paula, Denyer is a dangerous offender who targeted innocent women going about their business. He killed without remorse, and would have continued to do so if he hadn't been caught.

Lest we forget.

Chapter Eleven

FINGERPRINTS

Senior Sergeant Jim Falloon's office, on the seventeenth floor of the St Kilda Road Victoria Police building, looked out over some of the most spectacular parts of Melbourne's cityscape. His view included the Shrine of Remembrance and, in the opposite direction, Albert Park Lake.

In his many years in the Victoria Police Force, Falloon has seen a lot of changes, not the least of which has occurred in his own department, the Fingerprint Branch. Indeed, one of Falloon's colleagues recalls a time when a senior Fingerprint Branch member ridiculed the use of computers in their area of expertise. 'You'll never see computers used around here,' the senior member had said. Ironically, within six years of his erroneous prediction, the Fingerprint Branch had, at its disposal, an extensive network of computers that perform almost miraculous feats in matching fingerprints to suspects Australia-wide from offences ranging from credit card fraud to murder.

Senior Sergeant Falloon recalls his training to become an expert in the study of fingerprint analysis. The training took five years. Falloon began his study with five months of theory work, which was later interspersed with on-the-job training with recognised fingerprint analysis experts. Before going solo, Falloon was required to attend fifteen crime scenes with fingerprint experts who would guide the development of his investigative techniques and write reports on his progress.

At the completion of his five-year training, Jim Falloon passed an examination in Sydney and returned to Melbourne a fully-fledged expert. One week after taking up his new expert status, Falloon was called upon to attend his first solo major crime scene. It remains the worst job he attended in terms of bodily damage. A car, peppered with bullet holes, was parked in the emergency lane of the Burwood Highway. Crouched on the floor was a young woman with most of her face shot away by a jealous boyfriend. Her skull and her brain matter were sprayed all over the car's interior and such was the extent of damage, the victim was barely recognisable as human. Falloon later received, for inclusion in the police files, a photograph of the young woman taken at a theatre restaurant weeks before her death. She had been so beautiful, she could have been a model.

It was with such experiences and years of practical work behind him that Falloon attended a crime scene on Melbourne Cup Day in November 1983.

An elderly woman had been beaten to death in her home in a bayside Melbourne suburb. Jim Falloon had become used to such crime scenes. It was his job to discover any fingerprints in the elderly woman's home that may have been left by the killer, but he had to wait in line. Investigations proceeded only after the crime scene – in this case the elderly woman's home – had been photographed and videoed by members of the photographic and audio-visual sections. After the photos, the crime scene examiners had to search the house for evidence, and only then it was Falloon's turn.

Having waited outside the neat white weatherboard with a fresh coat of paint and a well-tended garden, Falloon finally went inside and noted that the interior was as neat as the outside of the house. Inside the house it was a typical elderly woman's domain; the furniture was old-fashioned and some of the nicer lounge-room chairs were even covered in plastic. The lounge-room floor was decorated with a rug embroidered in quaint floral arrangements from another era, and an upright wooden dresser with glass doors held ornaments collected over a lifetime. The dresser drawer was opened, showing a selection of cutlery, including a set of bone-handled knives.

In the kitchen, the table had a pale green laminex top with metal trim and chrome legs, with chairs to match. The off-white linoleum covering the kitchen floor was now smeared with a long vivid drag mark of blood. A broken pot-plant holder and plants and dirt lay on the floor by the back door. The trail of dirt, blood and disarray allowed Falloon and the Homicide detectives to follow the killer's path through the otherwise neat home.

On a table in a room adjacent to the kitchen, a worn green leather purse lay on top of an old metal tray. It was open and empty.

The body of 77-year-old Miss Rosalyn Burns lay on her bedroom floor. Half of her face was battered to a sickening bluish-black colour and her left ear was viciously torn. Miss Burns' body was clothed only in an old-fashioned, yellowing singlet, which was now heavily stained with her blood.

Rosalyn Burns had met her death in the midst of a frenzy of violence. She had been bashed and stabbed as she had feebly tried to defend herself against the fatal attack. One of the bone-handled knives from the dresser had been used. Her grey thinning hair plastered damply to her head didn't cover the deep gash to the left side of her skull. Her legs had lines cut into them and she had been assaulted with a bottle.

In death, the elderly woman lay, her dignity stripped away by her killer. Men she never knew now stared down upon her lying in her old-fashioned underwear. She was the archetypal innocent victim. The injuries to the old woman were horrific. Detectives hoped for her sake that she had died early on in the attack.

Jim Falloon quickly summed up the scene before him. His hardening to such scenes of tragedy, coupled with his extensive professional experience, meant that his primary concern was the acquisition of any evidence that may lead to the killer. In his job, there was no time to lament the loss of a woman's life.

Falloon proceeded to do the work he was trained for. He began in the kitchen area, which had a door leading outside. It seemed the killer had first encountered Miss Burns in the kitchen. A struggle had overturned the pot-plant stand. Blood stains in the kitchen area and on the linoleum made it obvious to the investigators that the initial attack had occurred near the back door. The bloodied drag marks on the floor suggested the killer had knocked the old woman down in the kitchen, and the trail of blood continued down the hallway and into the bedroom where the dead woman now lay.

Falloon dusted all the surfaces along this trail, items that the killer may have touched purposefully or in passing. Given that a bottle had been found close to the body, Falloon took his long-handled brush and applied the distinctive fingerprint dust to the surface of other bottles that stood in the wooden dresser in the neat lounge room. When a number of fingerprints appeared on the bottles enhanced by the fingerprint dust, Falloon photographed them with a Polaroid camera.

With the house securely shut to the growing crowd of onlookers outside, the investigators took a short break around the starting time of the horse race that has Victorians glued to their television sets – the Melbourne Cup. Someone turned on the elderly woman's television set and the investigating officers paused from their grim tasks for the few minutes it took for Kiwi to come from the middle of the pack to romp home and win the coveted trophy. When the race was over, they turned off the television and got on with the job of investigating a murder.

After the crime scene examiners had finished their inspection of the dead woman, Jim Falloon delicately dusted her body with a magnetic powder in the vain hope that fingerprints would be visible on her skin. This was a common procedure, although rarely successful. The best Falloon could detect were smudges on the victim's leg.

Falloon picked up the bottle next to the body with extraordinary care so as not to disturb any possible fingerprints. He dusted it and to his pleasure, and as he had suspected, the glass surface revealed a number of relatively clear fingerprints. He bagged the bottle and gathered the Polaroid photos he'd taken, and passed them into the care of two police officers for transportation to the Fingerprint Branch's offices, then housed in the old Russell Street police building.

Falloon and a colleague planned to use further technology to enhance the fingerprints on the bottle to produce a higher-quality impression.

During the long day's work, Falloon had periodically kept an eye on the gathering of spectators outside the white weatherboard house. He couldn't fail to notice a rather tall young man who had been watching the house all day.

While Falloon was still at the crime scene, his colleagues back at the Fingerprint Branch had received the photographs of the fingerprints and began manually processing them for a match against the six hundred thousand sets of prints the Branch had on file. The task wasn't quite as daunting as it seemed. All fingerprints are filed in order of their characteristics – loops, whorls, arches and composites. The fingerprints gathered at the scene that might have come from the killer were categorised as loops. Falloon's colleagues searched through the complex filing system, immediately discarding those fingerprints that their training and experience told them didn't match.

Searching through existing police records didn't guarantee a successful match. A match depended on one simple fact – the killer's fingerprints needed to be on file. Falloon had no idea whether the person who killed Rosalyn Burns had ever been fingerprinted before and had his detail entered into the database. The prints on file weren't just from people who had committed criminal offences; they also included anybody who had been fingerprinted for a pistol licence or for driving offences. Jim Falloon hoped that the killer fell into one of these categories.

Eventually Falloon's colleague, Sergeant Mark Ellwood, hit the jackpot. He matched prints from the scene with a set on record and within seconds, Sergeant Ellwood had put a name to the fingerprints – a 22-year-old man by the name of John Charles Housden. A check on his address showed that he lived one street away from Miss Rosalyn Burns.

Triumphantly, the information was telephoned through to the Homicide Squad officers. 'I've got you a name,' Ellwood said.

Falloon often says that the other investigators and experts may be able to tell you all about an offender – his strength, his build or whether he killed his victim in the kitchen or in the parlour with the dagger – but it is the Fingerprint Branch experts that can give you the all-important name.

While Jim Falloon was finishing his work at the house, Homicide detectives instructed local police to pick up the suspect and to bring him into the Russell Street offices. Falloon, too, made his way from the house to Russell Street when he heard that there had been a fingerprint match. Homicide detectives, in the interim, had searched police files and discovered the prior record for John Charles Housden for a minor offence. They also had a photograph of him on file.

Meanwhile, police went to the home of the young man whom they strongly suspected of beating and stabbing a defenceless old woman to death. When Falloon arrived at Homicide, the detectives showed him Housden's photograph.

'God, that's the tall guy who was watching the house all day!' he said.

Falloon was right. Housden had indeed been watching the house all day in what could be considered more than a casual interest in the outcome of the investigation.

John Charles Housden was an average looking young man, tall with dark hair and a weak chin. You could walk past him in the street and not give him a second glance. Detectives, who arrived at his house just before midnight on the day of the murder, immediately noticed a fresh red graze on the left side of his forehead.

Housden looked surprised at the appearance of police on his doorstep. The detectives took him to Russell Street police station for an interview, which Falloon was invited to sit in on. His interest in the case was understandable since he had spent seven hours at the crime scene.

John Housden denied everything. The detectives relentlessly pursued their line of questioning. Housden did not cooperate.

'How do you explain your fingerprints being at the scene?'

'I don't know,' Housden replied.

This game of verbal cat and mouse went on for nearly two hours. The break came at question number 122, when Housden made a startling statement.

'If I tell you anything, you'll hang me.'

Incredulous detectives explained to the young man that the state of Victoria and indeed the rest of the country had no death penalty – the last hanging in Victoria was in 1967.

'Oh well, that's all right then,' said Housden, looking relieved. 'I'll tell you everything ...'

Housden spent the next half-hour telling the detectives how he had gone to the old lady's home with the intention of breaking in and robbing the house. He had been surprised to find that not only was she home when he had expected her to be out, but she had been standing in the kitchen when he had walked through the back door.

According to the young killer, Miss Burns had immediately shouted at him to get out of her house and he had responded by punching her in the head a number of times. When the old lady fell to the floor, Housden continued the attack.

'What happened then?' asked one of the detectives.

Housden calmly described dragging her through the kitchen, down the hallway and into a bedroom and removing most of her clothing.

He had found a knife in the lounge-room dresser and returned to continue the assault.

Housden explained his process. 'I was panicking and thought I'd get a saw and cut her up and get rid of her.' He had abandoned that when he found it too hard – but the admission explained the raw straight lines cut into the old lady's legs.

After perpetrating such atrocities, the killer had found his victim's purse and had taken the $30 it contained.

The Homicide detectives asked Housden what he did next and the young man explained, matter-of-factly, 'I called a taxi from the kitchen and went down the pub.' Housden, it transpired, had the sense not to be picked up directly outside the victim's home; he had walked a short distance and had been picked up outside a local primary school.

Jim Falloon listened to the interview with great interest – especially when John Housden had given his occupation as a plasterer. Falloon knew that often manual labourers such as plasterers and bricklayers wore down their fingerprints so the impressions they left were usually less than clear. This information confirmed a suspicion he held because the fingerprint impressions at the scene showed signs of such wearing.

Falloon also reflected upon the irony of not finding any fingerprints on the telephone when Housden admitted using the phone in the kitchen to call the taxi. Every fingerprint expert knows that sometimes people leave prints and sometimes they don't. There are many variables and since the composition of fingerprints is mainly fats and water – often if the hands are too dry or the surface isn't porous enough, prints won't be found.

John Housden was charged with murder. He was photographed – both clothed and wearing only a pair of pale blue underpants. His body showed scratches, abrasions and bruises caused during his struggle with Rosalyn Burns. She had died fighting.

John Charles Housden received a life sentence for the murder of Rosalyn Burns. Ironically, Falloon was never given the chance to present his incriminating evidence in court because the judge felt that if the jury heard that Housden's prints were matched to his prints already on police files, they would automatically assume a prior criminal record – and such evidence would prejudice a fair trial.

Nonetheless, Senior Sergeant Jim Falloon regards the apprehension of John Housden so quickly and, as a direct result of the work of the Victoria Police Fingerprint Branch, as a major triumph.

Chapter Twelve

THE REMOVALIST

On a Tuesday in early August 2002, 56-year-old Janis tried to organise a removalist. She had just bought a new house and was making the move to the other side of town. The real estate agent had given her a fistful of brochures for everything anyone might need to move house. The first removalist she tried made an appointment to give her a quote, but didn't show up. She was relieved when she contacted another removalist company and the phone was answered by a friendly man.

'And how many people are you moving?' he asked.

'Just me,' replied Janis. 'I'm on my own.'

'My name is Mark Sutherland,' said the removalist. 'I'll come and give you a quote this afternoon.' He had a nice voice and a very friendly manner.

'Thanks,' Janis replied. She was grateful that one part of moving house might be made easier by the man on the other end of the line.

Later that day, Mark Sutherland rang Janis back.

'I'm running late. Can I organise a different time?'

Janis was busy and organised for Sutherland to come round later in the week, on Thursday evening.

The appointment was for 7 pm but Sutherland rang three times with various reasons for getting there late. When Janice finally heard the car pull into her driveway, she went to the door and opened it. It was a cold winter's night and she stood in the doorway to let in the removalist. *Come on*, she thought impatiently as he sat in his car and seemed to be looking through some papers. After several minutes, Mark Sutherland finally got out of his car and came to the door. He was slight of build, and had a receding hairline. He was perhaps mid-forties. Janis noticed that his cheeks were a bit blotchy and she wondered idly if he was a drinker. Sutherland introduced himself and was a friendly, good customer service type. He gave Janis a business card with his name on it and Janis offered him a cup of coffee.

'I'll have one if you're having one,' he said.

Janis, who had not long before eaten dinner and enjoyed a glass of wine didn't really want one, but she made herself one as well — just to be hospitable.

As they walked through her house, Janis pointed out various items that she was taking with her to the new house and Sutherland scanned his surroundings. Janis put her cup of coffee on a sideboard while they were talking and Sutherland commented on a decorative plate hanging on the opposite wall, drawing her attention to the other side of the room. The plate featured a 1940s picture of a beautiful young woman with Betty Grable hair and the writing next to the picture said, 'Gee, I wish I was a man — I'd join the Navy'. The curvaceous model in the picture was dressed in a Navy uniform.

'I used to be in the Navy,' Sutherland told Janis.

'Whereabouts?' Janis asked. 'My husband was in the Navy.'

'I joined in Western Australia.'

Janis, who'd been a Navy wife for fifteen years, thought he probably joined as a young recruit. 'What did you do?' she asked.

'I was an accountant in the Navy.'

Janis didn't say anything, but she felt that the removalist was big-noting himself. Accountants in the Navy weren't referred to as 'accountants'; instead, they were just called 'writers'. This was a minor detail, however, and she didn't give it a second thought. Sutherland also told her that he went AWOL but got an honourable discharge. Janis thought, *Couldn't hack it, huh?* But she didn't say it.

The two finished their coffee and Sutherland asked to take a look around the rest of the house. He looked in the bedrooms.

'Do you want us to pack your clothes?'

'No, I'll pack them myself,' Janis told him. Nonetheless, Sutherland checked the inside of all the wardrobes, which contained only women's clothing.

Sutherland then asked what was in the garage that had to be moved. Janis told him that the garage contained three boxes, a single bed and a ladder.

'I'll just take a look,' he said.

'Why?' asked Janis, forthright and a bit annoyed. 'I just told you what was in it.'

'I just want to take a look,' said Sutherland smoothly.

Janis took him out to the front of the house and opened the garage door. Sutherland stepped over to his car parked in the driveway and retrieved a torch which he shone around the almost empty garage. Janis thought this was strange but didn't say anything.

Back inside the house, Sutherland said he wanted a smoke and Janis, a smoker herself, said he was welcome to smoke inside, but he insisted on smoking outside in her courtyard, telling her that he smoked cigars and that they smelt.

'I don't mind,' she said. 'My dad smokes pipes and it doesn't worry me.' However, Sutherland seemed determined to go outside. Janis went out with him and got the distinct feeling he smoked the tiny cigar slowly as if he wanted her to go back inside rather than wait outside with him. Janis, however, did not want to leave him alone, and waited till he finished. Sutherland followed Janis back inside and she didn't think to lock the sliding door behind her.

When the house inspection was over, Janis and Sutherland sat down in the kitchen. Sutherland got out his quote pad and began writing out the quote. As she watched him, Janis began to feel sort of swirly in the stomach and said as much to the removalist.

'I don't feel so good,' she said. He didn't make any comment in reply, which Janis found vaguely rude.

It was about forty-five minutes since she had finished her cup of coffee and by this time, she just wanted the removalist to go. There was a football show on television that she wanted to watch and it was after 10 pm. When he handed her the written quote, Janis couldn't read it – partly because she wasn't wearing her glasses and partly because she was finding it hard to focus. After the quote was finished, Janis thanked him and walked him to the front door.

From her doorway, she watched Mark Sutherland drive away in his vintage Mercedes coupé. Janis could hardly keep her eyes open. As she climbed up the stairs, she felt a little unsteady on her feet.

She undressed, got into her pyjamas and crawled into bed. She turned on the television in her bedroom and began watching her footy show. But she was so tired. After only a few minutes, Janis couldn't keep her eyes open. Reluctantly, she turned off her program and fell into a deep sleep. She didn't hear the scraping sound of her garage door, or the smooth swish as her sliding door opened, or the footsteps on her stairs. And she didn't hear the man come into her bedroom and take off his clothes.

She didn't even know that he had climbed into bed beside her …

When Janis *did* become aware, she was lying on her side facing away from the bedroom door. She could sense someone lying beside her. Having slept on her own for many years, it was the feeling of someone else in her bed that jolted her into consciousness. Then she felt an arm slide over the sleeve of her satin pyjama top, reach around her. A hand took hold of her breast and then moved away. Her first reaction was to yell and scream, but a sense of self-preservation coursed through her. Janis turned her head and saw the removalist lying beside her. The way he was looking at her, Janis could only describe as 'lovey-dovey'.

'No …' she said. 'What are you doing here?'

'You left the door unlocked, I thought you wanted me to come back,' Sutherland murmured soothingly.

'No, not tonight,' she said and then added, 'maybe another time.' Janis was desperate to sound as if she didn't think anything was wrong. She was afraid of aggravating the naked man beside her, and if she made him think that there was a chance, he might leave her unharmed.

Mark Sutherland said nothing as he slid out of her bed. Janis didn't turn around but could hear him putting his clothes back on. She didn't say anything but in her mind she was screaming, *Just go! Just go!*

Janis heard him walk out of her bedroom and waited several minutes, all the while telling herself, *You have to get up! You have to up!* But even though her mind told her she should get up and check the house to make sure the man had gone, her body was strangely uncooperative. She felt like she was in a dream. Finally, she forced herself out of bed. Staggering through her house, Janis checked the front door and all the bedrooms to make sure Sutherland had really gone.

The next morning, Janis was woken by the phone ringing at 7.45 am. It was her ex-husband ringing from interstate.

'Are you just getting up now?' he asked, surprised. 'You'll be late for work.'

Janis couldn't believe she'd slept so late. She still felt so tired, like she'd taken a handful of Valium. And she couldn't shake the feeling. She didn't tell her ex-husband what had happened. She knew he would overreact and she just wasn't in the mood for a scene.

Downstairs, she noticed that the back sliding door was unlocked.

Driving to work an hour later, Janis felt unsteady behind the wheel, almost as if she shouldn't be driving. And then it hit her – the removalist must have put something in her drink. The way she felt just wasn't natural.

At work, Janis told her manager what had happened and announced that she was going to make an appointment to see a doctor. Even though Janis felt like she was acting normally, her manager thought she looked spaced-out.

At the doctors' surgery, Janis explained to the medical practitioner what had happened. He agreed that she may have been drugged but confessed that he didn't know which drugs to test her for and suggested she visit her local police station and ask their advice. And so Janis drove to the Brunswick police station. There were others at the reception desk and Janis was attended to by a young male constable. She quietly explained that she had been drugged and the doctor needed to know what to test her for. As she leaned against the counter-top, Janis felt herself go weak at the knees and she knew that whatever the removalist had given her was still in her system. The young constable disappeared behind the glass partition and Janis expected him to return with a policewoman. Instead, the young man returned with a note. On it was a list of six drugs that might be used in a drug-facilitated sexual assault.

Realising that the constable had little else to add, Janis, ever the take-charge person, told him that she would go back to the doctor and then come back to the police and start proceedings against the man once the results came back. And Janis drove back to the doctor for the referral and then on to the local hospital for the blood test.

Janis explained what had happened to her and two helpful nurses at the hospital advised her to have a urine test as well as a blood test, telling her that the results would come back more quickly. The nurses also advised Janis not to spend the night alone at her house, but to stay with a friend – advice that Janis took. One of Janis's female friends offered her a bed for the night and both women went around to Janis's house for her to get some overnight things.

Walking into her dark, empty house, Janis felt afraid – and then angry. How dare that man make her afraid to be alone. She lived alone and had done for some time. How dare he take that security away from her. But mostly, she felt tired. It was early Friday evening and all she wanted to do was sleep. Before she left her house to go to her friend's place, Janis followed her doctor's advice and carefully placed the cups from the night before in the fridge to preserve any evidence. He'd also told her to gather up her bed sheets for the police. For good measure, Janis also located Sutherland's cigar butt from the night before and wrapped it in cling-wrap.

In among all the drama of the day, Janis had a thought. She wondered whether Mark Sutherland was expecting her to contact him since in order to get him out of her bed, she had led him to believe he might have a chance with her at a later date.

On Saturday morning, Janis rang the Brunswick police again and spoke to the same young constable from the day before. She told him that she had the tests done and that the results would be back early the following week. On Sunday, she rang the police station again. She was really worried that if too much time elapsed, she might not be able to get Mark Sutherland charged with what he did to her. The female police officer she spoke to assured her that it didn't matter how much time elapsed, the police could still charge him. It eased Janis's mind. A bit.

On Tuesday, the test results came back positive showing traces of the drug flunitrazepam in her system. The results proved what Janis and her doctor had feared – that she had indeed been drugged.

Janis hesitated. Now she had proof that Mark Sutherland had drugged her, another thought occurred to her. She rang her solicitor and explained what had happened. She had one major concern.

'If I go ahead with this,' she asked, 'will I be on the television?'

'Of course not,' her solicitor told her, explaining that the identity of sexual assault victims was always kept from the media. It wasn't for her sake that Janis asked this. Both her parents were elderly and frail, and she didn't want them ever to find out what had happened to her. Janis told the solicitor that the local uniform police were going to handle it. The solicitor thought otherwise. It was a job for detectives at the Criminal Investigation Unit (CIU) – not uniform. This was serious. In fact, the solicitor knew one of the detectives there and he offered to ring for her.

Senior Detective Justin Schulze from the Brunswick CIU took the call and drove immediately to Janis's house with a team to gather evidence. Often when detectives are called to investigate an offence several days after it happens, the evidence has been contaminated. To Schulze's amazement, Janis had collected every bit of evidence that she thought police might need. She had placed the cups in the fridge, saved the cigar butt that Sutherland had smoked, and collected the sheets off her bed. Schulze was impressed by Janis's presence of mind. Janis, who was in her late fifties, had vowed that no-one would take advantage of her. She wanted the matter pursued with the full force of the law. The arrival of Schulze and his team meant for Janis that the cavalry had arrived.

What struck Justin Schulze, as he collected evidence from Janis's house, was how organised this offender seemed. It was as if he had refined the practice of gaining entry, drugging his victim, unlocking the doors, leaving, and then returning when the victim was incapacitated – in other words, to the trained eye of the detective, Schulze suspected that Janis wouldn't have been the removalist's only victim. Conversely, though, the removalist had made no attempt to hide his identity – his name, Mark Sutherland, was written clearly on the removalist quote form, and he hadn't bothered with a wig or a false moustache to hide his appearance.

Janis offered Schulze her statement. While she had been waiting around for the test results, she had made a careful written account of exactly what she remembered of the night the removalist came. In her job, Janis was used to attending meetings and made notes afterwards. She applied the same technique to the assault.

Janis went with Schulze to the Brunswick CIU office and made a statement. She was there so long that the detectives called out for pizza for dinner. At the end of her statement, Janis said quite clearly to Justin Schulze: 'Don't think I'm getting up in court to testify! I won't!' Schulze just nodded. The thought of saying all this again in front of a court and Sutherland terrified her.

Given that the name 'Mark Sutherland' could have been a pseudonym, the first thing Schulze did was to check the offender's name with other details that Janis had mentioned in her statement. She remembered the man driving away in an older-model Mercedes coupé, so Justin Schulze began there. He checked motor vehicle records and sure enough, there was a Mark Sutherland who owned the same model car. From the motor vehicle records, Schulze got an address for Sutherland in Tecoma, which was a suburb not far from Belgrave.

With evidence of the drug used in the assault on Janis, as well as the butt of the small Café Crème cigar, Schulze was granted a search warrant on Mark Sutherland's home. Schulze, together with Senior Detective Paul Tymms and Detective Sergeant Stuart Delbridge, drove to the Tecoma address to perform the search. When they arrived, Schulze pulled the police car into the driveway of Sutherland's neat double-storey home nestled in a bushland setting. The detectives walked to the front door and knocked.

'Mark Sutherland?' Schulze asked when a man in his early forties answered the door. He was slightly built, gaunt, and had short-cropped grey hair and rotting teeth.

'Yes,' the man replied, 'I'm Mark Sutherland.'

'We have a warrant to search your house in relation to the assault in Pascoe Vale,' explained the detective, watching Sutherland for any sign of flight, denial, or for that matter, violence. There was none.

'You're not obliged to say or do anything, but anything you say or do may be given in evidence.'

Sutherland nodded his head. He knew very well why the detectives were on his doorstep.

'Do you know which incident I'm referring to?' asked Schulze.

'Yes,' said Sutherland as Schulze, Tymms and Delbridge entered his neat, pleasantly decorated home.

'What happened?' asked Schulze, mildly surprised that Sutherland rolled over so easily.

'I put a drug in her drink.'

'Have you done this before?' Schulze had suspected right from the start that the offender was so slick that he had probably done this before. His hunch was right.

'Yep, two times. It's in my diary.'

Sutherland was quiet and cooperative. He showed detectives around his house while they bagged such evidence as Café Crème cigars matching the butt found at Janis's house, his diary, as well as Hypnodorm tablets – which contained the drug flunitrazepam that the doctors had found in Janis's blood and urine samples. Rohypnol is the trade name for flunitrazepam, which is now banned on the Australian market due to its misuse in drug-facilitated sexual assaults. However, products like Hypnodorm that contained flunitrazepam were still prescribed.

Schulze took Mark Sutherland into custody. They put him in the back of the unmarked police car and took him to the Brunswick CIU. It took an hour to drive from Tecoma to Brunswick and the detectives used the time to establish a rapport with the offender. It would help them later in the interview to know a bit of his history. Sutherland chatted casually about his house, the footy and, when the detectives drove past a certain road, Sutherland pointed to it and told the detectives that he'd had a car accident there in 1992.

Before the interview began, Schulze rang through to the Sexual Crimes Squad offices on the eighth floor of the St Kilda Road police complex. He was put on to a member of Sergeant Tony Silva's crew. Tony Silva was the overseer of all drug-facilitated sexual assaults and was fast becoming a veritable expert in this relatively new type of offence. Schulze described what Sutherland had confessed to and said that the case could get bigger. Schulze was given the go-ahead to handle the case for the time being, but was told to keep the squad updated.

In the small interview room, at the Brunswick CIU that used to be the old Brunswick courthouse, Justin Schulze and Paul Tymms sat on one side of the big timber veneer table and Sutherland sat on the other. Interviewing sex offenders is a tricky business. They *know* what they have done is legally wrong, but they don't *feel* it's wrong. Detectives have to mask their feelings of revulsion in order to let the offender think that they are offering a sympathetic ear. This is difficult but necessary; detectives want a confession. Schulze knew that because the squad had given him permission to take on the investigation, he had a huge responsibility. Things had to be done absolutely correctly, because with this kind of case no-one wanted to see it lost in court on a minor technicality.

After the obligatory caution, Mark Sutherland was happy to talk. Schulze listened as the suspect told how he'd gone to Janis's house and how he'd put a tablet in her drink.

'Why did you do it?' asked Schulze.

'So she would pass out and I could have sex with her,' he replied matter-of-factly. Sutherland then told the detective how he'd noticed the sliding door was unlocked so he would be able to get back into the house once Janis had gone to sleep. He said that if she hadn't woken up when he returned to the house, he would have had sex with her.

'Did you have permission to re-enter the property once you had been asked to leave?'

'No.'

Sutherland's admissions met the criteria for the Sexual Crimes Squad to be called in. If an offender enters a property illegally with the intent to assault, the offence is classified as an aggravated burglary and that, along with the drugging of the victim, meant that Schulze had to contact the Sexual Crimes Squad as soon as the interview was finished.

When they had spoken to him at his house, Mark Sutherland said he'd done this a couple of other times – just as Schulze had suspected when he'd first spoken to Janis.

'Tell me about the others,' Schulze said.

Sutherland described how he met a woman called Kimberly when she'd called for a removalist quote. He quickly learnt that she was recently separated and moving up north. Sutherland had called Kimberly back, and in the second conversation, she confided that she was currently staying with a friend but she needed somewhere more permanent to live. Sutherland had offered her a room at his house. Kimberly refused but over the following week, Sutherland continued to call her and repeat his offer. The young mother of two was desperate and finally agreed and moved into the bushland house in Tecoma.

The first night began well. Sutherland was nice and the home was certainly comfortable. After sitting around chatting, Sutherland produced a stash of marijuana which both Kimberly and her host smoked. And then Sutherland gave Kimberly a drink. Next thing, Kimberly began to feel dizzy and then fell onto the couch unconscious. Sutherland waited half an hour before removing her clothes and then anally and vaginally raped her. After he was done, he fell asleep next to her on the couch.

Next morning, Kimberly awoke feeling groggy with Sutherland lying beside her. Sutherland got up, had a shower and left for work. Kimberly, however, was too groggy to leave the house. When he got home from work, Sutherland was surprised to see Kimberly still there. That night, she agreed to sleep in his bed with him, but by the next day, she had taken her children and left.

The next victim Sutherland spoke about was Dana, a woman in her late fifties. Within days of his attack on Janis, Sutherland was at it again. Dana had rung for a quote at the same time Sutherland was organising to do the quote for Janis. He attacked Janis on

Thursday 8 August 2002 and arrived at Dana's house for a quote late in the evening on Saturday 10 August 2002. Sutherland inspected Dana's flat and then asked for a cup of coffee. Offering to help in the kitchen, Sutherland slipped a Hypnodorm tablet into Dana's drink. While they drank, they chatted and Sutherland smoked his trademark tiny cigars. Half an hour after drinking her drugged coffee, the phone rang and Dana got up to answer it. She had bumped into the walls in the hallway and nearly lost her balance. After she'd spoken on the phone, she asked Sutherland point blank whether he'd put something in her drink. Sutherland said he hadn't but turned the lamp off and moved to sit next to Dana, and then put his hand on her knee and asked for a kiss. Dana had refused and asked him to leave and he had. She locked the doors behind him, and then passed out unconscious on her bed. He didn't return.

In the face of what he'd done, Mark Sutherland tried to justify his actions. He said he couldn't meet women, or if he did, he couldn't hold on to them. He said pubs and loud music gave him sensory overload. He explained that in 1992, he'd had a serious car accident and it had left him with injuries for which he'd been paid a lot of money in compensation. Since the accident, he had been seeing a psychiatrist for an anxiety disorder that made it difficult for him to form and maintain relationships. As part of Sutherland's treatment, he was prescribed flunitrazepam, diazepam and clonazepam.

When the interview was finished, Sutherland was allowed to leave. Schulze knew that if he had charged Sutherland then and there, the committal hearing would have to take place within three months. Even with what he had, the detectives knew that the investigation would take a lot longer than that and they decided to wait until the investigation was complete before charging him. They also needed to identify any further victims.

When Sutherland had gone, Justin Schulze rang the Sexual Crimes Squad for a second time and this time he spoke to Tony Silva personally. Silva agreed that because of its serial nature, the case needed to be handled by his squad. He arranged to come straight out to the Brunswick CIU.

For the previous couple of years, Tony Silva had been assigned a special portfolio within the Sexual Crimes Squad – that of investigating drug-facilitated sexual assaults. Silva took on his new role with enthusiasm and applied for the Angela Taylor Memorial Scholarship to investigate overseas practices in this relatively new type of crime. Silva was confident that he would get the scholarship because of the emphasis policing policies were placing on violence against women – particularly in the area of drugging. Sure enough, the award gave him $14,000 to use to attend conferences in Los Angeles, Orlando, San Diego and Las Vegas. In the United States, Silva heard FBI experts and scientists from around the world discussing this new phenomenon. In Las Vegas, the problem was twofold. In the gambling mecca not only were drugs used in sexual assaults, but they were also used to separate unsuspecting gamblers from their money.

On the study tour, Tony Silva spoke to both local cops and district attorneys because in the American system, DAs were involved in the investigations and prepared the briefs, like detectives do in Australia.

Silva learnt that people reacted differently to the kinds of drugs used in sexual assaults. In 2000, a study was done that monitored participants' reactions to drugs traditionally associated with sexual assaults. Some of the participants reported confusion and difficulty with speech, and during the test they generally behaved out of character. One subject said that she remembered going to sleep after the drug was administered and waking up when the effects had worn off, but supervising staff had witnessed her walking and talking and generally appearing quite alert. Most subjects were less inhibited, and one tried to remove her clothing before the researchers stopped her. Some victims of drug-facilitated sexual assault reported losing consciousness and had no memory at all of what happened, while others described regaining consciousness for short periods of time – usually in response to pain stimuli. Some victims spoke of being paralysed, while other victims with complete memory loss had been observed as acting like they were mildly drunk.

The effects of the types of drugs used in sexual assaults were also amplified when used in conjunction with alcohol or cannabis, so if a woman was already drinking alcohol at a bar and had her drink spiked, the effect would be worse than if she were completely sober.

After his study tour, and several years' experience dealing solely with drug-facilitated sexual assaults, Tony Silva had become the squad expert. When he finally met up with Justin Schulze at the Brunswick CIU, Silva told him that the squad would take over the case against Mark Sutherland.

'You can take the case,' said the quietly spoken Brunswick detective, 'but I'm not letting it go.' Something about this case had convinced Schulze that this might well be the biggest case in his career.

'Fine,' said Silva, noting Schulze's white-knuckled grip on the case file. Silva sensed a tenacity about his younger colleague. 'How would you feel about coming into the squad? I'll assign a team to work on this with you.'

And with that, Schulze was seconded into the Sexual Crimes Squad.

One of the first jobs for Justin Schulze at the squad was to investigate Mark Sutherland's diary. Sutherland had explained that because of his impaired memory from the car accident, he'd written down names and addresses of women he'd drugged. The diary contained many women's names and Schulze began at the beginning and telephoned each woman in turn. He followed a set proforma so as not to bait or lead potential victims or witnesses. One phone call remains in Schulze's memory. It began in the same way as all the others: 'Hello, I'm Senior Detective Justin Schulze. Do you know a man called Mark Sutherland?' and then the woman on the other end of the line replied, 'Yes.'

'What can you tell me about him?' Schulze had asked.

'He drugged and raped me,' said the woman bluntly.

Schulze was amazed. With each subsequent phone call, the story was eerily familiar. The women Schulze spoke to told how they had rung the removalist company for a quote and Sutherland had come personally to do the quote. Many of the women agreed that Sutherland seemed really nice on the phone. One woman described him as 'having a woman's brain', meaning that he could immediately identify with women and was a sympathetic listener. When they met him in person, however, it was another matter.

One woman said, 'If you look at him, you'd see there's something not quite right ...'

This sentiment was echoed by many of the women. On the phone, Sutherland sounded great, but in person, he made women uneasy. One woman told of a lucky escape. She'd rung for a quote and Sutherland had asked her out to dinner. Wary of meeting a stranger for a meal, she agreed to meet him at a cafe. She let him describe himself and where he would be sitting so that she could observe him unnoticed before introducing herself. When she saw him in person, she told Schulze that she walked straight past him. To her, he looked freaky.

Sutherland's modus operandi became obvious. Sutherland would speak to women on the phone, establish them to be either single or single mothers, or that they were in a vulnerable situation. He would then organise to give them a quote after hours. He told them that it was normal practice for the company to quote after hours. This put the women at ease. He would attend, ask for coffee or a drink and then he would drug the woman's drink. Most of the drugged victims felt disoriented and couldn't remember what had happened. If they contacted him, he would admit that sex had taken place. He was so blatant and obvious about it. He didn't try to hide his identity, and he made them feel that they had come on to him. The women felt embarrassed, ashamed, or responsible. If the women became upset, Sutherland was immediately apologetic.

One of Sutherland's victims had told the detectives something that Sutherland had shared with her. He'd told her that he'd been married when he was younger and his wife had contracted cancer. Her pain was so great that in order for Sutherland to have sex with her, she would have to be drugged to the point of unconsciousness. She had died in 1985. Schulze knew that if Sutherland had drugged his wife in 1985 and had developed a penchant for drugging women, it was chilling to think that this might have been going on for seventeen years. Sutherland would later deny this ever happened.

Weeks after the attack on Janis, a friend phoned her and told her to turn on her radio to 3AW. Janis was just in time to hear the end of the news item naming Mark Sutherland as an alleged rapist who had been charged with a number of offences. Janis was shocked. She grabbed the phone directory and called 3AW and spoke to someone in the newsroom. She explained her situation and asked for the full bulletin. The obliging staffer read it out to her. She had been dumbfounded initially when she'd heard she wasn't Sutherland's only victim. She had thought of him as a weedy little man who didn't have the guts to go up to women in pubs and ask them out honestly. She had even thought he might be gay when they'd met. And now to find out that he had done this to a lot of women really shook her.

It was around this time that Janis paid a visit to her local courthouse at Broadmeadows ... just in case. She'd been adamant that she wouldn't get up in court and testify and Justin Schulze had suggested she go and have a look at a court in action. And Janis did. And then the next time she was in the city, she told herself she'd just nip into the Magistrates' Court and have a look. And she did. And then the County Court ... and then she received a letter calling her for jury duty. Janis wrote back and explained that she was a victim of sexual assault and that her attacker's case was going to court in the near future, but even that didn't get her out of jury duty. She was advised she must attend. So for the woman who was scared of courts, Janis ended up spending a lot of time in them. The jury duty – even though she wasn't picked to go on a jury – helped demystify the process for her. Around this time, she realised that she *would* testify in court. In fact, she realised that she would do anything in her power to make Mark Sutherland pay for what he'd done to her and all the other women.

What surprised Janis was that the men in her circle of close family and friends in turn quietly offered to pay Sutherland – who was not in jail – a visit. They usually suggested that the visit would include a baseball bat or a bikie. As tempting as the offer seemed, Janis had gotten to know Justin Schulze and his team of detectives and had complete faith that it would be all right and that justice would prevail. It was chilling how easy payback would be, but decent law-abiding people had to believe in something stronger than violence – they had to believe in the system.

Another surprising thing for Janis was that she found herself crying a lot. Normally she never cried. But at work or at odd times, she would notice her eyes were wet and would find herself in tears. She thought she had a handle on what had happened, but it turned out, she didn't. She began to see a counsellor.

Two of Sutherland's earliest victims to come to light were friends of his – it seemed that no-one was safe from his drink spiking. Donna and her teenage daughter had been friends with Sutherland for a number of years. Sutherland would occasionally spike Donna's drinks when they'd spend a Saturday evening together and she would wake up the next morning sweaty and sick to the stomach. He even offered to make Donna's teenage daughter a chocolate drink and spiked that too. She walked into a door while trying to get to her bedroom to lie down. Things became more serious when Donna had a drink with Sutherland one Friday evening in September 1991. Sutherland supplied the cans of alcoholic drinks and the two were sitting watching the football on television. Next thing Donna knew, she was in her bed and Sutherland was lying naked beside her, trying to pull her tracksuit pants down. In her dazed state, Donna punched out at Sutherland and told him to get out. He did and Donna passed out, not waking again till the next morning. She never heard from Sutherland again.

Sutherland's next victim, Genevieve, rang for a removalist quote. During the quote, Sutherland flirted with this woman in her early forties. His skilled questioning quickly revealed that she was single and lived with her daughter. Genevieve, happy with his quote, enlisted the services of the company he worked for. Ever helpful, Sutherland offered to deliver boxes for the move and arrived at her home at 9.30 the next evening. Genevieve was in bed asleep. She was recovering from surgery and taking pain medication. When her daughter went to wake her, Sutherland followed the girl into her mother's bedroom. He was carrying cans of bourbon and coke and offered her one. She drank it unaware that he had added another mixer – a Hypnodorm tablet. When she woke up the next morning, Genevieve found Sutherland asleep on top of her bed covers. She felt groggy and embarrassed. Sutherland woke up and apologised, saying that he must have fallen asleep while they were talking. From then on, Sutherland visited her every day to help her pack to move house. But there was a price.

On the day she moved, Genevieve welcomed Sutherland into her new house. Once again, he offered her a bourbon and coke and once again, he drugged it. But this time he didn't just fall asleep beside her – Mark Sutherland raped her. Waking the next morning with a headache that would last for days, Genevieve felt sore all over and physically worn out. Sutherland had left the night before, but he maintained regular contact with her. On the third occasion Sutherland raped Genevieve, she awoke the next morning, stood up and *knew* she had been raped. She was sore and had baby oil all around her genital area. There were oil stains all over the sheets as well. The last thing that she could remember was taking a bite out of a piece of pizza and drinking from a glass of wine the evening before – with Mark Sutherland.

Genevieve tried for days to contact her 'friend' and when he finally spoke to her, he admitted drugging her drink and having sexual intercourse with her. Genevieve screamed at him in anger. But for an offender like Mark Sutherland, it was like water off a duck's back.

Days after his third assault on Genevieve, Sutherland targeted another victim – a friend called Hannah who lived with her young primary-school-aged daughter. Sutherland supplied her with some of the cannabis he grew. On Wednesday 13 February, Sutherland visited and offered Hannah a coffee and her young daughter a chocolate drink. This time, he drugged two victims at once. A short time after drinking the drink Sutherland made for her, the little girl told her mother she felt sleepy and was going to bed. Moments later, Sutherland and Hannah heard a crash from the girl's bedroom, but when Hannah tried to go to her daughter's aid, she felt dizzy and unsteady on her feet. The daughter appeared back in the kitchen and then bumped into the pantry door and fell backwards. As Hannah tried to assist her daughter, the young girl began to convulse and thrash around before being violently ill. The panic-stricken mother was herself feeling very strange; she couldn't see properly and had trouble thinking clearly.

Hannah begged Sutherland to take her and her daughter to hospital. Sutherland carried the girl to his silver Mercedes and placed her on the back seat. By this time, the girl was thrashing her arms and legs about and was incoherent. With Hannah falling asleep beside him, Sutherland drove his victims around the streets. In one of her bouts of consciousness, Hannah recalled that Sutherland became upset and emotional telling her that he had drugged her drink to make her 'feel good' and that he had accidentally drugged the girl as well. Sutherland said that if they took the girl to hospital, then the mother could face custody repercussions since the girl had been drugged and the hospital might report her to the authorities. Hannah was terrified that she could lose her daughter and agreed not to take her to hospital. By this time, the girl had passed out completely. Sutherland drove around for hours before taking his victims home. After taking the unconscious girl to her room, Sutherland then sexually assaulted Hannah on her couch. She pushed him away and he left.

Early the next morning, Hannah woke on the couch wearing pyjamas that she didn't remember putting on. Sutherland phoned her at 7.30 am to see how her daughter was. He was extremely apologetic and promised that he would never do anything like that again. Sutherland also gently reminded Hannah that she could lose her daughter if anyone found out what had happened.

Like Genevieve before her, Hannah would also be drugged by Sutherland on several occasions. The next time he drugged her, he was interrupted by visitors before he could assault her, and he was apologetic after the event. Hannah ignored his entreaties for several weeks. He kept ringing her telling her he only gave her the 'feel good' powder because he wanted her to feel good. Finally, she forgave him.

On the third occasion, Hannah was home alone when Sutherland came for a visit. He offered to make her a cup of coffee, but by this time, Hannah was wary. Sutherland insisted and Hannah followed him into the kitchen in time to see him holding a clear film canister containing white crushed powder. Hannah asked him what he was doing. Sutherland blushed and quickly put the canister away. Hannah refused to drink the coffee he'd made her. Sutherland kept nagging, she kept refusing, and then he became upset and left.

Two days after he drugged Hannah and her daughter, Sutherland gave a quote to another single mother, Sarah. They established a rapport on the phone and Sutherland told Sarah that she sounded nice and asked if she would like to have a drink with him. Since she had a friend staying with her, Sarah thought there was no harm in having a drink with the nice-sounding removalist. She was wrong.

Following his usual pattern, Sutherland drugged Sarah's drink while she was in the toilet. The next thing Sarah knew was waking up the next morning wearing a pyjama top and nothing else. She was sore and knew that she'd had sexual intercourse. Later that afternoon, Sutherland phoned her to tell her what a great night he'd had. Reluctantly, Sarah asked: 'Did we do it?' Sutherland said: 'Oh Sarah! Don't you remember?' He went on to describe how she had come on to him and assured her that he had 'used protection'. Sarah declined a follow-up date, and instead went to see a doctor who told her that she could have been 'date-raped' but he didn't take any samples or even examine her. Sarah didn't go to the police because she blamed herself for what had occurred.

She had no idea that Mark Sutherland was master of the art of making women blame themselves.

Sutherland's next victim had a lucky escape. In May 2002, Sutherland arrived to do a quote for Shelley. He brought some cans of alcoholic mixed drinks and the two chatted about their backgrounds. Shelley told Sutherland that she had had a difficult time since separating from her husband, and Sutherland opened up and told Shelley about the death of his wife and his car accident. As they spoke, Sutherland flirted with Shelley, who was in her early forties. When he finished writing out the quote, Shelley agreed to have a vodka and orange drink and left her open can on the table when she went to the toilet.

When Shelley returned, she could hear her drink fizzing which made her think that the removalist might have put something in it. She was suspicious enough not to drink any of it, and when Sutherland went outside for a smoke, she tipped the drink down the sink, then put the empty can back on the table as if she had drunk it. By this time, Shelley wanted the removalist out of her house, but she was reluctant to confront him. She feigned tiredness with a yawn and Sutherland said, 'Don't worry, you'll sleep well tonight.' Sutherland kept talking and even invited Shelley to come and stay at his house for the night. She declined and told him to leave. Sutherland insisted she make him a coffee before he left, and then when he did leave, he sat in his car in the driveway. Shelley turned on all the lights in the house and rang a friend. After a quarter of an hour, Sutherland finally drove off.

As Justin Schulze pieced together a chronology of victims, he realised that the next three victims were the ones who Sutherland had originally confessed to. While some women gave statements willingly to the police, others would not. In all, Detective Schulze identified ten victims, but knew there were more out there. He was amazed to think that if Janis had not come forward in the first place, Sutherland may well have continued his pattern of drugging and raping women indefinitely. Only one of his other victims had contacted the police.

Now that he had as much detail from the victims as he could get, Schulze and a team of detectives had to piece it all together and then back it up with expert testimony. Schulze contacted doctors who had examined some of the victims, and others who were experts on the effects of amnesia-type drugs such as the ones Sutherland used. Bit by bit, folders were filled with statements and documents building a strong case against Mark Sutherland.

On Friday 25 October Mark Sutherland was brought back in for questioning in relation to three more victims. After his candid initial interview, this time, he chose to make 'no comment' responses to all of the detectives' questions. Schulze and Tony Silva decided to search the silver Mercedes coupé parked near the police station and Sutherland gave permission for the search. Inside the sports car, Silva and Schulze found cannabis, baby oil, a camera, and another diary.

Schulze then applied for a second search warrant to look for earlier diaries as well as more cannabis. The search revealed 21.5 grams of cannabis, more Hypnodorm tablets and also an unregistered bolt-action .22 calibre Birmingham rifle. The second search of Sutherland's Tecoma property failed to reveal any further diaries –

either Sutherland hadn't kept them, or they had been removed from the house.

Sutherland told the detectives that he cultivated the cannabis himself and that he sold it to others at $70 for seventy grams. When the interview was finished, Mark Sutherland was charged and remanded into police custody.

Sutherland had thought he was just coming for an interview, but at the end of the interview he was handcuffed and driven to the Melbourne Assessment Prison underneath the Melbourne Magistrates' Court. Sutherland was not going home.

In the early stages, Sutherland had indicated that he wanted to plead guilty, but at the committal hearing, he contested the evidence. As a consequence, some of the victims had to recount their experience in court. Giving evidence can be traumatic – especially for rape victims, who have to stand before a court and relate in minute detail what they have been through.

Sutherland tried to introduce the fact that his car accident had caused him to commit the offences and that he wasn't responsible for his actions. Listening to the excuse from the public gallery, Justin Schulze noted the ten-year lapse between the accident and the subsequent sexual assaults. It was always a possibility that an accused will claim some sort of disorder or illness as part of his defence but the ten-year gap in this case would make it quite a stretch.

Sutherland was committed to stand trial and refused to make a plea offer – so in other words, his victims might have to testify a second time. It wasn't until the day the trial started, two years later, that he finally made a plea offer to plead guilty.

Over the course of the wait, Justin Schulze had to keep in regular contact with all the victims to reassure them, keep them up to date. He knew that if the time gap was too long, there was a chance that victims could get so anxious and decide it was easier to just get on with their lives than to have to face testifying again. It wasn't unheard of for a rape victim to decide not to testify before a trial, which can in turn lead to charges being withdrawn by the prosecution. Schulze knew how important it was to keep the women informed and updated every step of the way. It was vital not only for his case, but also for their own healing processes.

For Schulze the court case, nearly two years after Mark Sutherland's arrest, was a culmination of many months' painstaking work. Sutherland appeared in court neatly groomed and presenting as an unimposing figure in a grey suit. He was forty-three years old with grey hair. He looked gaunt. Sutherland pleaded guilty to most of the charges.

In court, a whole row was taken up with Sutherland's victims. Janis was there; this was her day in court too, even though Sutherland had pleaded guilty. Walking into court, she hadn't realised that Sutherland was there sitting in the back. Someone alerted her to the fact and she turned around and stared at him till their eyes met and locked together. Such was her anger towards the rapist, she mouthed what was clearly a string of swear words at him. His resilience was weaker than her anger, and he looked away first. Janis felt triumphant! It was a victory – a small victory, but a victory nonetheless.

When Judge Smallgood sentenced Sutherland to fourteen years in prison (with a nine-year minimum), the detectives in the courtroom sighed with relief. Janis couldn't help herself. She clapped quietly. A court officer gave her a stern look and she told him through gritted teeth, 'Don't you tell me not to clap! I was one of his victims!' Since she was denied her opportunity to testify, and her victim impact statement was read privately by the judge, prosecution and defence, but not read aloud in court – a small round of applause was the only voice Janis had.

That evening, Janis and another of Sutherland's victims were interviewed for the nightly news. In between the sexual assault and the court hearing, Janis's mum and dad had passed away without ever knowing what had happened to their daughter, and so Janis agreed to be interviewed on television. The two women told the reporter that they felt the sentence was too short. Even so, Detective Schulze and his colleagues knew that an average sex offender received a sentence of around six years and was out in just over four years. Sutherland's sentence was relatively severe, showing the judge's condemnation of the nature of his crimes – even murderers serve on average around fourteen years.

After the sentencing, Schulze stopped by the Sex Crimes office in St Kilda Road to visit the detectives who he'd spent months working alongside. They were genuinely pleased with the sentence and Schulze was patted on the back and congratulated by his colleagues.

Versions of: 'Good on ya, mate! Great result!'

In this business, a victory for one is a victory for all.

Justin Schulze is at a bit of a loss to explain the actions of an offender like Mark Sutherland. While Sutherland could be kind and thoughtful to women, his actions were always calculated to put them in his debt. Schulze says, 'He'll do anything for you, but at the end of the day, you owe him something.'

In hindsight, Janis is glad she reported Mark Sutherland and stood up for herself. She knows that she has coped better because she had a hand in bringing a rapist to justice. She is proud of herself and knows that if she hadn't reported him, she would have spent forever wondering how many other women went on to suffer because of her silence.

Women were made vulnerable by Mark Sutherland and many didn't report him because they felt embarrassed or couldn't remember what had happened. If the victims confronted him, Sutherland was apologetic and vowed that this was the first time he'd ever drugged anyone and begged them not to tell the police. He had the lines down pat.

Sutherland described the drugs he gave to women without their consent as 'feel good' drugs and said that he just wanted women to feel more comfortable so that his chance of having sex with them was better. Whether he comprehended the terror experienced by a woman who wakes in the morning feeling disoriented and sore from sex she doesn't remember having, lying on stained sheets and having no memory of anything at all is debatable. Mark Sutherland drugged women – those he'd just met and friends alike. No woman was safe from his 'feel good' remedies – until, of course, the judge locked Sutherland away for at least the next nine years.

Chapter Thirteen

THE RYE CROSSBOW MURDER

Two men stood talking in a suburban garage.

'Have you got the cheque, Jimmy?'

'Yeah, sixty thousand dollars,' said Jimmy Pinakos, patting his breast pocket.

Ronald Lucas turned his back on his business associate and walked towards his garage workbench. Jimmy couldn't see what Lucas was doing. Lucas picked up the glossy black crossbow and turned towards Jimmy.

'On your knees,' he demanded.

Pinakos knelt down. Lucas pointed the crossbow at Jimmy's chest and fired. The arrow thumped into Jimmy's heart and he had only seconds to look shocked before he died.

While walking his dogs along Rye's back beach on a brisk afternoon on Tuesday 18 July 1989, a local man called John noticed a large package partly buried in a shallow hole near the beach car park. His dogs began sniffing and digging around the edges of the soft hole. John became concerned when he got close enough to smell the odour emanating from the bulky parcel. It smelt like something rotting. Worried, John pulled his dogs away and returned home. The more he thought about the package, its size and its smell, the more he began to realise that it might contain something sinister. He grew concerned enough to telephone the local police, offering to meet them in the car park and guide them to the package.

Rosebud police station logged John's call at 5.35 pm, and two police officers were dispatched to investigate. John stood waiting in the Rye back-beach car park as the police officers arrived.

It was probably nothing, thought Senior Constable Wayne Pattison, but when he stared down into the shallow hole and saw the protruding tarpaulin, he smelt the odour of death.

Within an hour, two Frankston CIB detectives, Senior Detective Colin Clark and Detective Sergeant Ray Air, met Pattison at the car park. Senior Detective Clark, too, was immediately assaulted by the smell of the partly buried object; but at this stage, even though the rancid package was certainly suspicious, the two detectives knew that it might just contain nothing worse than a buried pet.

Clark began to gently dig some of the sand away from the offending object and his labours soon revealed the entire top surface of a large bundle wrapped in a tarpaulin and secured with off-white masking tape. The smell was becoming unbearable and the detective regularly gulped breaths of fresh air up-wind of the putrid odour. Gently prising the bundle open, detectives Clark and Air stood staring down at the remains of a decomposing human torso.

The CIB detectives set the investigative wheels in motion. Homicide, forensics, photographics and coronial services were all notified and converged on the beach to perform their respective tasks.

The State Emergency Service provided lighting as the crime scene examination continued into the night. Melbourne homicide detectives, senior constables Mark Newlan and Nigel Howard, along with their senior sergeant, Sal Perna, got to the Rye back beach half an hour ahead of crime scene examiner Sergeant Brian Gamble. Gamble worked at the State Forensic Laboratory, in the aptly named Forensic Drive in the outer Melbourne suburb of Macleod. He'd worked a day shift, and was on call at home when the job came through.

Gamble's job was to collect any physical evidence that might help detectives solve their cases. He was required to make sketches of the crime scene, take detailed notes, prepare a written report, and examine the physical evidence – either personally, or by passing it on to the many experts who were employed or at disposal of the police Forensic Science Laboratory.

Gamble and three officers from the photographics and audio-visual section – senior constables Chris Paulett, Gary Wheelan and Steve Batten – arrived at the crime scene around 10.30 pm to begin a long night of investigation. Senior Constable Chris Paulett took photographs of the shallow grave site and the surrounding sand dunes, while the others videoed the scene before any further digging was attempted.

A little after midnight, the torso in its wrappings was removed from its sandy grave under the supervision of forensic pathologist Dr Shelley Robinson. It was transported by state-employed funeral directors to the Victorian Institute of Forensic Pathology's mortuary. Dr Robinson performed the post-mortem examination.

At the mortuary Dr Robinson took notes concerning the appearance of the package and noted the presence of maggots within the inner plastic wrapping. When it was unwrapped, the torso, which on closer inspection was found to be male, was laid on the metal slab and visually examined by Dr Shelley Robinson while Brian Gamble, Mark Newlan, Sal Perna and Nigel Howard looked on.

Senior Constable Chris Paulett took several photographs of the torso. The missing head, arms and legs had been cleanly severed. Despite the dirt and dried blood, there was a puncture mark clearly visible in the chest.

Senior Constable Mark Newlan looked carefully over the torso. He had seen over a hundred bodies in his role as a homicide detective and he remained professionally detached. To Newlan, a body – any body – represented the beginning of an investigation, and he had developed the technique of looking beyond the sheer horror of it so he could study the physical damage. He is, however, at a complete loss to describe the smell: 'Unless you've smelt a decaying body, you can't imagine how bad it is. It's putrid.'

When Paulett had finished taking photographs and Dr Robinson had completed her visual inspection, the torso was washed and prepared for the internal examination. Robinson cut around the small puncture wound in the chest and pulled open the flesh which, devoid of dirt and smeared blood, was a ghostly white colour.

Inside the wound, the doctor found a broken arrow.

The triangular tip was intact, but the bamboo shaft of the arrow was broken in half. The arrow, Dr Robinson informed the police officers, had pierced the right ventricle of the heart and, judging from the downward angle of the wound, had been fired from above the victim.

The small number of maggots inhabiting the remains were sealed in a jar of formalin to be sent to the CSIRO in South Australia, where scientists would test them in an attempt to find an approximate time of death of the murder victim.

After the post-mortem examination, Senior Constable Mark Newlan returned to his St Kilda Road office of the Homicide Squad to begin his paperwork, which would eventually fill several large folders. He worked through the night and at 7 am received a telephone call from a friend of his, Sergeant Mick Hughes, who worked at the Prahran CIB.

Hughes asked Newlan about the body find, which he had heard about on the morning radio bulletin on his way to work. He explained that he had a missing person on his files called Jimmy Pinakos, who had been missing since April. If the torso belonged to Pinakos, that would mean three months had elapsed since it had been buried there. Newlan told his friend that the torso at Rye didn't look decomposed enough to be three months old. Hughes told him to keep it in mind, nonetheless. Newlan drove back to Rye.

After catching a few hours' sleep, Sergeant Brian Gamble also returned to the Rye back beach to organise the sifting of sand around the burial site, and to complete diagrams and reports for the police and forensic files. Homicide detectives had organised a line search of the beach and the surrounding scrub to begin at first light. It made sense that if they had a torso, the rest of the body might also be in the area.

Ironically, despite the number of police searching the dunes along the foreshore, it was another dog, sniffing and digging in an area of bushland near to the beach, that led police to the second gravesite. The familiar foul odour alerted searchers that they had found more of the body. The process of photographing, digging and sifting began again. Another wrapped parcel was soon unearthed.

❖❖❖

Mark Newlan spent his morning flying around the crime scene in the Southern Peninsula rescue helicopter while he and other officers surveyed and photographed the scene from the air. The helicopter landed as soon as they heard that another parcel had been found.

Contained in the new find were two severed hands, two feet, and some other pieces of flesh from the arms and legs. Wrapped separately in a Safeway supermarket bag was the head.

In addition to the body parts, police officers found a grey tie with blue stripes, a white and blue pin-striped shirt and a pair of underpants.

Newlan was given the task of flying by helicopter back to Melbourne clutching the re-wrapped body parts. The helicopter landed at the Yarra heliport and Newlan was picked up by police car and taken, with his parcel, back to the city morgue.

By laying the parts on the slab, Dr Robinson and the detectives completed a macabre human jigsaw puzzle. The head, the hands and feet had been cleanly severed. Additional pieces were identified as portions of arms and legs.

When she examined the head, Dr Robinson noted a marked distortion of the facial features, but no apparent damage to the brain. The head was then sent to the Royal Dental Hospital in Melbourne for a forensic odontology examination – the teeth would be examined for later comparison with charts belonging to missing persons fitting the general description of the unidentified male.

Dr Robinson later concluded in her report:

> 1. Identification of the deceased was based on forensic odontological examination of the head. The head was found separately packaged and situated from the torso; however, there is no evidence to suggest that they are not from the same body, although the former was in a more advanced state of decomposition.

> 2. Decomposition changes obscured some pathological changes; however, it is likely that the penetrating injury to the chest (involving the heart) by the arrow was the cause of death.

> 3. It is also likely that the decapitation and dismembering of the body took place after death, with a sharp instrument such as a band saw; however, the exact time or course of events cannot be established on the basis of the pathological findings.

With the second find, which included the hands, Senior Sergeant Jim Falloon from the Fingerprint Branch was called to the mortuary. After gaining clearance from the State Coroner, Falloon put the putrid pair of hands into a bucket and took them to the Fingerprint Bureau offices so the fingertip skin could be removed and printed.

Falloon gently removed the skin from the fingertips, placed the ridged skin over his own fingertips and carefully rolled his covered fingers in the ink and onto a fingerprint card.

Unfortunately for those working in the nineteen-storey St Kilda Road building, the smell entered the air conditioning system and wafted through the whole building. As a direct consequence, severed hands and fingers were henceforth banned from the fingerprint offices as a health risk.

Identification from fingerprint comparison and dental records showed the deceased to be Dimitrios Pinakos, known to his friends as Jimmy. Pinakos, an insurance agent, had been missing since 20 April. The web of intrigue surrounding his disappearance began to unravel and Mark Newlan was able to tell his buddy Mick Hughes that his hunch was correct.

Dimitrios Pinakos was born in Greece in 1958 and immigrated to Australia with his family when he was still an infant. He soon anglicised his name to Jimmy and left school when he was eighteen years old. He worked for a time as an electrician and eventually bought his own small business. Jimmy Pinakos began selling insurance in 1987, and it wasn't long before he created his own corporate agency, Limnos Insurance, operating under the umbrella of the Melbourne Mutual Group.

It was in the offices of the Melbourne Mutual Group in St Kilda Road that Jimmy Pinakos met the man who would fire a crossbow arrow into his chest, carve his body into small pieces and bury him on the Rye back beach.

Ronald Lucas began working in the same St Kilda Road building in January 1989 with another corporate agency, also operating within the Melbourne Mutual Group. Although Ron Lucas did not share office space with Jimmy Pinakos, many people would later tell police that the two knew each other well and had held private meetings in the week before Pinakos's disappearance.

Ronald Lucas was deeply in debt. He had a habit of borrowing money – to buy cars, a house, a swimming pool, among other things – and making only a few payments before abandoning his financial responsibilities. Lucas was being pressed for money from a number of directions, particularly from his wife, who had set up house in Perth. Lucas had joined her there for a couple of weeks and then moved back to Melbourne. He had instructed her to have a swimming pool put in the backyard with promises to deposit money into her bank account. The money never arrived.

Lucas owed Westpac Bank over $2000, Diners Club $16,151, Statewide Building Society $80,000 for the mortgage on his Perth home (no payments had ever been made), $5209 on an unpaid MasterCard debt, and $2350 on a loan taken out by Lucas and his wife that was still outstanding. He also owed American Express $1462, and had recently borrowed $47,326 to buy a four-wheel drive vehicle. True to habit, he had only made one payment on the luxury vehicle.

In addition to his debts, Ron Lucas had a penchant for crossbows.

On Tuesday 18 April 1989, fellow worker Harry Triferis went to Jimmy Pinakos's office to collect his friend Ron Lucas to drive him home. In the office, Pinakos told Triferis and Lucas of a $60,000 development loan he had access to in a trust account. Access could only be gained if it were used for a mortgage. Triferis would later say that he had come in on the end of the conversation and that Jimmy and Ron had been discussing the money before he had entered the office.

Discussing being in possession of a large sum of money with a man heavily in debt turned out to be a fatal mistake. Jimmy Pinakos also probably did not know about a conversation that Lucas had had with Triferis a few weeks earlier – about how easy it would be to chop up a body and bury pieces in different locations so it would never be found. Triferis himself would not see the significance of the conversation for many months to come.

On Wednesday 19 April, Jimmy Pinakos and his brother William, with whom he shared a house, went to the bank and received a cheque for $60,000 made out to Lucas's wife. Understandably, William questioned his brother about the large cheque and Jimmy told him that he was going to swap it for $80,000 cash that very night.

Later that evening, William phoned Jimmy to ask how the deal had gone. Jimmy told him that it had fallen through because the 'bloke turned up dressed in a Rambo suit and armed with a crossbow'.

The next morning Jimmy Pinakos took the cheque to work. It was the last time William Pinakos would ever see his brother. That same morning Ron Lucas was visiting a friend boasting that he was about to collect money owing to him from many years earlier. Lucas even promised the friend $13,000 from the windfall.

Pinakos's hours were numbered.

Lucas met Jimmy in his office in the early afternoon. Harry Triferis's brother Peter saw Lucas leaving and expressed his concerns about Ron Lucas to Jimmy. Peter Triferis would later tell police that at first Jimmy refused to tell him about the deal he was planning with Ron Lucas, but further prompting led him to reveal that Lucas had offered him 'eighty thousand dollars of black money for a sixty thousand dollar bank cheque'. According to Peter Triferis, Pinakos told him that the deal was supposed to have taken place the night before, but that Lucas had arrived dressed like Rambo and armed with a crossbow. Apparently Ron Lucas had explained his strange attire by saying that he had to be careful, carrying that much money around. Pinakos had shown Peter Triferis the cheque and told him that another meeting had been arranged at Lucas's home at three o'clock that afternoon. Although Triferis made arrangements to meet Pinakos back in the office later in the afternoon, he would never see his colleague again.

Jimmy Pinakos instructed his secretary to telephone his mobile phone at exactly 3.15 pm and, for reasons he didn't explain, told her not to worry if he replied with the code word 'sweet'. He left the office and his secretary duly phoned him at 3.15 pm.

Pinakos answered and told her that he had yet to arrive at his destination and instructed her to telephone again at 3.40 pm. At the appointed time, she telephoned again and heard Jimmy say, 'It was all sweet.' A third telephone call about another matter at 4.30 pm was answered by Jimmy. He said that he was in Springvale. The secretary later told police that he sounded as if he was in fact in his car. This phone call was the last reported contact anyone admitted to having with Jimmy Pinakos. Pinakos was obviously nervous. He knew what he was doing was illegal, and perhaps the thought of earning $20,000 in one afternoon made him act as if he were in a gangster movie, using code words and disguising his location.

That evening, Ronald Lucas was an hour late for a 7.30 pm appointment. Even though his business diary revealed no prior appointments that evening, Lucas had excused his lateness by saying he was held up at another appointment. It is likely that in those unaccounted-for hours, Ronald Lucas killed Jimmy Pinakos with a crossbow and dismembered his corpse.

The following day, Lucas didn't arrive at the office until after midday, and left after two hours for an unspecified appointment.

William Pinakos, concerned about his brother's uncharacteristic absence, began to make inquiries. One of the first people he contacted was Ronald Lucas. Lucas told William Pinakos that Jimmy had been at his home the day before, but that he had received an urgent phone call and left abruptly.

After telephoning his wife in Perth to cancel his imminent trip to visit her, Ron Lucas telephoned Harry Triferis and confessed that he was in 'a lot of shit at the moment'. Concerned, Harry Triferis immediately contacted his brother Peter and related the strange conversation. Without delay, Peter Triferis went to visit Lucas who, he would later tell police, appeared to have been crying. Peter Triferis probed Ron Lucas for the cause of his worries. Lucas told him that he was having money problems and that the bank in Perth was pressing his wife for money.

Triferis raised the subject of the financial deal that Pinakos had mentioned, but Lucas denied knowing anything about it although he did admit inviting Jimmy over to his house to discuss a loan, but the terms didn't suit Jimmy and he had left.

When Peter Triferis left Lucas at 7.30 pm, he bluntly told Lucas that there was talk that he had killed Jimmy. On his guard, Lucas said that it was impossible because neighbours had seen Jimmy leave his house the previous afternoon. Neighbours would later deny this.

Later that evening, relatives of Ron Lucas arrived at his home to stay. They later told police that Lucas wasn't home when they arrived at 10 pm. It is likely that in the time between Peter Triferis's departure and the arrival of the relatives, Lucas drove the body to the Rye back beach and buried it across several locations. If this was indeed the case, then the dismembered body was in the garage when Peter Triferis visited.

When rumours began filtering back to Lucas that he was a suspect, he responded by leaving home and staying with friends for two days. Using a false name, he then bought a bus ticket to Adelaide, where he stayed with friends for three weeks.

Two days after Jimmy disappeared, William Pinakos found his brother's silver Porsche near a house in Prahran that he and Jimmy jointly owned – the same house where Jimmy had met Lucas dressed as Rambo. The Porsche contained Jimmy's briefcase, which, in turn, contained the $60,000 cheque. If Pinakos had been killed for the money, the murderer's plans had been thwarted. Perhaps Jimmy hadn't completely trusted Lucas and wasn't willing to hand over the cheque until he saw the cash. Whoever had killed Jimmy had gained nothing for his crime.

A neighbour later told detectives that he'd first noticed the Porsche the previous evening around midnight.

Lucas had also abandoned his Holden ute, which was found soon after the Porsche. Both vehicles were photographed and examined for fingerprints, blood and any trace evidence that might link Pinakos and Lucas. Nothing of evidentiary value was found.

Detectives also searched Lucas's home in Reservoir and found no evidence that anything untoward had occurred there. The home was full of furniture and the garage was cluttered with tools.

From Adelaide, Lucas travelled to Queensland and stayed with another friend for a week. Returning to Adelaide, he began working as a builder. He approached a friend inquiring where he could get some jewellery valued. He produced a gold chain and a single diamond, explaining that he had received the jewellery as payment for mercenary work in Malaysia. Both items together were valued at $19,945, but the jeweller informed Lucas that he could only expect to receive $5000 if he sold them. Lucas decided to keep the jewellery.

The friend, becoming increasingly concerned about Lucas and his strange stories and expensive jewellery, eventually contacted local police, who in turn contacted officers from the Adelaide Major Crime Squad. Melbourne detectives were notified and flew directly to Adelaide.

On 7 June 1989, Lucas arrived home from work and the detectives were waiting for him. They had a search warrant and had already searched Lucas's room, finding the gold chain and the diamond, as well as the bus ticket that Lucas had used to leave Melbourne.

Ronald Lucas was taken to the Adelaide Major Crime Squad office and questioned by detectives. Asked about the jewellery, which fitted the description of jewellery belonging to Jimmy Pinakos, Lucas had no satisfactory explanation for having it in his possession, thus giving detectives a reason to extradite Lucas back to Victoria to be charged with its theft. Finally back in his own state, Lucas was charged and bailed to report to the local police station every Monday and Friday.

Five weeks later, walking along the Rye Back Beach, a man and his dogs discovered the remains of Jimmy Pinakos buried in the sand behind the Rye back beach car park.

The day following the discovery of the two burial sites, Ron Lucas telephoned the Melbourne police officer who had arrested him in

Adelaide. He reported seeing a 'bloke hanging around' the night before and wanted police protection. Lucas also casually asked the police officer, 'What's the go with the body on the beach at Rye?' When the police officer asked why he wanted to know, Lucas replied that he was just curious.

That same morning, Lucas collected wages owing to him from a building site where he had been working and vanished again. He stayed in hiding with a number of friends until February 1990. He bleached his hair blond, used an alias, told people he was a doctor of biochemistry from Sydney, and began a liaison with the seventeen-year-old stepdaughter of the friend he was staying with.

Three days after Jimmy Pinakos's body was discovered, police carried out an exhaustive search at Ron Lucas's Reservoir home. Crime scene examiner Brian Gamble was called on again, accompanied by a team of forensic science experts. The investigation soon centred on the garage with its old carpet and its cement sheet walls. When detectives had checked the property months earlier, the garage had been full of junk; now it was empty.

Biologists Jane Taupin and Pam Scott tested the dirty carpet and walls for the presence of blood. They used Hemastix – a preparation that changes colour when rubbed against a blood stain – to test marks on both the walls and the carpet, which tested positive. The team of experts scoured the garage for any other evidence linking Ron Lucas with the murder of Jimmy Pinakos.

The house in Reservoir had changed hands since Lucas fled and the new owners had given police permission to examine it. However, even if permission hadn't been obtained, the Victorian Coroners Act gives investigators the right to 'enter and inspect any place and anything in it …' and to 'take possession of anything which the Coroner reasonably believes is relevant to the investigation and keep it until the investigation is finished'. Accordingly, when Gamble and his team discovered splatters of blood on the garage wall, they simply cut out a huge section of the wall and took it with them back to their laboratories. Large sections of the garage carpet were also removed.

❖ ❖ ❖

From the moment the body was identified as Jimmy Pinakos, Mark Newlan's investigation led clearly to the doorstep of Ronald Lucas. Suspicion and innuendo became fact.

On the day following the body's discovery and identification, Newlan went to another Reservoir home and was given the crossbow in its camouflage carry-case by a neighbour who had been storing it for Lucas. Newlan lodged it at the State Forensic Laboratory where Senior Constable Alan Pringle, a firearm and toolmark examiner, would test the weapon and its propensity to discharge its lethal arrows. Pringle found that the crossbow could only be fired after it had been loaded, cocked and with considerable pressure — 4.5 kilograms — applied to the trigger. In simple terms, the crossbow couldn't be fired accidentally.

David Black, another scientist at the forensic science lab, was given documents belonging to Ronald Lucas. Black analysed the handwriting on a Diners Club receipt from a Dandenong sporting goods store for the purchase of a Barnett brand crossbow and carry-case. He identified the signature on the receipt as that of Ronald Lucas.

Ronald Lucas was eventually apprehended in Cairns on 19 March 1990 as a result of information given to police by the stepfather of Lucas's young girlfriend. Lucas initially gave police a false name when he was picked up, but when detectives asked him to accompany them to the police station, he replied, 'I suppose this is about Jimmy.'

Detective Senior Constable Newlan flew to Cairns the following day. Within 24 hours, following a successful extradition hearing in the Cairns Magistrates Court, he made the five-and-a-half-hour flight by light plane to Melbourne with Ron Lucas.

This was Newlan's first chance to chat with his suspect. He found Lucas to be an amiable fellow, but with a childish habit of boasting about everything. Looking out the aeroplane window, Newlan asked Ron Lucas if he had ever done any parachuting. Lucas told him that he had made hundreds of jumps. Later, when Newlan spoke of diving, Lucas told him that he was a diving expert. Newlan reflected wryly that it seemed that there was nothing Ron Lucas wouldn't brag about — except, of course, killing Jimmy Pinakos.

In the murder trial of Ronald Lucas, new ground was broken in the realm of forensic evidence in the argument over the admissibility of the use of DNA testing for the purpose of linking Jimmy Pinakos with the scene of the crime, Lucas's garage.

When geneticist Alec Jeffreys discovered the means to isolate the elusive genetic material in 1984 at Leicester University, one of the first tests he performed was to see whether DNA patterns were inherited. His tests on family groups showed clearly that half the bands and stripes of DNA of offspring were from the mother and half were from the father. The courts were to argue this point at length because owing to the advanced state of decomposition of Jimmy Pinakos's body, DNA tests could not be conducted on his remains. The prosecution conducted a series of DNA tests on blood samples from Pinakos's parents and compared the resulting DNA profiles with blood samples taken from the garage. The results showed a sixty-five per cent probability that the blood in the garage belonged to Jimmy Pinakos. This was not certain enough for the court to accept as evidence.

To convict Ron Lucas, it was vital to link him with the body, or the body with his house. There was plenty of circumstantial evidence, but detectives were looking for solid forensic evidence to provide the vital link.

The Fingerprint Branch provided that link. Fingerprint expert Sergeant Sean Hickey carefully examined the material in which the body had been wrapped. On a piece of masking tape used to bind the tarpaulin, Hickey discovered a latent fingerprint. It belonged to Ronald Lucas.

The masking tape, with its still clearly distinguishable fingerprint, held pride of place in a display cabinet at the St Kilda Road Fingerprint Branch offices.

Ronald Lucas was found guilty in 1991 and sentenced to twenty years in prison.

A decade into his sentence, Ron Lucas made headlines again when he and a fellow inmate escaped from the Ararat jail in June 2001. The two climbed over a wire fence at 11.30 am and were seen roaming paddocks by farmers around 5 pm. The two had made it six kilometres from the prison, but since all roads were blocked and the manhunt included tracker dogs, it was only a matter of time before the men were apprehended.

Chapter Fourteen

SEXUAL PENETRATION
OF A MINOR

Wendy O'Shea joined the Victoria Police Force in April 1986. Ever since she was in primary school, she'd wanted to be a police officer. In her childhood innocence, her ambition was simply to help people. Wanting experience in the workforce before joining up, Wendy O'Shea was employed as a clerk for three years after leaving school. In hindsight, she feels that even joining the force at the age of twenty-one was probably too young. She believes that police recruits need to gain adult life experiences before becoming law enforcement officers, since the majority of people that officers deal with are adults.

O'Shea began her career in Melbourne's western suburbs and, before long, experienced most types of crimes – burglaries, assaults, car thefts and armed robberies were commonplace.

O'Shea spent twelve months in the Sunshine Specials – a plain-clothes division dealing mostly with thefts and drugs. She was part of a small team that did surveillance work and search warrants. Camaraderie was tight and she enjoyed her work.

In 1990, Senior Constable O'Shea went before the CIB board, passing both an interview and a written test. She was then eligible to train to become a detective. Entering Detective Training School in the old Russell Street police building, O'Shea spent an intensive twelve weeks studying the finer details of investigative methods, crime scene examination and law. When she successfully completed the course, she applied for and was accepted to fill a vacancy at the Sunshine Criminal Investigation Branch.

In early 1993, Wendy O'Shea was seconded to spend three months at the Altona North Sexual Offences Investigation Unit, which while still in its infancy had proved to be both effective and successful. Detectives worked with Community Policing Squad officers to deal exclusively with sex offences – both with victims and offenders. Statements were taken from victims, offenders were apprehended and charged, and the unit had established an excellent conviction record.

As a CIB detective, Senior Constable O'Shea investigated a number of sexual offences interspersed with her other cases. She had always felt that she couldn't give them the amount of attention they needed because of the caseload of other offences requiring her attention. O'Shea felt that detectives needed to spend time with the victims and her professional experience told her that if investigators didn't gain the trust of the victim and obtain a clear and detailed statement, the cases would often be lost when they eventually came to trial. The setting up of the Sexual Offences Investigation Unit had turned the tide of sex investigations for the better.

One of her early cases involved a middle-aged woman who had been viciously raped by her estranged husband on two occasions. O'Shea recalls discussions with the victim including intimate personal and sexual details. Indeed, she initially experienced a mild discomfort and explains that 'it felt like I was interviewing my mum'. It didn't take the young detective long to realise that working in the area of sexual assault required special talents – especially in human relations.

O'Shea arrested the woman's husband and charged him with aggravated rape. O'Shea believed that it took the laying of charges and the court case to finally convince the man that his estranged wife was not his for the taking.

The establishment of the Sexual Offences Investigation Unit at Altona North meant that the detectives at the new unit could devote all their time to investigating their cases. Complexities in law and statement-taking were made clearer because officers were dealing with sex offences all the time. Expertise was especially needed in the legal area because when charges were laid, they had to apply to the time the offence occurred, so if a middle-aged woman broke a twenty-year silence about sexual abuse occurring in the 1970s, her abuser had to be charged according to whatever laws applied at that time.

In her short three-month stay, O'Shea, together with a couple of other detectives, dealt with over fifty offenders. It didn't take long to become expert in the area of child sexual assault.

At the end of April 1993, a Community Policing Squad member, Senior Constable Damian Christensen, received a telephone call while working at the Sexual Offences Investigation Unit. The call was from a woman wanting information about her seventeen-year-old daughter, whom she believed had been raped. Senior Constable Christensen suggested that the daughter contact the unit herself and talk to the detectives. The following day, the young woman made a long-distance call from Sydney, where she was staying with her aunt.

She told Christensen that her aunt, who was a counsellor for sexually abused teenagers, had convinced her to talk to the police. Damian Christensen developed an almost immediate rapport with the troubled teenager, who agreed to return to Melbourne to meet with him. She refused his suggestion to contact New South Wales police and it appeared to Christensen that she had trouble trusting anyone, and that talking to him had been a big step for her.

On 3 May 1993, a young woman called Georgia entered the offices of the Sexual Offences Investigation Unit in the company of a friend to tell detectives the story of her lost childhood. She was casually dressed and slender with short-cropped dark hair. There was something about her that struck both Wendy O'Shea and Damian Christensen. O'Shea is at a loss to explain what it was exactly, but she feels that it was a combination of the young woman's incredible sadness and vulnerability, mixed with a somewhat tough exterior that drew the detectives to her.

Georgia initially didn't trust them. She would later tell Wendy O'Shea that it was only because she thought 'Damian sounded like a nice bloke' over the phone that she had made the decision to tell him her story – a decision that hadn't come easily.

As a detective, it was O'Shea's job to tell Georgia about the way the investigation would proceed. She explained to the scared teenager that she would have to give the officers a detailed statement about the sexual abuse she had suffered. An investigation would follow and then Georgia would have to testify in court. O'Shea told her that it wouldn't be easy, but other victims who had been through the same process were usually glad once the offender had been punished.

Georgia still didn't fully comprehend the extent of her own involvement in the process. She imagined she could tell the police about her severe and prolonged sexual abuse at the hands of her stepfather, and then leave the case in their hands. Ironically, Georgia's mother, who had initially contacted the Sex Offences Unit, had no idea that it was her ex-husband who was the perpetrator. Georgia had recently been raped by her boss at work and it was about this that the mother had contacted the unit.

Georgia, however, was not interested in talking about the recent attack. Indeed, it had hardly touched her – she was so used to being abused.

O'Shea and Christensen listened to her horror story.

Georgia told the two police officers that the violation had begun on her eighth birthday. Her stepfather, Mick, had come into her bedroom in the early hours of the morning and had gently woken his sleeping stepdaughter. He wished her happy birthday and told her that he had a special surprise for her. The trusting little girl got out of bed and walked over to Mick, who had sat down on a chair with his pants pulled down. Mick picked Georgia up and forced her down upon his erect penis. The child screamed as the incredible pain shot up to her stomach. Mick clamped his hand firmly over her mouth and she bit him.

Georgia quietly told the detectives that straddled over her stepfather, her feet couldn't touch the ground. She remembered thinking desperately that if only her feet could touch the ground, she could push herself up and stop the excruciating pain.

The young woman explained to O'Shea and Christensen that Mick had carried her, crying, back to her bed and told her that what had happened would be their special secret. He left the room and Georgia had curled herself up and cried herself to sleep.

In her naive, child's way of thinking, she believed that this must happen to all little girls on their eighth birthday.

Georgia finished her story abruptly by saying, 'And then he fucked me three or four times a week from the time I was eight until I was thirteen and I left home.' Georgia apologised to the detectives for using the expression 'fuck', but she explained that to her, sex or making love was between people who cared about each other. What Mick had done to her only qualified as a 'fuck'.

Detective O'Shea explained to Georgia that in order to take a statement that would be of use in court, the police would need as much detail as she could possibly remember – names, dates, places. It was a tall order, but absolutely necessary. O'Shea told Georgia to go home and think about everything that had happened to her and come back the next day. Wendy O'Shea saw that although the first session had only taken two hours, it had left Georgia physically and emotionally drained.

But the following day, she was back. This time with a different friend for support. Damian Christensen conducted the interview because Georgia trusted him. Christensen was not a detective, he was a Community Policing Squad officer, so it was Wendy O'Shea's duty to periodically enter the interview room and read over the statement as it progressed. As a trained detective, she guided Christensen in his questioning and told him which parts required more detail.

Horrific details of abuse were painstakingly drawn from the young victim. She told Christensen every detail she could remember from the five and a half years of sexual abuse at the hands of her stepfather.

Mick was a large, powerful man and he had initially been nice to her. Georgia had known him since she was six years old. He had married her mother and moved into the family home.

Mick proved to have an almost insatiable sexual appetite for the young child – the rapes took place three or four times a week until she had gone to live with her grandparents when she was thirteen and a half. A quick calculation totalled nearly one thousand sexual offences against the child – Mick would eventually be charged with only ten.

The nature of the charges that are laid against an offender have to be specific in order to give him the chance to answer them. It is not good enough to charge him with sexual penetration of a minor 'three or four times a week' for a number of years. Georgia had to remember specific times and places – a tall order for most people, let alone an abused, frightened child.

Georgia remembered the birthday incident and could give Christensen the exact date. She also remembered both times Mick had tried to force her to perform oral sex on him because both times she had vomited. He had given up trying, but had continued the sexual abuse, which, Georgia explained to the officers, was doubly terrifying because he would always cover her face when he was assaulting her – with either his hand or a pillow.

One time, Mick had sat down on the toilet and had tried to penetrate the child from behind by sitting her on his lap. He found that he was unable to and gave up trying. Georgia particularly remembered that incident because she had bumped her head in the attempt.

The statement, which would eventually run to twenty-five pages, was progressing well when O'Shea and Christensen stopped the interview on the second day. Georgia had sat through seven gruelling hours reliving her nightmare and she still wasn't finished.

She returned the third day with yet another friend.

Georgia told of the final years of her abuse. By the end of primary school, she began to realise that what was happening to her wasn't normal and was in fact very wrong. She listened to teachers warning students that nobody had the right to touch them inappropriately and she began to filter the message to her stepfather. Georgia began swearing at him and trying to resist. Mick responded by becoming increasingly violent towards her and the abuse continued. By this time, she was terrified of him.

He used a variety of methods to petrify the child. He made her watch while he drowned her kittens, and he killed chickens in front of her. Once he had even broken a chair across her back. Georgia told Damian Christensen about the last time Mick had sexually abused her; she had resisted until he smashed her into a wall. He raped her while she was semiconscious.

Georgia suffered emotionally from the continued and violent abuse. She never told her mother who, ironically, was a Community Services worker. Mick had cleverly turned her against her mother until finally, Georgia trusted no-one. To her mother, the only obvious factor in the family dynamics was that there were problems between Georgia and Mick.

Once, Georgia's mother suggested that Georgia and Mick take a drive and discuss their difficulties. Mick took his wife's advice and drove off with his stepdaughter. However, instead of resolving their difficulties, he raped her.

Over time, Georgia's behaviour at home became so bad that when she asked to move in with her grandparents, Mick convinced her mother that it was best for all concerned. Georgia's mother agreed.

When Georgia finally finished her statement, she read it through and signed it. She was drained, relieved and happy all at the same time. On her way out of the police station, Georgia stopped to thank Wendy O'Shea by giving her a hug. O'Shea remembers almost being driven to tears, so sincere was the thanks she received. O'Shea says today that the trust was so great, 'it was like she had handed us the package of her life'. O'Shea felt she had finally achieved her childhood ambition of truly being able to help someone. Georgia affected Damian Christensen the same way and he would later unashamedly admit to blinking away tears at times when she was relating particularly vicious incidents.

For three days, O'Shea and Christensen had listened to Georgia's story and taken her lengthy statement. On the fourth day, they sat down together to sift through the evidence. They had helped Georgia link times and dates necessary to prepare the charges against her ex-stepfather. Now the finer details required their attention. Georgia had described some of the sexual abuse as taking place in her stepfather's work van. They checked registration records to prove that he did indeed own a van of the type she described at the time of the abuse. She described the van as having a bench seat. It all had to be verified.

Georgia had described abuse taking place at a factory rented by her stepfather. The police officers checked leasing records.

On the fifth day, O'Shea and Christensen arrested Mick.

O'Shea and Christensen conferred before the arrest. They knew that every detail must be done absolutely by the book and that any personal feelings that they had formed about Mick after listening to Georgia's story must be set aside for the sake of professionalism. The first thing that struck Detective O'Shea about Mick was his size. In her experience, child abusers were usually weak, small men – the type of men who were reluctant to look you in the eye. Mick was different. He was a large, heavily built man standing over six feet tall.

He had long, curly blond hair and a beard. O'Shea could understand how frightened of him Georgia must have been.

Mick welcomed the officers into his home, which was a bus parked outside a factory. He was friendly, polite – and of course, he denied everything.

He was arrested and taken to the Altona North police station for questioning. O'Shea charged Mick with thirteen counts including sexual penetration of a child under ten years of age, attempted sexual penetration, assault, and possession of marijuana, which the officers had found in his temporary home.

Wendy O'Shea thought Mick was a smooth talker. He denied ever touching Georgia and he blamed her allegations on the messy divorce he had gone through with her mother. Financial settlement in the divorce had been a drawn-out affair with Mick demanding money from Georgia's mother. He dismissed the allegations. He said they were a result of spite.

Mick even went so far as to boast of his capabilities as a father. He explained that Georgia's mother had worked and he had been a house-husband until he had eventually bought a bus repair business. He described the meals he used to cook and the good care he used to take of Georgia and her siblings.

Wendy O'Shea and Damian Christensen interviewed Mick for over four hours and while he answered all of their questions, he also denied all the charges. It made no difference. Mick was then taken to the Broadmeadows Magistrates' Court, where the magistrate gave him bail with $1000 surety on condition that he report daily to police. He also was forbidden to have any contact with Georgia or her family.

In the months between Mick's arrest and his trial, Wendy O'Shea and Damian Christensen gathered their evidence as well as statements from Georgia's friends – particularly a young man whom she had confided in when she was fifteen.

One unfortunate incident during the investigation was the burning of a diary that Georgia had kept since she was ten. She had told O'Shea that she had written in the diary describing her abuse and her feelings at the time. As a child, Georgia had used code words – 'hurt' referred to the beatings Mick had subjected her to, and 'hate' referred to sexual abuse. O'Shea was more than disappointed to learn that her grandmother had accidentally burnt the book along with Georgia's old school books.

When the committal proceedings were held, Georgia was so terrified of Mick that she testified by closed-circuit television. Nonetheless, O'Shea and Christensen were impressed by her performance as a witness. She was candid and her memory for detail was excellent. So clear was the abuse in her mind, she never had to refer to her statement.

When the case came to trial in November 1993, one of the most gruelling aspects for Wendy O'Shea was having to support Georgia into the courtroom — ironically to give evidence in front of Mick as to why she couldn't give evidence in front of him. Wendy O'Shea recalls that Georgia was so frightened in his presence, she buried her head into the policewoman's shoulder and didn't look in the direction of her abuser. Wendy was almost supporting her entire body weight.

Over the two-week trial, Georgia's fear would manifest itself in a number of ways: she wouldn't get out of the court elevator until Wendy had checked the corridor to make sure Mick wasn't there, and even when she was giving evidence via closed-circuit television, she confessed to the detective that she felt almost as if Mick could reach through the screen and grab her.

Wendy O'Shea slowly realised that Georgia was not telling her the complete story. There were incidents that the girl had hinted at but wouldn't share — not even with the police officers who had become her friends. One such incident had occurred at the factory that Mick rented for his bus repair business. Georgia had told Wendy that Mick had forced her to watch one day while he masturbated another man. She remembered feeling relieved that while Mick was occupied with his male partner, he had left her alone. This was bad enough, but Wendy O'Shea felt that other things happened at the factory that Georgia couldn't bring herself to talk about.

Wendy O'Shea sat through the entire two weeks of the trial, offering her support to the young girl of whom she had grown so fond. O'Shea experienced some tense moments when Georgia was giving evidence from another room, but Georgia told her story as she always did — with honesty and feeling. O'Shea had never seen a jury as attentive as they were when Georgia spoke. It was also frustrating for the detective to hear Georgia's evidence because of all the elements of her abuse that she couldn't talk about. The judge had ruled that Georgia couldn't give the jury the impression that she had been abused on occasions other than those eight with which Mick had been charged – two of the original ten charges of sexual abuse had been dropped for lack of evidence. Georgia also couldn't mention that every time she was sexually abused, Mick used to lick his fingers to moisten her before penetration. The judge ruled that this act couldn't be linked to any particular incident and was therefore inadmissible.

O'Shea knew the full story and couldn't help thinking that the eight charges were but a tiny fraction of the overall litany of abuse that Georgia had suffered.

Perhaps the most poignant moment of the trial came when Georgia was giving evidence. The young woman tried to articulate her mixed feelings towards her stepfather. Through her tears, Georgia held her thumb and forefinger in front of her indicating a couple of centimetres and said, 'I still love him this much.' After all, he had been her father.

In contrast to Georgia, Mick made a poor witness. He slouched in the witness box, flippantly denying everything. After a court recess, Wendy O'Shea noticed he sat a lot straighter and she figured his barristers had told him not to look so casual in light of the serious nature of the charges.

Defence barristers had compiled a jury completely made up of men, perhaps in the belief that men would be more sympathetic to Mick, but Georgia made such a powerful witness that the jury took under two hours to find Mick guilty of all charges. He was sentenced to seven years in prison with a five-year minimum.

In his summing up, the judge told the defendant that what he had done to Georgia, she would live with for the rest of her life.

Georgia telephoned Wendy O'Shea a couple of weeks after the trial and told the detective that she had decided to live. She realised that she was faced with being either a victim or a survivor and she had chosen to survive. Next year, she told O'Shea, she would finish Year 12 at high school.

Wendy O'Shea smiled wistfully to herself and thought, 'What a nice kid.'

Chapter Fifteen

COLD CASES AND BIZARRE STORIES FROM HOMICIDE

Detective Senior Sergeant Jack Jacobs had been in the Homicide Squad for eleven years at the time of our interview. He said that most murderers were 'just normal people' and considering that in an average year, around one-third of the fifty-odd murders in Victoria are as a result of partner violence, he's probably right. Jacobs also believes that most murderers commit their acts of human destruction without realising the full consequences of their actions – a man commits family violence; another may be defending his drunken honour outside a pub; while another may simply lose his temper. According to Jacobs, murderers are just like everybody else and usually, in the cold light of day, can't understand why they killed.

Homicide detectives work in teams and follow investigations from the discovery of the body and its subsequent post-mortem examination, through to the apprehension of the killer and his or her trial. Some investigations take days, while some remain unsolved with detectives periodically reviewing them as cold cases – sometimes for years after.

A little-known aspect of the job of a Homicide detective is the investigation of suicides. Jack Jacobs said that detectives are called in to investigate any death that looks suspicious and many of them are eventually found to be suicide. They were known in the squad as 'half jobs'.

Australian police case files abound with horror stories of suicides that on first appearance were taken for homicides. In 1987, a New South Wales man in his forties killed himself by first cutting off the fingertips of his left hand with a pair of scissors, then five of his toes with a tomahawk. He began hacking away at his left arm before passing out and ultimately dying from loss of blood. His apartment looked like a slaughterhouse. Detectives investigating the death found a bloody handwritten will on the man's kitchen table and forensic scientists traced his trail of self-mutilation through the house. What appeared at first to be an execution by some sort of toe-cutter gang was found to be a suicide.

Another man ended his twenty-three years on earth by tying one end of a chain around his neck and the other to a tree. He revved up his Holden ute and simply accelerated forward. The chain severed his head, which rolled forward and landed on the car floor next to his bare feet. Bizarre – but suicide.

Detective Senior Sergeant Jack Jacobs was used to such scenes of self-inflicted carnage, which were interspersed with cases of genuine homicide. Over his years attached to the Homicide Squad, many cases remain as clear in his mind as if they were yesterday.

One particularly perplexing case early in Jack Jacobs' experience as a Homicide detective was the discovery of a body in bushland on the outskirts of Melbourne. Jacobs didn't realise that the case would haunt him and become one of the many cold cases that lie unsolved at the Homicide Squad. The male corpse, despite its partial decomposition, was largely intact and although there were no identifying papers, Jacobs was confident that the identity of the body would be established. Fingerprints, dental records and missing persons files usually provide police with the necessary answers. However, in this case, all of the usual channels were exhausted with no result. Jacobs was even sent to New Zealand to further his inquiries because clothing on the body was of a New Zealand brand. A post-mortem examination concluded that the man, who had died of stab wounds, was of Polynesian or part-Polynesian origin. Jacobs' victim didn't fit any missing persons files in the land of the long white cloud and to this day his identity remains a mystery. Without an identity, an investigation is virtually impossible. If detectives don't know the victim's name, they can't find out about his enemies, his last known movements, or his life.

In 1993, an expert in facial reconstruction was asked to try to reproduce the facial features using the victim's exhumed skull. The resulting replica was photographed and shown in the media in both Australia and New Zealand. No result.

Jacobs still finds it difficult to believe that a body can just turn up without anyone having reported the victim missing or anyone subsequently claiming him. Cases like this, however, are rare.

Another case that stands out in Detective Jacobs' memory is one he was called to a number of years ago in country Victoria. At the crime scene, the body of a teenage boy was found slumped against the front fence of a house where, earlier in the evening, he had attended a party. In the darkness, the teenager looked like he had fallen asleep, but when his friends found him there and rolled him over, they saw that he had been shot through the head. Homicide detectives were called in.

When Jack Jacobs arrived at the scene, he spoke to the young man's friends who told the detective that before the party, the teenager and his mates had been drinking at the local hotel. Outside the pub, the drunken youth had smashed a bottle of beer over his own head for fun, cutting his thumb in the process. A blood trail over a kilometre in length led from the pub to the party where the teenager went to bandage his thumb. He had left soon afterwards and had been found dead when his friends left the party.

The following day, a small-calibre rifle was found lying in a paddock around a hundred metres from where the young man had died. Forensic examination soon revealed that it was the same weapon that killed the youth – indeed, the weapon belonged to the teenager's father. Tests also showed the victim's own fingerprints on the gun.

Did he kill himself? How did the weapon come to be found so far away? If he did kill himself, then why? By all accounts, the teenager was a well-adjusted, normal youth with no apparent reason to commit suicide.

Detective Jacobs had been conducting an investigation in the country town for nearly a week when the big break came – by luck. Walking around the paddock where the gun had been found, Jacobs noticed a large German shepherd dog wandering about with a tin can in its mouth. He had an idea ...

Jacobs casually asked the farmer – who owned both the paddock and the dog – if it was common for the animal to collect such strange objects. The farmer told him that the dog had a habit of picking things up and carrying them around in his mouth; he did it all the time.

Detective Jacobs had the dog put to sleep – temporarily – in order for a forensic dentist to take a mould of its teeth and jaw. The teeth were a perfect match to the strange scratches found on the butt of the rifle. Case solved.

It transpired that the teenager had been temporarily mentally affected when he hit himself on the head with the beer bottle. Leaving the party, he had walked home, got his father's gun and then, for some reason, returned to the party. The young man had then sat down against the front fence and shot himself in the head. The dog had wandered by and picked up the gun and carried it to the nearby paddock. For a Homicide detective, truth can be much stranger than fiction.

Each of the fifty-seven operational Homicide detectives attached to the Victoria Police Homicide Squad may only average a handful of genuine homicides per year, but with cases like the aforementioned, these detectives are rarely idle.

Another suicide case, which took many investigative hours, was a cleaner's discovery of an elderly woman's body in a room at the Melbourne YWCA. The woman was staying at the hostel for a few days while on holiday from Perth. She was found lying on the floor with her hands tied behind her back. There was a noose around her neck and a small cut under her chin.

At first glance, it looked like murder although no-one staying at the YWCA had seen or heard anything suspicious. A post-mortem examination revealed that the woman hadn't died through strangulation – the noose was not tied tightly enough around her neck. The exact cause of death was never established and it was up to Detective Jacobs to come up with the answers.

Inquiries in Western Australia revealed that the elderly woman was considered lonely and 'difficult' and would take lengthy bus tours around the country. Suicide was considered a possibility.

The question facing the detectives was, could the woman have tied herself up in the manner in which she was found? Examination of the knots revealed that they were exactly the same as the knots used to tie her shoelaces. Detectives compared their own efforts to emulate the knots with the method used on the body and found that the elderly woman could have tied herself up. Did she tie herself up in a strange attempt to make a suicide bid look like murder? Was this her last attempt to get attention? Did she will herself to death? The verdict was suicide but the mystery of how and why remains.

A little discussed form of death is known as autoeroticism. Some people enhance sexual pleasure during masturbation by cutting off their oxygen supply at the point of orgasm. Unfortunately, some who practise this cut off their oxygen supply permanently. Due to the nature of death, these types of body finds can often, at first, appear to be sexual murders.

The circumstances of autoerotic deaths lead relatives to sometimes try to cover up the circumstances before calling police – preferring others to think that the victim suicided rather than died accidentally while masturbating. Jacobs says that a typical autoerotic death scene will have the victim – male or female – with their genitals exposed, some kind of masturbation aid and most importantly – an escape route. The noose, used to cut off the blood supply to the brain, might be padded with a towel – for comfort, not suicide.

One family couldn't come to terms with the autoerotic nature of their son's death when he was found hanging from the ceiling with a rope padded with a towel. His fly was undone and his penis was exposed. He had been standing on a chair, which he had accidentally kicked over. Perhaps it is the sexual nature of the death or the needless waste, or even the element of the dangerous masturbation practice that makes this type of death harder for families to deal with.

Victims of autoerotic deaths are sometimes found in their bedrooms and the noose is often a dressing gown cord. The danger of this type of practice is that if anything goes awry, the person dies. In Jacobs' experience, some victims have tied dressing gown cords around their necks and the other end to a bedroom door. A number of victims have simply lowered themselves onto chairs in order for the noose to tighten. Death has occurred when the chair has tipped over or the person loses consciousness and is unable to remove the noose. Invariably, autoerotic deaths result in a coronial finding of death by misadventure – not suicide. The practice has obvious dangers but because of its intimate nature, it's probably not the type of activity that people feel they can ask a friend along to just in case anything goes wrong.

Jack Jacobs recalls another case where death was brought on by sexual activity. A daughter in her late teens arrived home to discover her mother lying on her bed, dead. Her underpants were pulled down and a hairbrush had been inserted in the woman's vagina. Her nipples both had clothes pegs clamped on them. Horrified, the daughter telephoned police. It appeared to her that her mother had been killed by a sex fiend. Forensic pathologists found that the woman had died of an aneurism during masturbation. It was Jacobs' unpleasant duty to break the news to the distraught daughter.

Often the job of the Homicide detective is not as daunting as it seems. Basic steps are followed with each new case. The detectives work by a process of elimination. Could the death be from natural causes, suicide, an accident or misadventure? If these elements are discounted, then the detectives are left with murder.

This elementary procedure served Jacobs well when he was called to investigate the discovery of a man's body in a vacant block that was used as a short-cut between two suburban streets. The veteran detective noticed that vegetation around the body was flattened and broken, showing obvious signs of recent disturbance. The dead man's clothing was in disarray and it was heavily soiled with dirt and grass. Blood had seeped onto the ground from a number of injuries to the back of the man's head. Jacobs noticed that several rocks near the body were stained with blood and, on closer inspection, he found hair attached to the dried blood.

First appearances suggested that the man had been battered to death by someone using the rocks, but appearances in this case were deceiving. Crime scene investigators revealed that the rocks hadn't been recently moved from where they lay and there was no evidence of a second person being at the death scene.

An in-depth investigation revealed that the dead man had been an epileptic and had gone for a walk to calm down after having an argument. Apparently, he had wandered through the vacant block and had an epileptic seizure. Falling to the ground and convulsing violently, the man had hit his head a number of times on the surrounding rocks and had died as a result of head injuries sustained during the seizure. The initially suspicious death was eventually found to be one of natural causes.

Detective Jacobs spoke at length about the privacy of the victims.

In one case, his inquiries revealed that a victim had a baby in her youth. He says that the family had no idea and he kept her secret because it bore no relationship to her murder. Jacobs is conscious of the delicate nature of such information and only reveals what he has to in order to further his investigation. His rule of thumb is: where possible the privacy of the victim is respected, but the investigation comes first.

Some murders are never solved, and Jack Jacobs has had his share of these. He still receives phone calls from the son of the victim in one case that he has worked on for many years. In 1984 a strange series of events led to the murder of a woman in the outer Melbourne suburb of Ferntree Gully. The victim was an attractive woman in her forties who looked years younger. She lived with her two children and worked in Belgrave. In the week before her death, strange things began happening to her car. On a number of occasions, she would have rocks thrown at her as she was driving on Monbulk Road on her way home from work. Her windscreen and radiator were smashed. Other cars had also been targeted but this woman's car was hit by rocks on three separate occasions. It could have been a random attack, but then similar incidents began happening at home. On various mornings she would go outside to find her tyres punctured, paint thrown on her car, the windscreen wipers were bent, and the car aerial broken.

The terrified woman contacted the police, who provided her with escorts to and from work. By the end of the week, the woman said she didn't need a police escort because a friend had offered to follow her home. The friend left her a few streets from her house. After pulling into her driveway, the woman had to make a number of trips into the house to unload things from her car. At some time during the unloading, she was murdered.

The woman's body was found at the back door to her home. She had been stabbed to death so viciously that large sprays of blood covered the surrounding areas. Jack Jacobs says that by the time the investigation was over, he felt he knew the woman better than even her closest friends – without ever having met her. He explored every avenue of her life looking for clues to the identity of her killer.

One aspect of the investigation focused on the possible connection between the recent attacks on the woman's car and her murder.

Despite the long investigation, Jacobs could never positively establish the link. He says that in most cases, the establishment of a motive will lead you to the killer, but in this case there was no apparent motive. The woman had no enemies, no criminal connections – nothing. Years later, when her son rang the Homicide Squad, Jacobs had little to report.

After so long in the Homicide Squad, Jack Jacobs has seen his share of bodies. They no longer bother him – except for the odd occasion when the harsh reality breaks through the carefully maintained exterior. On one such occasion, Jacobs admits candidly that he broke down and cried when the body of a young girl reminded him of his own daughter of a similar age. The worst aspect of his job is when a parent suicides and 'takes the kids with them'. Child murder is never easy, even for the most hardened detectives.

One of Jacobs' most stressful periods in the Homicide Squad was in the aftermath of the Ash Wednesday bushfires of 1983. His duty was to prepare an inquest brief on the twenty-eight fire victims. One man he met in the course of the investigation had gone back to his house in search of his wife and daughter. Their charred bodies were later found and Jacobs realised that the man had walked straight past them without knowing. Tragedy surrounded the detective, but the reality didn't hit him until months later when he saw the same man on a television program talking about the bushfires. Jack Jacobs broke down and wept with the incredible sadness of it all.

In his days as a senior sergeant, Jack Jacobs was not an operational detective. His seniority meant that he now had a supervisory role within the squad with more regular hours.

Jacobs says that it is not unusual for Homicide detectives to suffer burnout after only a couple of years in the squad. For operational detectives, seventy-hour weeks are typical, and family life can become severely strained. Nonetheless, being a Homicide detective has always been regarded as a pinnacle of police work by many.

Chapter Sixteen

OAKLEIGH 206

Life might be like a box of chocolates, but so is any police nightshift cruising around the suburbs of Melbourne – you never know what you'll get. The south-eastern suburb of Oakleigh is known more for its Greek food, period homes and ageing population than its crime rate. But there are often exceptions. On 28 November 1997, a woman took her two young sons down to the Oakleigh train track and laid them on the line in a murder–suicide bid. The train driver didn't see them in the dark – until it was too late. All three were killed.

With this recent tragedy fresh in their minds, Senior Constable Mark Wheller and Constable Tom McMahon report to work the 6 pm to 2 am shift on a Friday in early December 1997. Their call sign is Oakleigh 206.

It is Mark Wheller's last shift in uniform. Come Monday, he will cross the car park of the Oakleigh police station to join the Oakleigh CIB as a detective. Wheller has been waiting a year and a half for a detective vacancy in what is an extremely competitive field. His progress to the CIB is a culmination of nine years in the job.

Tom McMahon, on the other hand, was a latecomer to the police force. Like Mark Wheller, he is in his late twenties, but McMahon only joined the job eighteen months ago. Before that, he worked as a fitter and turner, mowed lawns and did security work.

The first call of the evening is at 6.07 pm. A report of youths fighting has come through the police communications centre, D24. Wheller and McMahon hurry to the marked police car and drive quickly to the address given. As often happens, there is no sign of the fight by the time they arrive and the incident is noted as GOA – gone on arrival.

For tonight, Mark Wheller is the driver and Tom McMahon rides shotgun filling out the running sheet. He notes the GOA and Wheller drives on, and the cruising begins.

McMahon, idling at traffic lights on Dandenong Road, notices that a man in a white van pulled up alongside the police car is gesturing to him. He winds down the window and listens to a garbled account of a scrape the driver had with another vehicle.

'I've already reported it to the police station,' the man finishes after Wheller has missed his green arrow to turn.

'Yep, you've done all the right things then,' McMahon calls out the window. Some people just like that extra reassurance. While that interchange is going on, Wheller smiles to himself, noticing two teenage girls waiting to cross Dandenong Road. They had stepped off the curb, saw the police car, and stepped back up on the curb again, reluctant to cross against the lights. It is a common thing. The presence of the police car makes people nervous and they change their behaviour – thus proving effective such concepts as 'proactive policing' and 'police presence'.

Like all police, Mark Wheller and Tom McMahon are veritable eagle-eye experts. They see things that the untrained observer just doesn't see – like spotting drunk drivers, stolen cars, kids with criminal records and people walking along railway lines – the latter being what McMahon spies when Wheller crosses a level crossing. After the triple fatal the week before, they take no chances. But by the time the police car speeds down to where the people were, they are gone.

At 6.26 pm, D24 directs Oakleigh 206 to stand by for a domestic. The information the two officers are given is that a woman has reported a theft and her ex-boyfriend is the culprit. She wants him charged but he has been drinking and might fire up. A couple of police vehicles hover in the general area for backup.

At 6.30 pm, Tom McMahon notices a red late-model Magna parked facing the wrong way in a side street off Warrigal Road in Oakleigh. A young man is sitting in the driver's seat smoking a cigarette. Wheller pulls over, gets out of the police car and asks him what he is doing. The man is just having a smoke but Wheller checks his licence and registration against the police computer via D24. McMahon notes the details on his running sheet. All checks out and the man makes his way into a nearby block of flats.

At 6.34 pm, Oakleigh 206 is called to a house in a street off North Road. D24 informs the two officers that the matter concerns an intervention order. The man will meet them near the corner of North Road. A young man called Aldo, with shoulder-length greasy dark hair and a dyed orange fringe, emerges from a small hatchback and walks over to squat down by Tom McMahon's passenger-side window. He breathes the smoke from his cigarette in the police officer's face while explaining that his ex-fiancée has an intervention order against him and he wants to pick up some CDs from her house. An intervention order cannot be breached unless in the presence of a police officer so McMahon and Wheller follow the hatchback and park outside the house where his ex-girlfriend Nadia lives.

Wheller knocks on the door while McMahon hovers near Aldo, who is in the company of two tall women who appear to be keeping check on his anger. Tom McMahon later explains that the duty of two police officers in such cases is one officer stays with the woman and the other with the man in case things turn nasty.

Nadia walks out through the screen door and stands on the porch. She is very nervous, shaking, and her feet are slightly turned in like a child. She wraps her arms protectively around herself. She has peroxide-blonde short-cropped hair and a tattoo on her upper arm. A tiny tabby kitten brushes playfully against her ankles.

Aldo tells McMahon, 'I want my CDs back. And the PlayStation.'

Nadia hesitates. She whispers to Mark Wheller that she will give back the CDs but if she gives back the PlayStation, she is worried that he won't then return some of her stuff that he still has. It is a stand-off.

Aldo yells from the fence, 'I've got my life back!'

Nadia's voice is weaker. 'Me too,' she says.

And then the arguing begins. The couple are oblivious to the police officers and Aldo's tall women who stay near the fence while he walks quickly over to face his ex-girlfriend. He accuses her of going out with his best friend and in the next breath tells her that he is over her. She trembles. There is fire in her eyes, but her body language is uncertain.

Wheller and McMahon stand awkwardly in the middle of this angst.

'I had the baby terminated,' she says in a quiet voice.

'Where's the receipt?' he demands coldly. 'I won't believe you unless I can see the receipt. They never would have let you keep the kid anyway because you've got a bad back. They would have given it to me.'

Nadia flinches as Aldo's voice gets louder. He is losing control and the tall women at the fence yell at him, 'Calm down; she's not worth it.'

Accusations fly. He screams. She dissolves into tears and rushes back into the house. Wheller follows her. McMahon stays close to Aldo, whose anger is palpable. The tiny kitten is chasing shadows in the garden and Aldo bends down to try to pat it. The kitten jumps out of his reach and the young man with the dyed fringe turns to Tom McMahon and tells the police officer that he gave Nadia the kitten.

'Am I allowed to take half?' he asks, his voice dripping venom. 'I'll take my half and leave her the rear end.'

Tom McMahon says nothing but looks grim. Mark Wheller and Nadia emerge from the house. Wheller is carrying a stack of CDs and hands them to Aldo. The issue of the PlayStation will wait until Nadia receives her belongings back in return. As the two officers turn to leave, Nadia asks them to ask Aldo if he is going to Transformers – a local nightspot in Moorabbin.

'I am going there with my friends tonight and I just want to know if he's going,' she says miserably.

'Yeah, I'm going to Transformers tonight,' he sneers, 'it's *my* club. I was going there before she did.' Wheller conveys this to Nadia, who looks worried.

And so they part company and McMahon and Wheller walk slowly back to the police car and wait until Aldo and his tall women have driven off.

'They use us as referees,' Mark Wheller says as he starts the engine. The domestic interchange has taken half an hour of police time and it won't be the only time this shift a couple uses the two young police officers to referee their battles.

One of the duties for Oakleigh 206 on this Friday shift is to try to pick up a young man who has failed to appear in court; a warrant has been issued for his arrest. The only address police have for him is his parents' house in Springvale South. The two officers don't hold much hope of finding him but head for the address anyway.

En route, travelling down Clarinda Road, Tom McMahon is the first to spot an old mustard-coloured Corona swerve on the road ahead. The driver could be drunk and from the back, he looks small. It could also be a case of unlicensed driving. There is a fine-mist drizzle and the road is damp and slippery. Wheller speeds up in pursuit. The Corona turns right at a roundabout and heads towards Old Dandenong Road. By the time the police car catches up with it, the Corona is turning into the driveway of a fairly rundown house adjacent to a market garden. Wheller pulls the police car into the driveway, blocking the entrance. A young woman and a young man emerge from the front and back passenger side doors and walk quickly into the house, completely ignoring the police officers. Wheller walks over to the passenger side and asks the driver to get out of the car. The driver, called Justin, slides over the seat to the passenger side to get out because his door won't open. Considering the appearance of the car, this is just one of a long list of things that is wrong with it. Tom McMahon was right about the driver – he looks young and is small in stature.

McMahon notes the details of the car on his running sheet and radios the registration and Justin's licence through to D24. Justin is just eighteen – although he doesn't look it – and is on P plates, only one of which is displayed. Wheller reaches in to the back seat and pulls the small breathalyser from a big blue case that also holds batons, penalty books, torches and a Melway street directory. Justin blows a double 0 reading but he doesn't get off that lightly.

Wheller asks him to get back in the car and turn on the headlights. He suspects that the car is unroadworthy and in need of a yellow notice of report sticker – better known as a 'yellow canary' – on the windscreen. Justin climbs back in through the passenger door and works the lights at Wheller's direction. Only one indicator light is working. There are no brake lights. One headlight is out. All four tyres are almost completely bald, which probably accounted for the swerving that brought the car to police attention in the first place. In short, the car is a death trap. Mark Wheller tears the yellow canary sticker from the penalty book and reaches into the police car to activate the windscreen squirties. He then dampens the back of it and walks over to paste it onto the Corona's windscreen. Police officers never lick the back of the stickers because they are made in prisons and there is no telling what the prisoners will mix in with the sticking gum, knowing police officers might lick them.

Justin looks miffed. His teenaged friends slowly filter out of the house and watch their mate. They drink alcohol from cans and joke to themselves. Another mate off the road, picked on by coppers. But they have never seen the carnage that an unroadworthy car can cause and they are too young and carefree to ever imagine themselves victims of failing brakes and fatal collisions.

Twenty minutes later and it's on to the Springvale South arrest warrant. The house is a 1980s dilapidated brick veneer. A fat black and white cat crawls out of the way of the two officers as they make their way to the front door. The driveway is empty and the house looks deserted. Mark Wheller rings the bell and listens at the door. A television sounds from inside but there is no sound of human movement. Both officers walk up the driveway and peer over a wooden gate. There is no-one around. The fugitive is safe for the moment.

Dinner time at Oakleigh tonight means pizza from one of the local pizza parlours. Tom McMahon — a self-confessed fitness addict — laments that, as nice as it is, the pizza will mean an extra workout at the gym or an extra-long bike ride.

At 8.21 pm, Wheller and McMahon are out cruising the main shopping drags of Oakleigh. They spy the younger brother of a teenager who has been in a lot of trouble with the law. Both officers know that the little brother is a potential master's apprentice. He is languishing outside one of the banks near the mall. At fourteen, Russell is streetwise and has a rogue's smile.

'Evening, fellas,' he says, leaning down to the passenger window of the police car. He says he's going to a party.

'Who are your mates?' McMahon says, nodding back towards the older teenagers that Russell was talking to.

'They're friends of me brother. Don't know their names,' Russell says innocently.

McMahon and Wheller get out of the police car and call to the other boys, who are happy enough to allow themselves to be patted down in a search for weapons or drugs. Russell's brother has already graduated to armed robberies. His trick is to pull on a balaclava and wave knives at other teenagers for their pocket money. This time the kids are clean and are sent on their way, knowing that the police will be keeping an eye on them.

Throughout the evening, D24 is constantly crackling in the background. McMahon and Wheller converse but always remain tuned in to the events that run like stories with beginnings, middles and ends. House alarms, fights, domestics, then the 'job's right' signal that all is well. One of the house alarms falls within the jurisdiction of Oakleigh 206. It is one of the more common jobs for the police patrols. Big concrete house. Yapping dog next door. Neighbour standing huddled in a cardigan by the front fence. She thinks the family is on holidays. Wheller and McMahon walk up the paved driveway amidst the high-pitched whining of the house alarm. Another dog begins a frenzied yapping and the officers know that the likelihood of there being an intruder in the house is slim. If the dog barked the minute they set foot on the property, chances are it would have been barking at an intruder. And it wasn't. The house itself is like Fort Knox. The neighbour asks if the officers can turn off the alarm. They can't, they explain patiently. The alarm will probably reactivate itself. It can take anywhere between fifteen minutes and half an hour.

'They all think we have some sort of magic key,' McMahon muses as he and Wheller drive off.

Fifteen minutes later, Oakleigh 206 is driving slowly around the Chadstone shopping centre car park. It is mainly a police-presence thing. People see the police and are a bit less likely to break into cars or steal them.

Back in the Oakleigh shopping drag at 10.15 pm, McMahon spies a driver ahead without headlights turned on. This is worth investigating because often drunk drivers forget their headlights. The car turns into Queens Avenue and Wheller hits the flashing lights button. This turns out to be a very embarrassed woman who had simply raced up to the local shops for milk. McMahon does the licence check and she is what she claims to be. They send her on her way.

At 10.30 pm, there is a D24 call that sounds more urgent than the ones that have come before it. There is trouble at a convenience store in East Bentleigh. It is outside the Oakleigh district boundaries, but these become elastic if police colleagues need backup. Convenience stores can become havens for youths with nothing better to do when other amusements close for the night. And they are particularly vulnerable. They are often staffed by only one or two young people and can become targets for fights or robberies. But halfway down North Road, D24 downgrades the call to 'not urgent' and Wheller U-turns back to Oakleigh.

Other potential areas for trouble are train stations. McMahon and Wheller, driving at a snail's pace past Oakleigh train station, notice three teenage boys standing under a street light. Wheller brings the car to a halt and McMahon winds down his window and calls them over.

'Where have you guys been?' he asks pleasantly. They look a bit nervous.

'Um, we've been to Chadstone and Hungry Jacks and we're waiting for my dad to pick us up,' one of them replies in an accent that is not Greek or Italian and McMahon can't place it.

'What's the accent?' he asks.

'We're from Iraq,' they say.

'Wow,' says McMahon, 'I've never met anyone from Iraq before. How long have you been here?'

'Two years,' they say.

'Gee, your English is good. Did you study it in Iraq?'

'No, we learnt it here.'

McMahon says pity about the trouble over there and the boys say they like Australia just fine. McMahon lists their names for his running sheet and Wheller drives on.

An abandoned car and a licence check for a pizza delivery boy take up the next twenty minutes. Then on to Valley Road. Two teenage boys are walking along the dark footpath. Wheller pulls over beside them and McMahon does the names and address routine for his running sheet. They have been to Trackside and they, like the Iraqis, are initially nervous. McMahon is expert at putting them at ease.

'Do you go to school?' he asks. One does and has just finished Year 11. He got a good school report. The other quit school to work at the Waverley Gardens Cinema. He gets to see movies for free. They are both walking home.

'Take care, boys,' says McMahon.

'You too, fellas,' they say, waving goodbye.

Then D24 requests for a patrol car to do a car check in Valley Road. It is metres from where the Oakleigh 206 is already. Wheller swings the car around and pulls up behind a green Commodore. A resident has rung the police to say that the Commodore has been there all day and he thinks it might be stolen or dumped. Wheller gets out to look through its dirty windows while McMahon checks the registration over the radio. It hasn't been reported stolen. Wheller returns to the car and reports that the ignition doesn't look like it has been tampered with. There is a handbag on the back seat. The car is registered to a woman in Dandenong.

At 11.35 pm there is a call back to the big brick house with the yappy dog. The alarm has gone off again. Same neighbour at the gate, but this time the alarm has been turned off. The officers knock at the door and a young teenager answers. He just got home and accidentally activated the alarm. Wheller tells him that the alarm went off earlier and the young man looks a bit worried. He is home alone.

More cruising. The industrial areas are quiet apart from the few businesses that work through the night. The brothels are quiet too – but they usually are.

Wheller makes his way to Clayton. Past the sex shop, which is lit up and looks busy even close to midnight. Then on to Clayton train station. No Iraqis here, but Wheller spies something a little more interesting. On the other side of the platform to where the marked police car is, there is an amorous couple sitting on a bench under the bright station lights. She is around twenty with long blonde hair and a very short skirt. He is wearing only trousers.

'Hey, look at that!' says Wheller. The young woman is sitting writhing on the knee of the young man. 'Guess what they are doing!' The two officers laugh at the audacity. They laugh even harder when McMahon points out that the couple is performing right underneath the station security camera. In a graceful movement born of practice, the young woman extricates herself from the young man and he pushes her head down into his lap. The act lasts a further minute before the man throws back his head. The earth obviously moved for one of them. The platform is otherwise empty of people and the two police officers can hardly believe what they have just witnessed.

'If you drive around long enough, you see all kinds of things,' says McMahon. The man stands up and passionately embraces the young woman, who is a tad unsteady on her feet. The act was obviously consensual – which was the only concern of the two police officers. Had there been others around, the couple could have been charged with offensive behaviour but since Wheller and McMahon aren't offended, and the couple remained clothed during the act, there is no point in ruining their moment. And then comes the time of reckoning. The young man spies the marked police car from across the platform and gives the officers a cheery wave. The girl does the same just as the train pulls in. From the lights of the carriage, Wheller and McMahon spot police colleagues from the Transit Police in the end carriage. If the couple tries a repeat performance, Transit is there.

Back at the Oakleigh police station, five or six officers with overlapping shifts congregate in the front office and discuss the murder–suicide the week before. A couple of them worked the shift and spent hours at the scene guarding the bodies while forensics and accident investigators did their work. A female officer tells the others the details. Apparently the dead mother had hired a private investigator to follow her husband. She wrapped the suicide note in the private investigator's bill. The officer is angry. She saw the bodies first-hand and says that no mother has the right to do that to her children. The biggest worry, though, is that one of the little boys had his eyes open. This could mean that he was conscious when the train hit. The officer had tried to find out through the proper channels whether the children had suffered or not. All things considered, she thought they probably didn't. There was evidence of pills and vomit near the boys. She hoped that they were doped or drugged or dead before the train hit. It would help her cope with what she saw. But the wheels of officialdom are slow and it would be another couple of weeks before she would find out that the two boys were indeed heavily drugged before the train hit and could even have been already dead. But for now, she is just venting her feelings. It was just so tragic.

At 1.40 am, the shift is near its end. Tom McMahon and Mark Wheller begin to wind down for the night when D24 beckons. There is a domestic in Drummond Street, which runs parallel to Atkinson Street where the police station is. It has been a slow night, so the divisional van accompanies the marked police car to where a small crowd has gathered on the nature strip not far from Dandenong Road. Wheller and McMahon quickly get to the bottom of the problem.

Most of the people are spectators who live in the nearest house. They heard screaming and called the police. An attractive, well-dressed blonde woman in her late twenties stands on the nature strip crying. An older well-dressed man tries to comfort her like you would placate a child having an embarrassing tantrum in public. The man tells the officers that he and his wife were at a party a couple of houses up and they had an argument. She walks off down the street and he follows a couple of metres behind in the car. Mark Wheller asks if they have been drinking and the man admits both have.

'I just want to walk home,' says the woman in a tearful voice. She is a bit overwhelmed by the crowd, the two police vehicles and the four police officers surrounding her. Their argument has now blown out of all proportion.

'Obviously you've had too much to drink to be driving,' says Wheller.

'I only drove a couple of metres,' says the man.

'I just want to walk home,' says the woman.

'Where do you live?' asks Wheller.

'East Bentleigh,' sniffs the woman.

'It will take you hours to walk there,' says Wheller.

'I don't care,' says the woman.

'I'll walk with her,' says the man.

'Do you mind if he walks with you?' asks Wheller.

'Okay,' says the woman, drying her tears.

The man and the woman look embarrassed now that they have both calmed down. Mark Wheller takes the man's car keys and tells him they can be collected in the morning – but this is unlikely. Both Wheller and McMahon know that the majority of people, like this couple, who have their keys confiscated are too humiliated to collect them in the morning. They use their spare set and prefer to forget all about it.

Everybody goes on their respective ways. McMahon will hear the next morning that the well-dressed man tried to outsmart the police by using his spare key to drive home. The van crew hovered around the corner suspecting that he might do this. They waited and sure enough, he appeared soon after, got into his car and drove off. He only made it a hundred metres up the road before they pulled him over. He blew well over .05 and lost his licence.

And so the shift is over and Wheller and McMahon drive back to the police station, grab their gear and head off. With a couple of domestics, a couple of licence checks, an arrest warrant who wasn't at home, a yellow canary, a coupling on Clayton station, and a man called Aldo who wanted to cut a kitten in half – all things considered, it had been a pretty quiet shift.

ABOUT THE AUTHOR

Vikki Petraitis has been writing since the early 1990s and her best-selling book *The Frankston Murders*, about serial killer Paul Denyer, has become a classic in the genre. Vikki is a popular speaker and presenter. She runs workshops for students of all ages, and her author presentations are sought after by her growing fan-base of true crime podcast enthusiasts. Vikki appears on panels and at comic debates and has been a judge for the Ned Kelly Awards. She is currently working on her PhD in Creative Writing and teaches short courses in creative writing. Her last book, *Cops, Drugs, Lawyer X and Me*, was released in February 2020. Vikki has made her first ten-part true-crime podcast series for Casefile called *The Vanishing of Vivienne Cameron*. She is working on her second series called *Searching for Sarah MacDiarmid*.